The Poetic Imagination in Heidegger and Schelling

Bloomsbury Studies in Continental Philosophy

Bloomsbury Studies in Continental Philosophy presents cutting-edge scholarship in the field of modern European thought. The wholly original arguments, perspectives and research findings in titles in this series make it an important and stimulating resource for students and academics from across the discipline.

Some other titles in the series:
Adorno, Heidegger, Philosophy and Modernity, Nicholas Joll
Between the Canon and the Messiah, Colby Dickinson
Castoriadis, Foucault, and Autonomy, Marcela Tovar-Restrepo
Deconstruction without Derrida, Martin McQuillan
Deleuze and the Diagram, Jakub Zdebik
Deleuze and the History of Mathematics, Simon B. Duffy
Derrida and the Future of the Liberal Arts, edited by Mary Caputi
and Vincent J. Del Casino, Jr
Derrida, Badiou and the Formal Imperative, Christopher Norris
Derrida: Ethics Under Erasure, Nicole Anderson
Emmanuel Levinas, Abi Doukhan
From Ricoeur to Action, edited by Todd S. Mei and David Lewin
Gadamer and Ricoeur, edited by Francis J. Mootz III and George H. Taylor
Heidegger and Nietzsche, Louis P. Blond
Immanent Transcendence, Patrice Haynes
Jean-Luc Nancy and the Question of Community, Ignaas Devisch
Kant, Deleuze and Architectonics, Edward Willatt
Levinas, Storytelling and Anti-Storytelling, Will Buckingham
Lyotard and the 'figural' in Performance, Art and Writing, Kiff Bamford
Michel Henry, edited by Jeffrey Hanson and Michael R. Kelly
Performatives After Deconstruction, edited by Mauro Senatore
Place, Commonality and Judgment, Andrew Benjamin
Post-Rationalism, Tom Eyers
Rethinking Philosophy and Theology with Deleuze, Brent Adkins
and Paul R. Hinlicky
Revisiting Normativity with Deleuze, edited by Rosi Braidotti
and Patricia Pisters
The Movement of Nihilism, edited by Laurence Paul Hemming,
Kostas Amiridis and Bogdan Costea
The Time of Revolution, Felix Ó Murchadha

The Poetic Imagination in Heidegger and Schelling

Christopher Yates

B L O O M S B U R Y
LONDON • NEW DELHI • NEW YORK • SYDNEY

Bloomsbury Academic

An imprint of Bloomsbury Publishing Plc

50 Bedford Square	1385 Broadway
London	New York
WC1B 3DP	NY 10018
UK	USA

www.bloomsbury.com

Bloomsbury is a registered trade mark of Bloomsbury Publishing Plc

First published 2013

British Library Cataloguing-in-Publication Data
A catalogue record for this book is available from the British Library.

ISBN: HB: 978-1-4725-0888-1
ePDF: 978-1-4725-1352-6
ePub: 978-1-4725-0640-5

Library of Congress Cataloging-in-Publication Data
Yates, Christopher S.
The poetic imagination in Heidegger and Schelling/Christopher Yates.
pages cm. – (Bloomsbury studies in Continental philosophy)
Includes bibliographical references and index.
ISBN 978-1-4725-0888-1 (hardcover: alk. paper) – ISBN 978-1-4725-0640-5
(ebook (epub) – ISBN 978-1-4725-1352-6 (ebook (pdf) 1. Heidegger, Martin, 1889–1976.
2. Schelling, Friedrich Wilhelm Joseph von, 1775–1854. 3. Imagination (Philosophy)
4. Kant, Immanuel, 1724–1804. I. Title.
B3279.H49Y38 2013
193–dc23
2013015413

Typeset by Deanta Global Publishing Services, Chennai, India
Printed and bound in Great Britain

For Christen

Contents

Abbreviations

Note: What follows is a list of abbreviations used for frequently cited works, including the original authorship dates and the abbreviation assigned to the corresponding German text. Page citations throughout will be given as English/German unless otherwise noted. In cases where the work under discussion is clearly identified I do not include the in-text abbreviation. See bibliography for full citations.

Kant

CPR   Immanuel Kant, *Critique of Pure Reason* (1781, 1787). Cited by A/B pagination according to convention, where 'A' refers to first edition, 'B' to second edition.

CJ   Immanuel Kant, *Critique of Judgment* (1790). Cited according to Pluhar's English translation, followed by pagination of the *Akadamie* edition: *Kants gesammelte Schriften* (Berlin: Königlich Preußische Akademie der Wissenschaftlen, 1902—).

Schelling

German pagination refers (unless otherwise noted) to the standard *Friedrich Wilhelm Joseph von Schellings Sämmtliche Werke*. Ed. Karl Friedrich August Schelling. Stuttgart-Augsburg: J. G. Cotta, 1856–1861. (SW, numbered consecutively across the two series of collected works). See bibliography for further editions.

LDC   *Philosophical Letters on Dogmatism and Criticism*. (1795). SW1.

UHK   *Of the I as a Principle of Philosophy, or On the Unconditional in Human Knowledge* (1795). SW1.

T   *Treatise Explicatory of the Idealism in the* Science of Knowledge (1797). SW1.

STI   *System of Transcendental Idealism* (1800). SW3.

P   "Presentation of My System of Philosophy" (1801). SW4.

FP   "Further Presentations from the System of Philosophy" (1802). SW4.

B   *Bruno, or, On the Natural and the Divine Principle of Things* (1802). SW3.

US   *On University Studies*. (1802). SW5.

ART   *The Philosophy of Art* (1802–1803). SW5.

PA   *Concerning the Relation of the Plastic Arts to Nature* (1807). SW3.

F   *Philosophical Investigations into the Essence of Human Freedom* (1809). SW7.

C   *Clara: Or on the Relationship Between Nature and the Spirit World* (1810). SW4.

AW   *The Ages of the World* (1815 version). SW8.

NPS   *On the Nature of Philosophy as Science* (1821). SW9.

PM   *Historical-critical Introduction to the Philosophy of Mythology* (1842). SW11.

Heidegger

German pagination refers (unless otherwise noted) to the *Gesamtausgabe* (GA) (Collected Edition) published in Frankfurt am Main by Vittorio Klostermann.

PRL   *The Phenomenology of Religious Life* (1920–21). GA60.

HCT   *History of the Concept of Time* (1925). GA20.

BT   *Being and Time* (1927). GA2.

BPP   *The Basic Problems of Phenomenology* (1927). GA24.

MFL   *The Metaphysical Foundations of Logic* (1928). GA26.

PIK   *Phenomenological Interpretation of Kant's Critique of Pure Reason* (1927–28). GA25.

KPM   *Kant and the Problem of Metaphysics* (1929). GA3.

ER   *The Essence of Reasons* (1929). GA9.

OET   "On the Essence of Truth" (1930). GA9.

IM   *Introduction to Metaphysics* (1935). (GA40). German pagination refers to the Niemeyer edition of 1953. N.

OWA   "The Origin of the Work of Art" (1936). GA5.

OWA1   "On the Origin of the Work of Art: First Version" (1935). German pagination refers to the edition appearing in *Heidegger Studies* 5. HS

HEP   *Hölderlin and the Essence of Poetry* (1936). GA4.

ST   *Schelling's Treatise on the Essence of Human Freedom* (1936). GA42.

ST2   Appendix (course notes 1941–43) to *Schelling's Treatise on the Essence of Human Freedom*. GA49.

BQP   *Basic Questions of Philosophy: Selected "Problems" of "Logic"* (1937–38). GA45.

CP   *Contributions to Philosophy (Of the Event)* (1936–1938). GA65.

AWP   "The Age of the World Picture" (1938). GA5.

N1   *Nietzsche, Volume I: The Will to Power as Art* (1936–1937). GA43 (see GA6.1).

N2   *Nietzsche, Volume II: The Eternal Recurrence of the Same* (1937). GA44 (see GA6.1).

N3   *Nietzsche, Volume III: The Will to Power as Knowledge and as Metaphysics* (1940). GA47 (see GA6.1).

N4   *Nihilism* (1939). GA48 (in part; see GA6.1).

IP   *Introduction to Philosophy—Thinking and Poetizing* (1944–45). GA50.

PMD   "... Poetically Man Dwells ..." (1951). GA7.

AS   "Art and Space" (1969). GA13.

Introduction

In 1920, Martin Heidegger (1889–1976) begins a lecture course on *The Phenomenology of the Religious Life* by announcing that philosophical concepts are "vacillating, vague, manifold, and fluctuating." He then declares that it, in fact, belongs "to the sense [*Sinn*] of philosophical concepts themselves that they always remain uncertain" (PRL 3/GA60 3). Some twenty-five years later, at the outset of a course entitled "Introduction to Philosophy: Thinking and Poetizing," he observes that "historical humans always already stand within philosophy because they do so essentially" (IP 1/GA50 90).[1] Together, these statements suggest that the human being, in spite of his/her rational perspicuity or blithe indifference, stands within a domain of thought in which the purported markers of illumination are necessarily kinetic, and provisional—one could say, essentially preliminary. But this account is a descriptive reckoning, not a concession to relativism, skepticism, or nihilism. It bears witness to the sojourn of reflective human dwelling and evokes something of the 'virtue' exercised in remaining awake and attuned to those basic questions that, following Friedrich W. J. Schelling (1775–1854), seek to know things—be they entities or matters—in accordance with their own necessity.

This book is an attempt to keep watch with Heidegger and Schelling as they remain alert to the dynamic potential and elemental standing of a matter that is as much in question for philosophy as it is in practice for poets and artists: the *imagination*. It is a project that concerns the poetic imagination in these thinkers—in their field of conceptual navigation and in the manner of thinking they bring to this domain. The phrase 'poetic imagination,' although a necessary heuristic, denotes something different from a hard and fast conceptual matter that these thinkers will chisel and polish with the ready instruments of rational command. Perhaps, alternatively, we hear the phrase in the same register we hear the conjunction appending the title to Schelling's 1809 treatise, *Philosophical Investigations into the Essence of Human Freedom and Matters Connected Therewith*, as though the poetic imagination denoted a semblance of secondary concerns. But what is true of Schelling's text is true of decisive stages in the thought of Heidegger and Schelling—that the imagination as a 'matter connected' is, in fact, something integral to their courses of inquiry. But before elucidating the meaning of 'poetic imagination' in this regard, a more immediate question presents itself: Why Heidegger *and* Schelling? Accustomed as we are to treating Heidegger in concert with Edmund Husserl, Jacques Derrida, Immanuel Kant, and possibly Aristotle and Plato, and to treating Schelling in concert with J. G. Fichte, G. W. F. Hegel, and possibly the mystical tradition, this pairing may well strike an anachronistic and unlikely chord.

Schelling and Heidegger indeed appear to inhabit the summits of 'mountains most separate.'[2] Schelling is the protean German Idealist for whom the Absolute is the unconditioned, infinite, living system by which being is rendered in terms of rational necessity. Heidegger is the thinker of fundamental ontology for whom the question of the meaning of being is to be treated phenomenologically in the form of *Dasein*, and poetically in the shape of *Ereignis*. Heidegger's '*Destruktion*' of the history of Western ontology is, it would seem, an offensive against the totalizing ambitions of Schelling's Idealism. However, the inadequacy of such summations belies the more specific inadequacy of assuming a standard, readily delineated distance between these two thinkers, for they are, in fact, much closer than the categorization of philosophical schools or movements may permit. Indeed, if compared on the basis of their fundamental concentration on the imagination, one realizes how Schelling, and Heidegger's paths of thinking are deeply intertwined, even to the extent of their shared willingness to think the very limits of metaphysics and to risk the enactment of a new style of *thinking* itself. Moreover, if considered in light of Heidegger's own reading of Schelling, one sees that the crossing of these paths, though marked by distinct tension, and distance, is of profound importance to the formation of Heidegger's thought after *Being and Time* (1927).

As a starting point, then, this project wagers on the fruits to be won by an unlikely and uncommon comparison. Of course, what Heidegger himself says of comparing [*Vergleichen*] here applies—that "the two 'things' to be compared are somehow already equated with one another insofar as they are selected and presented as what is to be compared . . . [T]here is already something the same [*Gleiches*] that is perceived about the two things, although it is mostly undetermined and evanescent" (IP 42/ GA50 137). If, following Paul Ricoeur, one asks of this project *D'ou parlez vous?*, the answer is that I speak from a horizon wherein something of the 'same' is sensed in these thinkers, is accredited by Heidegger's own 1936 lecture course on Schelling, and though initially 'undetermined,' this kinship appears rooted in the manner in which both thinkers come to conceive of the poetic imagination. Accordingly, to carry out this comparison I will address not only their explicit treatments of the imagination in the wake of Kant and at the limits of metaphysics, but also the dynamism this problem affords their own paths of thought. For the imagination, I will argue, is not simply an isolated problematic for these thinkers, but rather the whetting stone by which they sharpen their own philosophical inquiries and hone their sense of the deeper necessities these inquiries serve.

My approach to the topic will follow a systematic and exegetical course, and will stay close to the historical ordering of the texts under consideration. My argumentation will be clarifying with respect to the centrality and reorientations of the imagination in the stages of Schelling and Heidegger's paths; it will be dialogical in the attention I give to Heidegger's encounter with Schelling on the question of freedom, ground, and creative measure; and it will be provocative in contending that the poetic imagination delimits both the 'end' of metaphysics and the shape of the 'crossing' to another beginning for thought. Though I intend the resulting shape of this project to be a contribution to contemporary discussions of aesthetics, it is not an interrogation of what Heidegger and Schelling have to say about imagination and poetry *on the basis* of interests delimited by contemporary conceptual points of reference.[3] Heeding Heidegger's own appraisal of philosophical concepts, my project is better understood as a retrieval of the basic questions and dispositions that run antecedent to (and to some extent in anticipation of) today's aesthetic touchstones—I have in mind matters such as the meaning of artistic works, expression, form, symbol, beauty, and the intrinsically creative shape of reason. Of course, contemporary aesthetics, like recent Continental philosophy, is always already in dialogue with a tradition in which the matter of imagination is of principal concern, and the efforts toward conceptual delimitation and discovery are, at least in part, hewn through a mindfulness to that Kantian critical spirit, which wants to know on what basis we enjoy an experience of objects, and engage in a conceptual ordering of their meaning. Accordingly, we must lay a certain ground for this project by asking a question we cannot answer in full: How has the imagination faired in a critical tradition prone to regard it as reason's affective double?

In his eminent novel, *Les Misérables* (1862), Victor Hugo furnished the conscience of Europe with this study of his main character: "He set himself up as a tribunal. He began by arraigning himself . . . If a millet seed under a millstone had thoughts, undoubtedly it would think as Jean Valjean did." One thought that comes to pass in this prolonged self-arraignment on the threshold between grace and the abyss is a peculiar reflection on thought itself. With Valjean, writes Hugo, we attain a state in which "We no longer see the objects before us, but we see, as if outside of ourselves, the forms we have in our minds."[4] If, through Valjean, Hugo allows human conscience to make its case, it was the concern of Immanuel Kant, through his *Critique of Pure Reason* (1781/1787), to do the same for human cognition. In both cases, the author and the subject of the 'tribunal' are modalities of the same entity (man for Hugo, metaphysics for Kant), and in both cases the critical itinerary is born from a spirit of necessity that will plumb the depths of self-examination so as to adjudicate justly the possibilities inherent in the 'forms' of the mind. In this way Kant will be not simply the historical, but also the thematic point of departure for the present inquiry. For it is from within the domain of his critical project that philosophy is recalled to the puzzle of imagination, and it is in the ontological aftermath of his transcendental turn that Schelling and Heidegger stake so much on this mystery.

That the scrutiny of critique should examine the question of the imagination is a necessity already familiar to the Western tradition before Kant.[5] In turning to this tradition, however, one finds a state of affairs in which the imagination is almost always already in question without ever quite resting in an established mode of signification.[6] The matter famously arises, for example, when in Book VI of the Plato's *Republic*, Socrates and Glaucon endeavor to arraign the educational emphases befitting those qualified to rule in the *kallipolis*. The result is an indictment of the imagination on two fronts. First, they determine that the love of learning appropriate to a philosophical nature must privilege "some feature of the being that always is and does not wander around between coming to be and decaying" (485b). The capstone of such being is an object pursued by all but understood by few: the good. The good is "more beautiful" (κάλλιον) than knowledge and truth, and "superior" to being in "rank and power" (508e–509b). And even though Socrates has appealed to *beauty* in order to disclose the necessity of a level of intelligible forms, and has already characterized philosophers as those who "love the sight of truth" (507b; 475e), the sun and line analogies are a case against the visible (equated with *doxa*) in favor of the intelligible. Hence the hierarchy that places understanding (*noêsis*) above appearances, and also the adjacent predicament that those guardians suited to "keep watch over everything" and be "keen-sighted rather than blind" must 'see' by way of forms, not images, for what may be first in the order of vision is lowest in the order of understanding (484c). When Socrates remarks "nothing incomplete is the measure of anything" (504c) it is not simply a reflection on the authority of their 'tribunal' "or a dig at Protagoras, but is a hint toward the inadequacy of the ocular imagination to the demands of dialectic and, ultimately, justice. But sensibility, and with it the imagination, remain marked by a curious tension. Early in Book VI, Socrates opposes the blind and ignorant to the *painters*—those who "look to what is most true" in the exercise of their craft (484d). And yet in Book X the painter, like the poet, is treated as a maker of imitation (*mimēsis*)—in effect, an imitator of appearances, and thus "far removed from the truth" (598b).[7] Whether a painter or a poet, the craftsman of imitation "knows nothing about that which is but only about its appearance" (601b), and so fails to exhibit the love of learning privileged in Book VI. Turning to the *Sophist*, we find this caution treated in the Stranger's comments regarding the imitative practice manifest in the canny images spoken by the sophist. Sophistry disguises itself as philosophy, John Sallis explains, by way of an "image-making [that] produces . . . only something that *seems* (ψαίνεται) to be like its paradigm." This product "can appropriately be called a semblance (ψαντασμα), and the τέχνη that produces such images the Stranger calls semblance-making or phantastic (ψανταστική) τέχνη."[8] A true likeness or image, by contrast, is an εἰκών, although the task of distinguishing which imitative work is underway remains beset by the concealment of the productive work. The distinction between ψαντασμα and εἰκών is not necessarily reducible to false/true imaginations, but rather informs the nascent sense in which imitative production, or imagination, is a τέχνη shrouded in difficulty even as its meaning is underway. We may in the least observe that to speak of true understanding, with Plato, is to speak of paradigms, and thus to involve questions of sight and production, likeness and image, in the discourse concerning wisdom, justice, and artistry. Returning to the *Republic*, the tensions surrounding imitation hold, and are more generally manifest in the kind of liberating 'vision' which sees through an image to an original.[9] Plato's case for 'original' understanding continues to entail an ascent in vision, though not the vision of the artist or poet. "Even in antiquity," observes Friedrich Schiller, "there were men who were by no means so convinced that aesthetic culture is a boon and a blessing, and were hence more inclined to refuse the arts of imagination [*den Künsten der Einbildungskraft*] admission to their Republic."[10] In short, sensibility and imagination are employed in the case against imagination as the currency of imitation and opinion, where such currency poses shortcomings for any understanding trained not only on being, but also on the good that exceeds it.

Still, though we are speaking here of 'imagination,' it is important to bear in mind the lack of a decided, anterior signification belonging to the term in the Greek context. Remaining on this terrain of cautionary development, we might also note that to occupy a position 'removed' from the truth does not, however, render 'the imagination' (in the broad sense) anathema to the function of knowing. As Aristotle, and Aquinas after him, concede, "*the intellect can't operate without images* [ψαντασμασι]"[11] In *De Anima*, Aristotle surmises: "If imagination [ψαντασία] is that in virtue of which an image is formed in us . . . it [may be] some power or habit by which we discriminate, whether truly or falsely," although "most imaginations turn out to be false."[12] The possibility for the Platonic distinction between ψαντασμα and εἰκών is not explicitly entertained here; but the larger necessity for thinking 'in' likenesses, together with the caveat about falsehood, comprise a core tension that will pass into the disposition of the metaphysical tradition. When Plutarch recounts Cicero's effort to "compose and translate philosophical dialogues and to render logical and physical terms into the Roman idiom" the first term noted is *phantasia*.[13] Cartesian intellectualism, Spinozistic rationalism, and Leibnizian dogmatism, to be sure, exhibit the modernist wrangling with this state of affairs, with Descartes assigning the imagination (*imaginatio*) to the mediation between mind and body, Spinoza casting it as a shortcut to logical contradiction, and Leibniz balking at the deceptive, if persistent, status of images masquerading as rational ideas. But it is David Hume's summary empiricist account of the mimetic fiction that in one swoop establishes the representational centrality of imagination yet assails reason's purported autonomy on this very basis. In his *A Treatise of Human Nature* (1739–1740)[14] the imagination is that psychological vulnerability by which metaphysical reason contrives to translate distinct perceptions and impressions into unified entities. Likening the mind to a "theatre" and contending (contra Plato) that "thought is still more variable than our sight," Hume holds that the imagination is an intrinsic "bias" by which thought makes the mistake of attributing *identity*, for example, to what is in effect merely a sequence of perceptions. Conceptions of self, soul, substance, and cause arise from the "smooth and easy" connections of reason that "disguise the variation" in impressions, advance a "customary association of ideas," and thereby "gives rise to some fiction or imaginary principle of union."[15] By catching the imagination in this subtle work, Hume believes, we are pressed back upon a position of skepticism in which we must confess the contingency of metaphysical principles and exchange the ambitions of Descartes' 'foundation' for the modesty of a "labyrinth."[16] Removed from truth we may well be, but the illusions of subjectivism are all we have.

To say, as Kant does, that Hume "interrupted my dogmatic slumber"[17] is not only an admission of the questionability of *a priori* principles (such as cause/effect), but also suggests a more specific alertness to the difficulties attending any treatment of the imagination. Within the scope of the critical project, as we shall see, the positive accounts of the transcendental imagination do not escape moments of apparent hesitation—as though the precautions of Plato and Hume still sound from the margins of Kant's architectonic and have only to point to the rising enthusiasm of idealism in the 1780s as evidence for continued firmness. A brief look at the broader context of Kant's *Anthropology from a Pragmatic Point of View* (1798), which spans more than thirty years surrounding the critical project, illustrates Kant's hesitating resolve on the matter. He observes, on the one hand, how the "*power of imagination* swarms in one who studies by candle-light in the still of the night . . . or wanders about in his room building castles in the air. But everything that seems important to him then loses its entire importance the following morning after a night's sleep."[18] And yet, he will later position this 'power' in the heart of *genius*—which "flashes as a momentary phenomenon, appearing at intervals and then disappearing again; it is not a light that can be kindled at will and kept burning for as long as one pleases, but an explosive flash that a happy impulse of the spirit lures from the productive power of imagination."[19] In the first reference, the imagination 'builds' its images (*bilder*) by candlelight in the dim reveries of night. But in the second reference it illuminates a greater flash of poetic discovery. There are then two 'lights' by which we see the imagination at work and two distinct 'depths' from which this power arises. When, in his *Prolegomena*, Kant describes the science of transcendental philosophy as "shrouded in obscurity," and the Schematism of the Pure Concepts of the Understanding as "indispensable,"[20] he may well have had in mind the peculiar nature of this light and the function it serves amid the faculties.

The foregoing survey of our theme is not exhaustive, but affords a backdrop against which our study of the imagination, and the question of the poetic imagination specifically, will stand out in sharp relief. What follows is a brief account of how I will navigate this investigation of a matter that is at once obscure and indispensable.

Chapter 1 furthers the aforementioned account by examining the status of the imagination within the domain of Kant's critical project. Primarily oriented toward the *First* and *Third* Critiques, I highlight the nature of *aisthēsis* in intuition, his appeal to the transcendental, and productive imagination as a fundamental synthetic power of the subject, and the expansive repurposing of imagination in judgments of taste and the sublime. More than a mere elucidation, I establish the bases from which Schelling and Heidegger derive a Kantian point of departure for their own attunements to imagination at times in which their own decisive and distinct paths of philosophical questioning enter periods of pronounced refinement. To position these paths, I emphasize how (i) for Schelling, the Kantian imagination provides intuition with a means of approaching the Absolute and unifying theoretical and practical philosophy; and (ii) for Heidegger, Kant's 'root' comports with the itinerary of fundamental ontology in reawakening the question of the meaning of 'being' (*Seinsfrage*) in a way that seeks to avoid the Modern metaphysics of subjectivity and representational thinking, as well as the long-standing prejudices that ascribe to being superlative universality, indefinability, and conceptual self-evidence.

Chapter 2 investigates the expansive scope of the imagination as a matter for the ambitions of system and the problem of identity in Schelling's early work. Highlighting the accelerating poeticization of this faculty in conjunction with Schelling's treatment of intuition, spirit, nature, and history, I argue that his passage through self-consciousness, identity, and indifference is constituted by a heightened communication between the terrain of *Einbildung*'s productivity and reason's own aesthetic possibilities. Aesthetic intuition, artistic genius, unconscious production, and absolute reason are matters situated within a movement from transcendental reflection and Fichtean subjectivity to the mark of *Ineinsbildung* in a grounded system. The drive to position reason in the standpoint of absolute identity is, beyond the mere assumption of intellectual intuition, a strenuous appeal to the elemental life of creative production, and poetic consciousness.

Chapter 3 brings us to the intersection of Schelling's 1809 treatise on *The Essence of Human Freedom*, a work of thought that reexamines the grounds for a living idealist system and, so doing, crystallizes the matter of imagination both as a force of ontological creation and as a hindrance to the style of inquiry bent on delimiting the horizon of essential becoming. To underscore how this text represents a highpoint in Schelling's relationship to the imagination, as well as a point of tension with respect to the poetic possibilities of philosophical reasoning itself, I will elucidate the importance of the divine imagination in Schelling's account of God's self-revelation, the poetic framework for Schelling's ground/existence distinction in this account, and the priority of the 'word' in sustaining the inspired unity of the 'whole.' I will also argue that the work of *measure* Schelling ascribes to this 'word' signals an increasingly inspired and aesthetic bearing of thought that rivals the assumptions of imagination in representative and mechanistic modes of metaphysical inquiry. In this way, the imagination is not simply thematized as integral to the matters of ground and existence, but is indeed exercised in the dialogical and poetic performance of a path of thought closely attuned to the directives of its subject.

The treatise of 1809 is also an intersection through which Heidegger returns to the fore of our discussion. The aim of *Chapter 4* is to examine the significance of Schelling's study for Heidegger in his 1936 lecture course on this text and the milieu of idealism in which it stands. Though the matter of imagination is not as explicit in this course as it was in the *Kantbuch*, I will show that it comprises both the promise and peril of the fugal impulse Heidegger finds in Schelling's turn toward the limit of metaphysics. The necessity for fundamental ontology deduced in his reading of Kant is, in his reading of Schelling, radicalized toward a deduction for the being-historical thinking so often ascribed to Heidegger in this period. If, as I argue, he celebrates the impulse in Schelling toward the abyssal yet creative instantiation of Dasein in the jointure of ground and existence, Heidegger will also identify in Schelling's domain of measurement the very embodiment of idealism's ultimate impasse for thought. Elucidating his reading thus wins for us a means of exploring how and why the imagination lacks the luster it enjoyed for the Heidegger of 1929. Oriented by material from his later Nietzsche Lectures, I show that Heidegger's reluctance in this later period owes to a more specific concentration on the obfuscations of what he calls the poetizing essence of reason—the all-too-figurative and commanding reliance on an ontology of will in which the creative character of reason sees its own reflection. Heidegger thus reads Schelling in a moment wherein he is counting the cost of the Kantian creative inheritance, and looking to untwist the concealing drama of poetizing measures into the more revealing and projective measures of poetic imagination.

From this point of intersection in Chapters 3 and 4, *Chapter 5* explores the translation of our theme into the questions of essence and origin so decisive for Heidegger in the aftermath of his "On the Essence of Truth" (1930) and *Introduction to Metaphysics* (1935): poetry, art, and the depth of measure attending the event of the truth of Being in the strife and bestowal of its instantiating field of openness. If I allow the imagination to have a certain resonance in these matters that themselves aspire to surmount the 'productions' of reason's poetizing craft, this does not mean I protest too much on behalf of a theme that is very much in question, but neither am I content to gloss Heidegger's retreat from the imagination (properly speaking) as a minor episode in a larger tale of 'turning.' By focusing on his *Hölderlin and the Essence of Poetry* (1936) and "The Origin of the Work of Art" (1935/36), I indicate the elements through which Heidegger intends a reorientation and retasking of the poetic imagination as the very touchstone for thought's inceptual 'leap' into another beginning; namely I address Heidegger's concern to resolve the dilemma of production by way of the creative bestowal of projection, his specification of the fugal event as an event of poetic and artistic work, his opposing the measure of poetic naming and workly strife to figurative representation and aesthetic reductionism, and his effort to retrieve in the endurance of poetic work a basis for Dasein's resolute dwelling and thought's questioning. In short, these texts accentuate how the imagination is both *questionable* with respect to ascertaining what a poetic work discloses, and *question-worthy* with respect to composing the clearing of truth as the openness of beings and the founding of Beyng in a work. To speak of a poetic imagination in this milieu now means to speak of the life of measure and creative possibility signaled in Schelling's 'impulse' but untwisted from his 'impasse.' Finally, and in view of this same sensibility, I turn to two later texts that evidence how the task of thinking, for Heidegger, is to carry the best elements of Schelling's 'impulse' beyond his metaphysical 'impasse' by recalibrating the gage of philosophical questioning, essential measuring, and *aesthēsis* in an attunement to Beyng's *word*: *Ereignis*. A curious yet indicative passage from his *Contributions to Philosophy (Of the Event)* (1936–38) will reveal the projection of the *Da* of Da-sein to be the grounding exposure to imagination as the domain of transfiguration. The return of imagination in this text is by no means explicit, but by accounting for the priority of *measure* at the helm of what is to be *creative* thinking we shall observe how Da-sein's instantiation in/as site of *Ereignis* consists in a work of saying, configuration, and measure-taking justifiably termed 'the poetic imagination.' A brief look at Heidegger's "Poetically Man Dwells" (1951) then confirms how thinking and being comprise a path of questioning and dwelling shaped by the artistry of poetizing projection, and thus an active recovery of imagination as a domain of inceptual *poiesis*.

I conclude with some brief reflections on the development of our theme, the importance of Schelling for Heidegger, and how regarding Schelling and Heidegger as philosophers of the poetic imagination may assist and instruct contemporary interpretations of their thought.

***

My deepest thanks are extended to John Sallis, Richard Kearney, Jason Wirth, and Bernard Freydberg for their critical feedback on, and support for, this project.

The Kantian Breakthrough

My primary goal in this chapter is to ascertain the function and standing of the imagination in the architecture of Kant's *Critique of Pure Reason* (1781/1787) and in the aesthetic terrain of his *Critique of Judgment* (1790). This task is by no means equivalent to reporting on positions made plain in the material. What *is* evident is that Kant's transcendental turn includes a surprising reinstatement of the imagination as mediating intuition and understanding, an appeal to the transcendental or productive imagination as a fundamental synthetic power of the subject. I will highlight the role of this power within the *aisthēsis* of intuition, but will elucidate important tensions between Kant's treatment of the nature of synthesis in the A and B versions of his Transcendental Deduction, as well as the work of imagination in the Schematism. In the third *Critique*, I argue, the initially uncertain standing of the imagination is displaced into a pronounced repurposing of the power in the judgments of taste and the sublime. Here we find a new resolve to embrace and delineate the function of what was (arguably) the "unknown root" (A15/B29) of knowledge in the first *Critique*. This expansive horizon of the mediating, synthetic power is, I contend, a decisive matter of engagement for Schelling and Heidegger during periods fundamental to the direction of their philosophical itineraries. For Schelling, the Kantian imagination provides the basis for connecting theoretical and practical philosophy and arming intuition with a means of approaching the Absolute. For Heidegger, it furnishes a justification for the necessary work of fundamental ontology in extending the impulse of the *Seinsfrage* such that the continued recovery and repetition (*Wiederholung*) of this constitutive question will find in 'imagination' a name for a central preconceptual element, which the common structures of evidence and judgment have forgotten or failed to formulate properly, and which must be remembered in a decisive way. I will note how, in each case, our thinkers turn to Kant for a retrieval of the imagination, but assign to it a scope of necessity and possibility beyond the letter of Kant's project.

The elemental art of Kant's *Critique of Pure Reason*

The term "imagination" first appears in the *Critique of Pure Reason* (CPR) in a brief and negative light. In §7 of the Transcendental Aesthetic, Kant speaks in the voice of those who might oppose the *a priori* status of space and time as "the pure forms of all sensible intuition," maintaining instead their "inherent" absolute reality

(A39–40/B56–7). According to such a view, "the *a priori* concepts of space and time are merely creatures of the imagination [*Einbildungskraft*], whose source must really be sought in experience, the imagination framing out of the relations abstracted from experience something that does indeed contain what is general in those relations, but which cannot exist without the restrictions which nature has attached to them" (A40/B57). Though indirect and unthematized, the plausible remark by such "men of intelligence" (A36/B53) exhibits an assumed association between 'imagination' and error, perhaps fantasy, and thus places a subtle question mark beside the term. How would Kant, when pressed, treat the imagination, its 'framing,' and relation to experience or otherwise? How might his critics respond when Kant will allow, for example, that some intuitive representations "can very well be the product merely of the imagination (as in dreams and delusions)" (A226/B278), and yet will also assert that all empirical knowledge "involves the synthesis of the manifold by imagination" (A201/B246)? Behind such a question, and before attempting any investigation of Schelling and Heidegger's positions on the theme, lies the need to identify those steps in Kant's inquiry that give rise to the imagination as a discovery, a matter of hesitation, and a persistent point of possibility in transcendental philosophy.

In his effort to establish a science that will determine the possibility, principles, and extent of all *a priori* knowledge, Kant checks the driving momentum and irresistible "charm of extending our knowledge" (A4/B8) by rethinking the ground and authority of metaphysical thought. In so doing, his subject matter is, in part, not the nature of things, but rather "the understanding which passes judgment upon the nature of things; and this understanding . . . only in respect of it's *a priori* knowledge" (A13/B26). Delimited thus, the negative and positive aspects of his critical project stand as two sides of an overarching *necessity*. To satisfy the metaphysical necessity for *a priori* synthetic knowledge, while nevertheless remaining "within the bounds of possible experience," is to excavate "that transcendental truth which precedes all empirical truth and makes it possible" (A146/B185) and thereby introduce "the system of all principles of pure reason" (A13/B27). But to speak of transcendental truth also requires a form of argumentation that will disclose a shift in the locus of validity, and the objectivity of objects, to the side of consciousness in its constitutive work. Such argumentation, says Kant, will lead to "knowledge which is occupied not so much with objects as with the mode of our knowledge of objects *in so far as this mode of knowledge is possible a priori*" (B81). This focus on the structure of experience in terms of the *a priori* components of cognition (after the manner of the function of judgments with respect to the truth of objects) treats both the conceptual and the sensible elements of knowing without surrendering reason's capacity for determination.[1] And Kant's revolutionary measure, along such lines, consists in his stricture that the conditions "required for such determination are not, however, to be found in experience, and the concept itself is therefore transcendent" (A571/B599).

To exhibit the necessity of synthetic *a priori* knowledge by way of transcendental argumentation, and thereby disclose the underlying operations within any knowledge of objects of possible experience, Kant must provide a survey of the available terrain. That he names the leading division of CPR "Transcendental Doctrine of Elements" (*Transcendentale Elementarlehre*) already indicates the pronounced adoption of what

John Sallis calls an 'architectural metaphorics.' Kant's project, says Sallis, "is to prepare for the construction of the edifice of metaphysics" and to instigate this preparation by way of what Kant calls "an estimate of the materials."[2] Though, as Bernard Freydberg observes, "[t]he language of the CPR is the vocabulary of Kant's tradition, especially its rationalist side," the metaphorical disposition places the security of this very tradition in question.[3] What the material estimation intends, explains Sallis, is not "the construction of a new metaphysical edifice," but primarily a reckoning with what Kant calls "a ground that is completely overgrown" (Axxi).[4] Beneath the tangled thicket of metaphysical language and dogma lies a ground in need of recovery, of uprooting, one could say, if its structure is to stand. The architecture depends on the excavation, much the same as a system of pure reason depends on a transcendental movement before/beneath empirical experience to the level of cognitive capacities or roots—most famously, to the "two stems of human knowledge, namely, *sensibility* and *understanding*, and the 'unknown root' from which they may commonly 'spring'" (*aber uns unbekannten Wurzel entspringen*) (A15/B29).

In view of such a "phenomenon of depth"[5] beneath any edifice, the notion of a subjective and *a priori* 'grounds' for a necessary unity of appearances, and an original synthetic unity within the cognitive powers of the mind, testifies to an elemental itinerary that means to excavate conditions and possibilities—or rather, the transcendental conditions for the possibility of empirical knowledge. The common orientation for following this itinerary is of course the collaborative work of the faculties: sensibility, understanding, judgment. As Kant explains: "Sensibility gives us the forms (of intuition), but understanding gives the rules" (A126); and *judgment* is the event of relation and subsumption by which "given modes of knowledge are brought to the objective unity of apperception" (B141) such that the designs of these intrinsic powers may be stamped with a valid structuring of a given state of affairs. Delineating the precise function of these powers within the scope of their transcendental interrelation is the matter on which the constitution of knowledge depends. We will come soon to the question of the elemental status of the *imagination* as a faculty, as the productive force of synthesis within/beneath the transcendental unity of apperception, and as the schematizing link by which sensible intuition and concepts of the understanding converge in the transcendental doctrine of judgment.

But it is important to note that before Kant treats imagination in any strict sense, there is already an emphasis on the activity of 'form' or formation in the function and essence of *intuition*. To begin the elemental study with a Transcendental Aesthetic is, in part, to echo Plato's own initial approach (in the *Republic*) to 'truth' and 'the good' by means of aesthetic experience—namely matters of sight, light, and beauty. That is not to say that Kant (or Plato for that matter) means to assure safe passage to the summit of the rational on the provisional stepping-stones of the empirical, but that a 'complete measure' of knowing must embrace the aesthetic constitution of the knower. With this opening in view, Kant underscores the receptive passivity of sensibility and the flow of the manifold into the matrix of intuition. More specifically, he contends that the *form* of an object's appearance lies "ready for the sensations a priori in the mind, and so must allow of being considered apart from all sensation" (A20/B34). Consciousness is thus aesthetic, not simply impressionable, in its basic activity.

Insofar as intuition is "the representation of appearance" (A42/B59) the capacity to form/figure signals the fundamental role of *aesthēsis* within cognition. To attain true knowledge, this disposition to form and representation will require that the manifold of pure intuition be synthesized "by means of the imagination" (A78–9/B104). Prior to examining such synthesis, one must appreciate how the capacity to form or figure, in the immediacy of representation that defines intuition, is of course rooted in the *pure intuitions* of space and time. Briefly stated: *space*, as necessarily prior to any perception of an object, enframes the external appearance of objects such that they are valid as representations; *time*, as the "intuition of ourselves and of our inner state" (A33/B50), is that inner sense that contains the simultaneity of appearances against the backdrop of infinity. But there is a limiting factor alongside these elements: "The true correlate of sensibility, the thing in itself, is not known, and cannot be known, through these representations; and in experience no question is ever asked in regard to it" (A30/B45). Here it is important to recognize that Kant's account of aesthetic intuition—within such a phenomenal limit—worries not about being twice or thrice 'removed' from the 'truth.' The assumed status of the thing in itself poses a limit point for sensibility (as well as understanding), but intuition and the elemental artistry of sense are, in fact, intrinsic to the determination of "transcendental truth" (A146/B185). What then is the place of imagination in this larger determination?

The A Deduction: Imagination in the work of synthesis

On the other side of the Aesthetic stands the Transcendental Analytic, and with it the translation by/in the *understanding* of the intuitive material into the material of thought. But to elucidate this translation we must remain in the "the dark origin" or depth of its juncture,[6] and this means attending to the matter of *synthesis* within which the imagination stands out in sharp relief. To do so, it is vital not to lose sight of the relational context in which Kant presents sensibility and understanding; the temptation, and the source of much consternation in the literature, is to treat them as utterly distinct epistemological apparatuses—two continents within cognition that must be surveyed in isolation from one another, and then bridged by a narrow platform. Kant's own presentation tends to invite such an analysis insofar as we follow him down through intuition, up through pure concepts, and back and forth by way of the Schematism *en route* to the possibility of empirical knowledge. But to assume that the divisions of his text comprise a ready grid for his subject matter is to take a dynamic relation, render its elements static, and deprive oneself of the alertness to transcendental relations within which synthesis is understood. Returning to the notion of 'grounding' in both its logical and earthen aspects, intuitions and concepts are elements of the same soil, wherein synthesis is the agent of growth.

Kant explains that transcendental logic "has lying before it a manifold of *a priori* sensibility, presented by transcendental aesthetic, as material for the concepts of pure understanding" (A76–7/B102). The traditional positioning of potentiality and actuality is clear, but turns on a necessary *activity*: "But if this manifold is to be known, the spontaneity of our thought requires that it be gone through in a certain way, taken up, and connected. This act I name *synthesis*" (A77/B102). Synthesis is thus introduced as a necessity from the retrospection of knowledge: it *must* be the case. But the necessity hastens into a fact: "Synthesis of a manifold," he explains, "is what first gives rise to knowledge" (A77/B103). And what is required by the spontaneity of thought, once secured, nevertheless rebounds on thought with a further, more obscure, necessity: "Synthesis in general, as we shall hereafter see, is the mere result of the *power of imagination*, a blind but indispensible function of the soul, without which we should have no knowledge whatsoever, but of which we are scarcely ever conscious" (A78/B103, my emphasis). Kant's 'hereafter' is a promise to clarify and defend this necessity; one that even the most reluctant readers of Hume would have met with suspicion.[7] The imagination, it seems, is what accomplishes the synthesis of the manifold upon which the concepts of the understanding and "knowledge properly so called" depend (A78/B103). For a tradition that privileges sight and presence and is loathe to shadows, Kant has embraced a fundamental, figurative blindness. Such an imagination is already irreducible to an imitative facility trafficking in likeness or semblances (and is, obviously, a transcendental as opposed to artistic or sophistic visual or linguistic power), though it retains its 'productive' cast. To trace Kant's 'hereafter' elucidation of this necessity within synthesis I will remain close to the text, beginning with the Transcendental Deduction of the A edition. In so doing, I will highlight how Kant's descriptive account of synthesis as a condition for the possibility of knowledge allows him to identify the imagination in terms of its original and originating activity, and accordingly to title it *transcendental* and *productive*.

By way of introducing "The Deduction of the Pure Concepts of Understanding" in Book I of the Analytic, Kant recasts the relational elements of the mind in a three-fold division centered on the synthetic operation:

> There are three original sources (capacities or faculties of the soul) which contain the conditions of the possibility of all experience, and cannot themselves be derived from any other faculty of mind, namely, *sense*, *imagination*, and *apperception*. Upon them are grounded (1) the *synopsis* of the manifold a priori through sense; (2) the *synthesis* of this manifold through imagination; finally (3) the *unity* of this synthesis through original apperception. All these faculties have a transcendental (as well as an empirical) employment which concerns the form alone, and is possible *a priori*. (A95)[8]

The appearance of the imagination in these remarks would appear to forestall any dualistic reading of sensibility and understanding. At the very least, it is an invitation to regard the imagination as a necessary route—a passage through which the manifold of intuition may be "taken up into consciousness" (A116) as a synthesis that will then be unified in apperception. On the basis of the A Deduction (the "subjective deduction," Axvi–xvii), this route must be understood as a subjective cognitive power required by the larger demands for unity and combination on the side of understanding. To justify the application of the categories to the manifold, that is, the transcendental unity of apperception must be cast as a story of syntheses vectoring toward the unity of self-consciousness in cognition. All of this of course takes place on the level of the *a priori*, which means that any eventual employment of synthetic *a priori* judgments will owe a substantial debt to the depth of imagination. The representations absorbed through intuition will reach the understanding only if there is this "synthesis through imagination" (A119) to which apperception may assign a unifying principle. The unity of representations in 'my' consciousness, as it were, becomes synthetic and therefore graspable by the understanding on the basis of a production via the imagination. Kant explains:

> This synthetic unity presupposes or includes a synthesis, and if the former is to be *a priori* necessary, the synthesis must also be *a priori*. The transcendental unity of apperception thus relates to the pure synthesis of imagination, as an *a priori* condition of the possibility of all combination of the manifold in one knowledge. But only the *productive* synthesis of the imagination can take place *a priori*; the reproductive rests upon empirical conditions. Thus the principle of the necessary unity of pure (productive) synthesis of imagination, prior to apperception, is the ground of the possibility of all knowledge, especially of experience. (A118)

To be clear, this characterization of the imagination is not an empirical survey of concrete modalities within consciousness (as though such a thing were possible), but is an account of a dynamic that must by *necessity* come to pass on the level of conditions already delineated according to outer and inner intuitions. The dependence of apperception on its *a priori* ground, specifically the "*a priori* combination of the manifold," allows Kant to describe this "synthesis of the manifold in imagination" as "*transcendental*" (A118). Argument on the basis of conditions of possibility is not, however, argumentation reducible to hypotheses. The place/status of the transcendental imagination, and its productive synthesis, is not a supposition, but is demonstrable within the transcendental framework on the basis of what the Aesthetic has shown, on the one hand, and what is mirrored by the empirical, or reproductive, imagination, on the other. Kant's broader construal of imperative necessity is evidenced the following statement: "The empirical faculty of knowledge in man must therefore contain an understanding which relates to all objects of the senses, although only by means of intuition and of its synthesis through imagination" (A119). This says: to know objects objectively requires pure concepts of understanding (the categories), and these in turn require a sense manifold to combine, which itself depends on the productive synthesis of the imagination. A more precise, 'elemental' rendering of the same point explains that the "*unity of apperception in relation to the synthesis of imagination* is the *understanding*; and this same unity, with references to the *transcendental synthesis* of the imagination, the *pure understanding*" (A119). Understanding is thus disclosed in terms of the relationship between apperception and imagination. Even if one were to work from the 'grounded' level of empirical or reproductive imagination in terms of the association of appearances (as in the Humean critique), this same transcendental necessity arises:

> Since the imagination is itself a faculty of *a priori* synthesis, we assign to it the title, productive imagination. In so far as it aims at nothing but necessary unity in the synthesis of what is manifold in appearance, it may be entitled the transcendental function of imagination. That the affinity of appearances, and with it their

association, and through this, in turn, their reproduction according to laws, and so [as involving these various factors] experience itself, should only be possible by means of this transcendental function of the imagination, is indeed strange, but is none the less an obvious consequence of the preceding argument. For without this transcendental function no concepts of objects would together make up a unitary experience. (A123)

When Kant 'titles' or 'entitles' his operating concepts, it amounts to his placing a signature of necessity beneath them. That he does this for the 'imagination,' the 'productive imagination,' and the 'transcendental synthesis of imagination' no less than three times in the A Deduction (and three more in the B Deduction) is telling. Whatever hesitations and qualifications will arise, it is correct to say that the terrain of *a priori* necessity places *Einbildungskraft* and *Erkenntnisse* in close proximity. And it is with such proximity in view that Freydberg goes so far as to contend: "When the most rigorous look is taken at the Kantian text, it must be conceded that it is imagination-driven, even if imagination is seldom thematized. Both synthesis and the connection of concepts and judgments to sensation are its unique work."[9] Kant himself appears to concede as much when he allows that the "pure imagination, which conditions all *a priori* knowledge, is thus one of the fundamental faculties of the human soul" (A124); and when, in the B Deduction, he declares imagination to be "a faculty which determines the sensibility *a priori*; and its synthesis of intuitions, conforming as it does to the *categories*, must be a transcendental synthesis of *imagination*" (B151–52). In this way, we know the imagination by virtue of the effects of synthesis, but what we know of synthesis follows from the function of other necessary factors constituting the drive toward unitary experience. When, for example, Kant explains that *pure apperception* "must be added to pure imagination, in order to render its function intellectual" (A124), he signals how the essence of this productive/transcendental element is vital to consciousness with respect to how it may be *employed*.[10]

Understood by virtue of such employment, a certain ambiguity begins to shadow this abiding necessity, obscuring our efforts to treat the imagination in its singular function. Resurfacing from his descriptive excavation of the imagination, Kant observes that the "the formal unity of experience, and therewith all objective validity (truth) of empirical knowledge," and indeed even the unity bestowed upon the "synthesis of imagination," is ultimately grounded upon the *categories* (A124–25). That the productive imagination is vital to the possibility of pure concepts of understanding remains without question, but the culmination of the A Deduction executes a step beyond these depths of synthesis toward the integrity of original apperception and the "connection and unity (in the representation of an object)" (A130) furnished by the categories. Can one speak of the indispensability of the faculty of imagination—of its creative, synthesizing, formative work—in terms of reason's intrinsic, elemental capital, or only in the terms of a discourse calculated to deduce the categories? Must the latter, larger discourse attenuate the former? And this, as we shall see with Heidegger, begs the larger question of whether the imagination carries the transcendental project beyond itself, or whether it remains simply one layer of synthesis and mediation in the larger outgrowth of cognition.

The B Deduction and its aftermath: Imagination
in the drift of combination

If in the A Deduction the activity of the imagination is disclosed as a necessary function of the soul obtaining within the *synthesis* of the manifold, the B Deduction privileges the work of *combination*, thus treating imagination more from the side of understanding and the unity of apperception. I will now highlight how such combination, regarded as a spontaneous act, appears to eclipse the emphasis on the productive imagination's activity/effect with a more direct elaboration of apperception's synthetic unity. To account for and assess the ambiguous status of the imagination resulting from this drift, I will address the effects of an escalating need for determinability in Kant's discussion, namely the isolation of sensibility, the lacuna of imagination, and the partitioning of synthesis.[11] I will then compare these findings with an interpretation of the Transcendental Schematism and determine the character of possibility attending the matter of imagination in the broader extent of the first *Critique*.

Since Kant will follow this rigorous justification of the categories (as applicable to the manifold of intuition) with an account of transcendental judgment relying heavily upon cognitive connectivity or connections, it is unsurprising that he will prepare the way with a discourse of *combination* that serves the spirit of determination. Any residue of obscurity still attached to the work of synthesis must then be polished clean, redirected toward the structural integrity befitting a consciousness that is a priori equipped to employ its understanding in a valid manner. For this reason the B Deduction opens with a distinction between sensibility and understanding on the precise basis of combination. Though the manifold of representations is given in intuition through the form of affectivity, sensibility cannot exercise combination. As itself a power of representation (not that of the manifold proper), combination is an "act of spontaneity," which "must be entitled understanding" insofar as it "cannot be given through objects" (B129–30). More specifically, combination "is representation of the synthetic unity of the manifold" (B130–31). The singularity of such combination is, again, unsurprising, as the A Deduction already alerted us to the operations of unity on the side of understanding. What is surprising, however, is that Kant does not (in his initial discussion) here cite the crucial work of the transcendental synthesis of the imagination in rendering the manifold open to combination. Instead, he moves the spontaneous nature of combination further from sensibility and closer to the unity of apperception—what he entitles "the *transcendental* unity of self-consciousness" (B132)—stretching the mediating synthesis of the transcendental imagination so thin so as to appear almost irrelevant. Observe the lacuna in the following assertion: "[Combination] is an affair of the understanding alone, which itself is nothing but the faculty of combining *a priori*, and of bringing the manifold of given representations under the unity of apperception. The principle of apperception is the highest principle in the whole sphere of human knowledge" (B134–35). The absence of any mention of the productive imagination in terms of such a 'bringing' is odd. And when, continuing, he speaks of the unity of apperception as "synthetic" (B137) one wonders if this is meant to capture what was the synthesis previously performed by the imagination (see A95 noted earlier). The inevitable sense of 'activity' within any work of 'synthesis' has prompted Kant to move his emphasis toward the combination and spontaneity of an understanding safely anchored in "the principle of the original synthetic unity of apperception" (B137). As noted, Kant did hold in the Analytic of Concepts that it is the understanding that 'brings' the synthesis to concepts (A78/B103), but he also emphasized the synthesis itself *as an act* "by means of the imagination" (A79/B104).

The question of 'elsewhere'

There are two immediate ways to account for this ambiguity. The *first* is to say that the B Deduction's strict concern with an 'objective' demonstration incorporates the 'result/effect' (*Wirkung*) of the transcendental imagination without needing to revisit the matter. If so, the transcendental synthesis is not jettisoned, but has given way to the 'synthesis' attributed to *apperception* by virtue of the escalating need for its 'unity' to shoulder the burden of objectivity in judgments. Kant emphasizes his alertness to this necessity in stating: "This [objectivity] is what is intended by the copula 'is'. It is employed to distinguish the objective unity of given representations from the subjective. It indicates their relation to original apperception, and its *necessary unity*" (B142). We may surmise that any mere mention of *Einbildungskraft* could be misinterpreted as empirical ('reproductive' in the strict sense), and thus an erstwhile stress on the transcendental architecture. When describing the categories as rules for understanding, Kant specifies their power in terms of "the act whereby it brings the synthesis of a manifold, *given to it from elsewhere in intuition*, to the unity of apperception" (B145, my emphasis). If this account of the ambiguity is to hold, so much depends on this gift 'from elsewhere.' If it is a placeholder for the productive imagination then we have our clarification. If, however, it expresses an immediate leap from manifold to combination then, as a *second* explanation, we must understand all synthesis as a work of understanding, and wonder whether the faculty of imagination was, in effect, wholly consigned to the passivity of sensibility all along. This second possibility gains traction when Kant proceeds to draw the distinction between sensibility and the unity of apperception in terms of the *concepts of the understanding*: "The synthesis or combination of the manifold *in them* [the concepts (my emphasis)] relates only to the unity of apperception, and is thereby the ground of the possibility of *a priori* knowledge, so far as such knowledge rests on the understanding" (B150). If this 'synthesis' speaks for all synthesizing operations, then it appears as though the subtlety of 'bringing to' has given way to the 'determinations' of the understanding, and the 'formative' operation of the categories have indeed eclipsed the synthesizing work of the transcendental imagination.

Having left the reader in a state of uncertainty, Kant offers his own (*third*) explanation. In §24, well past the midpoint of the Deduction, he treats the problem of *synthesis* directly, noting:

> This synthesis of the manifold of sensible intuition, which is possible and necessary *a priori*, may be entitled *figurative* synthesis [*figürlich*] (*synthesis speciosa*), to distinguish it from the synthesis which is thought in the mere category in respect of the manifold of an intuition in general, and which is entitled combination

through the understanding [*Verstandesverbindung*] (*synthesis intellectualis*). Both
are *transcendental*, not merely as taking place *a priori*, but also as conditioning the
possibility of other *a priori* knowledge. (B151)

Does this distinction answer what has become the riddle of imagination? From within
the larger framework of our initial 'elemental' configuration, we are now able to
isolate the constitutive work of the synthesis in which the transcendental *imagination*
is primary, and the synthesis in which the *combining* work of the understanding is
primary. Having introduced this distinction, Kant reinstates the imagination as a
power of the soul, calling it "the ability to represent an object into view without
it being present"[12] (B151). This appears to amount to a measured clarification of
sensibility and understanding in their distinct roles, their intimate relationship, and
in terms of their point of contact within the activity of synthesis. However, the matter
is far from settled, for what is delineated by way of two-tiered synthesis unravels once
more in terms of imagination and presses us back on the confusion of the first two
accounts.

With this new distinction in mind, let us see to what extent the imagination returns
'from elsewhere.' Initially, it appears to stand as a chiasma between the two levels of
synthesis, provided the figurative synthesis takes place on the edge of sensibility. Since
the imagination is exercised in accordance with sensible intuition, Kant asserts that
it "belongs to *sensibility*" (B151), thus delimiting it within the intuitive faculty. And
yet, owing to the "spontaneity" inherent in any act of synthesis, he is also compelled
to characterize the imagination as a determinative faculty (performing its work in
view of the categories). The figurative synthesis 'is' the "the transcendental synthesis of
imagination" viewed with respect to its service to the unity of apperception and is not
to be confused with intellectual combination (B152). Viewed thus, the imagination is
"a faculty which determines the sensibility *a priori*" (B152). Accordingly, Kant terms
the transcendental synthesis of imagination "an action of the understanding on the
sensibility" (B152). But this would appear to say: the figurative synthesis (though
not intellectual) is an action of the understanding *on* sensibility, performed with the
aid of what belongs *to* sensibility (the imagination). Even if adequate, the conceptual
negotiation is bewildering, and all the more so when Kant then reassigns the signification
of his title, "*productive* imagination [*die produktive Einbildungskraft*]," to the action of
understanding (B152). He justifies this reassignment as a safeguard against confusing
the productive and reproductive [*der reproduktiven*] (empirical) imaginations, but as
there is little chance of such confusion at this stage one wonders if his aim is to deflect
the discussion away from the question of the status of the imagination as a faculty in
and of itself. Indeed, what is of interest to Kant in this section is the *quality* of the act
associated with imagination—that it is spontaneous—not its nominative location or
power. Put differently, he is content to treat the coefficients of imagination, though
with little comment on the variable itself. In short, the best resolution available thus far
is to say that the transcendental synthesis of imagination is not *intellectual*, but belongs
to *sensibility* on the basis of its conditions, and belongs to *understanding* on the basis
of its exercise.

Nonetheless, Kant's direct treatment of synthesis leaves him entangled in a
difficulty, the resolution of which will ultimately come at the price of renewed

ambiguity concerning the imagination. By attributing the transcendental synthesis to an 'action of the understanding,' he has inadvertently made room in the understanding for a term typically associated with sensibility. For this reason, he must insist that this synthesizing action does not imply the understanding is itself *intuitive*. He thus provides a concentrated view of synthesis, elucidated in terms of combination, which allows inner sense (sensibility) and apperception to remain distinct. So doing, however, the understanding's proprietorship over transcendental synthesis entails a further slippage of the imagination toward combination and concepts. Indeed, he countersigns once more what was the 'faculty of imagination' under the name of the understanding: "Thus the understanding, under the title of a *transcendental synthesis of imagination*, performs this act upon the *passive* subject, whose *faculty* it is . . ." (B153). And he characterizes the transcendental act of imagination as the "synthetic influence of the understanding upon the inner sense" (B154), thus tipping the scales toward the authority of combination over figuration. Combination of the manifold, to be sure, is a power lying beyond the realm of sensibility, and so it is the understanding that "*produces* it, in that it *affects* that sense" (B155). What is left for the imagination, however, is simply the "synthesis of apprehension," an empirical reflection of the figurative synthesis, and an act obtaining "under the title of imagination" though conforming necessarily to the (intellectual) "synthesis of apperception" under the title of "understanding" (B160–61 note b).[13] And insofar as both events consist in "one and the same spontaneity," the indebtedness to the understanding is all but assured once more. Kant expresses this very point by continuing to delimit what remains proper to the imagination in terms of apprehension alone: "Now it is the imagination that connects the manifold of sensible intuition; and imagination is dependent for the unity of its intellectual synthesis upon the understanding, and for the manifoldness of its apprehension upon sensibility" (B164–65). In short, though we should not expect the A and B versions of the Deduction to constitute one unified project, we are compelled to admit that this justification of the categories leaves the imagination in an uncertain light. It is a lens through which synthesis, combination, spontaneity, and unity may be magnified by the light of understanding, but a lens that, when examined in its own light, has none of the determinability it is meant to serve. One wonders whether the imagination's synthesis is only transcendental on the basis of intellectual combination, or if there is indeed an *a priori*, creative, unifying capacity within or alongside of intuition itself?

Time-bound mediation in the Schematism

If the exposition of the transcendental elements of *a priori* cognition leaves the imagination in a position of crucial function yet uncertain status, "The Schematism of the Pure Concepts of Understanding" (the first chapter in Kant's 'Analytic of Principles') positions the transcendental synthesis of imagination in terms of the events of subsumption and judgment. What problem necessitates this further return of the imagination from 'elsewhere'? To speak of the "employment" of "elementary concepts [*Elementarbegriffen*]" is to speak in reference to the *transcendental doctrine* of judgment (B169), and thus to come to the matter of that correctness or validity on which the application of concepts to appearances stands: "the possibility of synthetic judgments" (A154/B193). As it is the activity of the understanding, through its categories, that translates all the elemental work of synthesis and combination into the mode of judgment, and because sensibility is required for this work and its translation, Kant calls the schematism "the sensible condition under which alone pure concepts of understanding can be employed" (A136/B175). The condition provides the grounds for judgment as a mode of 'subsumption,' a term right away freighted with a matrix of necessity and relation. Under general conditions, subsumption requires a point of homogeneous relation between the object and the containing concept. The problem for transcendental judgment is that the pure concepts of understanding are heterogeneous to their objects, sensible intuitions. "How, then," Kant asks, "is the *subsumption* of intuitions under pure concepts, the *application* of a category to appearances, possible?" His answer rests with identifying a mediating term, a "third thing, which is homogeneous on the one hand with the category, and on the other hand with the appearance, and which thus makes the application of the former to the latter possible" (A138/B177).

As we remain on the level of transcendental operation, Kant describes this mediating entity as a "representation." Unique to the governing necessity that this representation be homogeneous to two heterogeneous elements, however, is that it reverses the general order of synthesis, combination, and unity thus far sustained in Kant's larger discussion. To attain a mediating "*transcendental schema*" that is "*intellectual*" in one respect and "*sensible*" in another is to disclose a matter by way of regression to parts rather than progression to the whole of elemental possibility. Kant's instigating regressive move is to pass from the *understanding*, which "contains the pure synthetic unity of the manifold in general" to *time*, "the formal condition of the manifold of inner sense" (A138/B177), and thus to time as the *a priori* host of the manifold. (Heidegger will make much of this time-related imaginative synthesis.) As Kant later explains, "[t]here is only one whole in which all our representations are contained, namely, inner sense and its *a priori* form, time" (A155/B194). Time is homogeneous to the category as well as appearance, and thus works as a point of mediation in the formal sense. Though not itself a representation, time indicates a formal sensible condition to which the employment of the understanding is bound— what Kant terms "the *schema* of the concept"—and thus a condition that may serve to guide the "*schematism* of pure understanding" (A140/B179).

Before addressing the question of imagination in this context, it is important to acknowledge that here we turn a rather difficult corner in Kant's argumentation. As we have begun to see, he not only must halt the activity of judgment (presumably spontaneous) so as to catch a mediation underway, but also must then exhibit the manner in which this schematizing relation obtains. This amounts to the disclosure of an occurrence of mediation within an event of subsumption. Though by many accounts this would seem a rather hypothetical venture in the operation of transcendental reflection, Kant's reference to the Aesthetic (namely time as form of inner sense) wins for him a case in which a sensible form is, so to speak, necessarily conceptualized. Time is unique insofar as it is the pure intuition in which objects are intuited and concepts are pressed into activity. The transcendental subject works 'in' time with objects intuited 'in' time. Time is homogeneous 'as' a condition for sensibility and understanding. In the Second Analogy, Kant will summarily declare that the "synthetic faculty of imagination . . . determines inner sense in respect of time-relation" (A189/B233). If time is the 'condition' for thinking the possibility of the transcendental schema, then in what way does the imagination constitute its 'art'?

Though schematism belongs to the understanding, a given schema, says Kant, "is always a product of *imagination*" (A140/B179, my emphasis). We are already familiar with such a tension, and remain curious to know how the product of one faculty can belong to another. One might regard the comment as a more specified way of echoing Aristotle's contention that "without images understanding is impossible."[14] But, again, we have already learned that what makes the imagination necessarily 'productive,' for Kant, is not images *per se* (which would be reproductive and empirical), but its service in furnishing a "connection" (A189/B233) or unity by which intellectual synthesis, combination, or the understanding more generally, may determine sensible objects. Without the imagination there is no synthesis of representations, and thus no synthetic unity, which means ultimately no transcendental judgment (cf. A155/B194). Since the progression of conditions is a story of figuration and connection, a mere 'image' will not suffice. But what distinguishes a schema from an image, and what has a schema to do with the imagination?

When Kant insists that "the schema has to be distinguished from the image" (A140/B179), he has in mind the nature of a schema to represent a "method" or form of, for example, multiplicity, and not a singular intuition. "No image," Kant explains, "could ever be adequate to the concept of a triangle in general. It would never attain that universality of the concept which renders it valid of all triangles" (A141/B180). On the basis of their representational power in the imagination, schemas have a conceptual bearing. Kant's example locates the discussion in the context of Aristotle's consideration of the triangle 'drawn' as an image within the understanding.[15] Here Aristotle cites the inherent need for such an imaginative sketch, provided "the mind understands it only as a quantity."[16] In his commentary on this text, Aquinas explains that Aristotle is attempting to maintain a tension between the understanding's need to "*conjure up* before our eyes an image of *determinate* size"—the need for a 'particular' representation—and yet still recognize that such determinacy does not apply to the 'concept' of what is sought.[17] Imagination, in this way, aids the understanding provided the understanding qualifies it: an image of a triangle produces a determinate representation, from which the quantitative determinacy (and not the sketch proper) yields a conceptual determinacy that may be used in proofs. Kant's distinction between schema and image is meant to simplify this confusion, while at the same time emphasizing the relationship between rule and unity furnished by the schema. In keeping with the formal condition that is time, the schema's mediating necessity requires that it be a representation of what exceeds the imaged—in the case of a triangle, "a rule of synthesis of the imagination, in respect to pure figures in space" (A141/B180). The same holds for schemata of the pure concepts of understanding:

> It is simply the pure synthesis, determined by a rule of that unity, in accordance with concepts, to which the category gives expression. It is a transcendental product of

imagination, a product which concerns the determination of inner sense in general according to conditions of its form (time), in respect of all representations, so far as these representations are to be connected *a priori* in one concept in conformity with the unity of apperception. (A141–42/B180–81)

Ambiguities remain, but what is significant for our present purposes is that Kant has based his account of the schematism on the mediating privilege of 'pure synthesis,' and has in turn based such synthesis on the effect of the imagination. Schematism itself belongs to the understanding, but, quite apart from a 'bringing to' *of* the understanding or an 'intellectual synthesis,' the mediation depends on "the transcendental synthesis of imagination" (A145/B185). Transcendental judgments' need for a homogeneous/heterogeneous principle of mediation between the categories and objects of representation echoes understanding's need for a figurative/intellectual synthesis. Both are bound to the imagination as the aesthetic point of delivery for the manifold—a point of intrinsic figuration and synthesis that is productive beyond the bounds of sensibility's passivity, yet not so active as to be determinative in its own right.

Between the visionary and inventive

If we follow the movement of the first *Critique* through judgment to the Transcendental Dialectic, we find a higher, more practical, formulation of these same tensions. When, for example, Kant speaks of "The Ideal of Pure Reason" he has in mind the manner in which the assemblage of cognitive powers, delimited by critique, may attain to the complete *determination* of given appearances and the regulative principles of actions. An ideal, in this sense, "must always rest on determinate concepts and serve as a rule and archetype, alike in our actions and in our critical judgments" (A570/B598). The critical and practical (ethical) bearing of such archetypes evidences the more constructive, indeed ambitious, tenor of these later remarks. We are no longer on the terrain of the elemental, but have ascended to the hard-won edifice of pure reason's possibility. And here Kant returns once again to the matter of imagination—in this case, as a counter-example to reason's ideal:

> The products of the imagination are of an entirely different nature; no one can explain or give an intelligible concept of them; each is a kind of *monogram*, a mere set of particular qualities, determined by no assignable rule, and forming rather a blurred sketch drawn from diverse experiences than a determinable image—a representation such as painters and phsyiognomists profess to carry in their heads, and which they treat as being an incommunicable shadowy image [*Schattenbild*] of their creations or even of their critical judgments. (A570/B598)

On the surface this says: what is born from the imagination is as obscure as the process precipitating it, and thus an inadequate measure for the determinacy of reason. Pure reason must be on guard against the whims of the sensible. And yet, if viewed from the side, the counter-example is simply a comparison: there *is* an obscure work of the imagination, and though it may not suffice as a resource for ideal archetypes, it may well serve another, possibly artistic, end. When Kant later considers the place of *hypothesis* in pure reason he turns once more to the imagination: "If the imagination is not simply to be *visionary* [*schwärmen*], but is to be *inventive* under the strict surveillance of reason, there must always previously be something that is completely certain, and not invented or merely a matter of opinion, namely, the *possibility* of the object itself" (A770/B798). The remark sustains the practical concerns introduced in The Ideal of Pure Reason, and we must not mistake this 'imagination'—this 'inventiveness'—for the transcendental imagination or its synthesis. But there is a resemblance of signification in the terms "*schwärmen*" and "*Schattenbild*," as if to imply that theories and opinions, like artistic representation, skirt the edge of reason's creative employment without meeting the criteria of determinant measures. This does little to suggest an embrace of the imagination on the constructive side of the critical project, but neither do these allusions amount to a statement of its full exclusion. The creative or inventive imagination is left, at this stage in Kant's discourse, in a position of qualified possibility.

Repurposing imagination in the *Critique of Judgment*

If, under the measures of the first *Critique*, the imagination and its artistic products or inventions attain a mere monogram or sketch, there is in the *Critique of Judgment* (1790) the rather astonishing discovery of a "momentum" (184/315) whereby the imagination is "free," released to a new level of interaction with the understanding and capable even of carrying understanding beyond the determinations of the concepts into the constitution of *genius* (185/316–17). Art, says Kant, is a "production through freedom" based in reason (170/303), and the fine art of the genius arises as means "for producing something for which no determinate rule can be given" (175/308). In this case, the rule or measure of the painter, poet, or composer is prescribed by nature in accordance with a "talent" (174–75/307–08) that is trained by trial and taste to produce an object in the excess of the rational concept. This is a remarkably different species of 'possibility' than the *Schattenbild* of the first *Critique*. It speaks to a creative imagination, which in fact "aesthetically expands the concept itself in an unlimited way" (183/315), 'quickening' [*beleben*] the cognitive powers (185/316–17) rather than threatening them. When Kant regards such possibility within the framework of imaginative presentations he terms *aesthetic ideas*, he speaks of the imagination as a "productive cognitive power" that is "very mighty when it creates, as it were, another nature out of the material that actual nature gives it" (182/314). There is no reason to believe he does not mean the same productive imagination discussed in the first *Critique*, but he is orienting it toward a new scope of animation. Several intervening discoveries are required to disclose the 'ideas' presented by the imagination of, most notably, the poet—whose talent equips him with the "inner intuitions" necessary to "venture . . . beyond the limits of experience," emulating the "example of reason" so as to furnish expressions of elements "with a completeness for which no example can be found in nature" (182–83/314). How is it that the imagination becomes this aesthetic agent of arousal and quickening, and might *judgment* itself (not simply genius) exhibit an adjoining level of possibility?

At play in the judgment of taste

The elucidation of the Schematism under the transcendental doctrine of judgment in CPR, together with the motion or effect of the imagination in furnishing the requisite schemata, presents a fitting bridge to CJ's grounding considerations. Kant's larger question remains that of his initial elemental and constructive itinerary: How are synthetic judgments possible *a priori*? However, the bridge consists in the traversal of a new discovery concerning judgment, and with it a new terrain of inquiry. Where the Schematism brought the productive imagination to bear and support the weight of validity in determinative judgments, Kant is now focused on the conditions of possibility for *reflective* judgments, and *aesthetic* judgments in particular. Of primary interest is the manner in which this traversal leads to the unique arraignment of the judgment of *taste*, and herein the status of the imagination in the function of permitting an object to be termed 'beautiful' without surrendering any objective universality in the determination. Kant asks:

> How is a judgment possible in which the subject, merely on the basis of his *own* feeling of pleasure in an object, independently of the object's concept, judges this pleasure as one attaching to the presentation of that same object *in all other subjects*, and does so a priori, i.e., without being allowed to wait for other people's assent? (153/288)

Kant is aware that the scope of the question already threatens to undo the rigor erected in the service of understanding's determinate employment within the transcendental doctrine of judgment. How could the integrity of subsumption—so intrinsic to the correct connections between concepts and sensibility—withstand this dalliance with a 'feeling' somehow beyond the domain of a containing concept? Is this not indicative of an enthusiastic profession masquerading in the subject as a communicable measure? What prevents such judgment from borrowing on the currency of hypothesis and inventing its own critical authority? Kant's specific answer, according to the "Analytic of the Beautiful," is that the *purposiveness* of a given thing's *form* supplies the judgment with the *a priori* condition required for determinant validity (27/187). This distinct, nonpractical purposiveness Kant characterizes as the "attainment of an aim," and such attainment is experienced as the subjective feeling of pleasure (27/187). As a result, the given thing is called "beautiful," and "our ability to judge by such pleasure (and hence also with universal validity) is called *taste*" (30/190). It is sufficient at present to highlight how these movements center on a crucial emphasis concerning *form*, and thus entail a significant burden upon, and provocative reappraisal of, the *imagination*.

We have already noted the underlying and imperative nature of 'form' within the *a priori* terrain mapped by the Transcendental Aesthetic. There the form of an object's appearance stood 'ready in the mind' as a capacity for representation and thus proximate to the imagination's task of synthesizing the manifold of pure intuition. A similar elementary relationship of *aesthēsis* remains in the judgment of taste, though the critique at hand is situated in within the larger task of reconciling the *a priori* legislation of the understanding (for nature) with that of reason (for freedom). Since the question of taste entails a specific class of objects, its treatment is less concerned with identifying the transcendental elements in their general positioning, and more intent on accounting for their work in a rather focused application. This means, as we will see, that the 'form' of the object will constitute the basis of 'pleasure' insofar as it remains in play (or motion[18]) through apprehension, but without a restriction to the operations of sensibility. For this reason we do well to recall the elemental role of form and imagination in the work of cognition, but must understand that Kant's 'reflective' appeal to them is now as much a matter of justifying this new species of judgment as it is a question of their elemental capacities. The judgment indeed concerns an object of intuition, but not with a view to determinate cognition (29/189), and so turns on a translation or specification in Kant's treatment of form (and with it a different aesthetic orientation). Aesthetic judgment, Kant explains, "is a special power of judging things according to a rule, but not according to concepts" (34/194). Such judgment "contributes nothing to the cognition of its objects" (34/194), but nevertheless remains reliant on the "spontaneity in the play of the cognitive powers" (37/197), and based on a mediating *a priori* principle in its application to art. How does this new emphasis on form pertain to an affiliated reorientation in Kant's understanding of the imagination?

Returning to the matter of *purposiveness* in a judgment "whose determining basis *cannot be other* than *subjective*" (44/203), the formal means by which the judgment is performed are meant to safeguard against any misguided inclinations of *interest* on the part of the subject. "Interest," says Kant, "is what we call the liking we connect with the presentation of an object's existence . . . But if the question is whether something is beautiful, what we want to know is not whether we or anyone cares . . . about the thing's existence, but rather how we judge it in our mere contemplation of it (intuition or reflection)" (45/204). An authentic feeling of pleasure thus depends on a formal, nonmaterial apprehension in sensibility (44/204). A valid taste for beauty, as it were, depends on the strict 'presentation' of the object in much the same way as a logical–determinative judgment depends on the strict presentation of the synthesis of the manifold before the combining work of the understanding and the unity of apperception. Kant means to highlight this *resemblance* when he notes plainly: "I have used the logical functions of judging to help me find the moments that judgment takes into consideration when it reflects (since even a judgment of taste still has reference to the understanding)" (43/203n1). But the measures assuring the presentation belonging to taste are not delineated by the accelerating emphasis on determinability observed in the B Deduction, which likewise suggests that the imagination in taste need not suffer the obfuscations attending its productive, synthesizing aspect in the first *Critique*. In the first "Introduction" to CJ, Kant explains that in "an aesthetic judgment of reflection . . . the basis determining [it] is the sensation brought about, in the subject, by the harmonious play of the two cognitive powers [involved] in the power of judgment, imagination and understanding" (413/224). Such status for the power of imagination may have been anticipated by Kant's comments on synthesis at CPR A78/B103, and his inclusion of the imagination among the "three original sources" of the soul at A95, but this notion of *harmonious play* ("the mutual harmony of imagination and understanding," 412/224) denotes a qualitative equality that is altogether new.

In §9 of "The Analytic of the Beautiful," Kant explains how this harmonizing activity is connected to the aforementioned matters of presentation and pleasure at the very center of taste's determining basis:

> The cognitive powers which are set into play by this presentation are thereby in free play, because no determinate concept restricts them to a particular rule of cognition. Hence the mental state in this presentation must be the feeling of the free play of the presentational powers in connection with this presentation and directed to cognition in general. Now if a presentation by which an object is given is, in general, to become cognition, we need *imagination* to combine the manifold of intuition, and *understanding* to provide the unity of the concept uniting the [component] presentations. This state of free play of the cognitive powers . . . must be universally communicable; for cognition, the determination of the object with which given presentations are to harmonize (in any subject whatever) is the only way of presenting that holds for everyone. (62/217)

Freed 'from' concept 'for' harmonious play with understanding, the imagination and its effect (*Wirkung*) must still serve the purposes of communicability. Insofar as beauty "is nothing by itself" without reference to subjective feeling (63/218), its determination depends on a mental state and not on a conceptually determined characteristic of the object. But for this necessity, in turn, to attain a justifiable mode of communicability (paralleling the objective validity of logical–determinative judgments) it must find its resource in the *harmony* of the powers and not in an intellectual schematizing. Ever the criterion for determinability and validity, 'unity' in this case, consists not in the application of the categories but rather in the "quickening" and "reciprocal harmony" of imagination and understanding (see 63/218–19). Specifically, the imagination presents the form of the object—its purposiveness—carrying it up into a play with the understanding and ultimately referring it not to subsumption but to the potentially pleasurable feeling of contemplation (see 68/222). To say that taste's "determining basis is therefore merely the purposiveness of the form" (69/223) is to ground the judgment on an apprehension performed by the imagination, though without any determinative concept. This amounts to a considerable work of the imagination. As John Sallis observes: "the reflection from which the harmonious interplay can issue is not performed by some agency that would supervene on the process; rather, it is already underway with the very apprehension, provoked, induced, by the apprehension of form in the imagination . . . in the apprehension imagination is in play already, from the outset, in interplay with understanding."[19] In sum, Kant has allowed the imagination to perform a central work in assuring the formal nature of the judgment, the authenticity of the feeling of pleasure that is/is not evoked by the object, and thus the determination of beauty. One would expect that such a result is beset by the limitations of the subjective, aesthetic nature of it. However, the determination's 'resemblance' to a logical judgment is further sustained when Kant says the determination has a universalizable objectivity (62–3/218). The work of the imagination herein, then, is of such a rigor and authority that it is rescued from the dim shadows of mere inventiveness and could not be further from anything like phantasy.

The supersensible imagination

Like the judgment of taste, that of the *sublime* consists in a reflective judgment that is singular yet universally valid, and in which the imagination acts as a "power of exhibition" that may ultimately 'further' reason without having recourse to determinate concepts (97/244). The difference between the judgments consists in their presentations, and hence in the qualitative aspect and movement of the imagination. Kant explains: "The beautiful in nature concerns the form of the object, which consists in [the object's] being bounded. But the sublime can also be found in a formless object, insofar as we present *unboundedness*, either [as] in the object or because the object prompts us to present it" (98/244). Beyond the qualitative presentation of beauty in excess of understanding's determinate concepts, the sublime's quantitative presentation exhibits "an indeterminate concept of reason" (98/244). Both judgments contain 'likings,' however, what was 'pleasure' and 'play' under taste is "seriousness" and "admiration" under the sublime. If in taste the imagination was oriented toward purposiveness, the sublime judgment apprehends and feels something in nature that at first seems "contrapurposive . . . incommensurate with our power of exhibition, and as it were violent to our imagination" (99/245). Nature arouses the imagination, that is, by way of chaos, exceeding the scope of presentable 'form' yet agitating our judgment in a way that nevertheless further attunes the "purposive use" of the imagination (100–01/246–47). As the imagination comes to recognize its own limits when faced with the excess of nature (mathematically or dynamically), an altogether new level of schematizing obtains—the difference between the sensible and supersensible is disclosed, the subject is in turn agitated, and the imagination begins to extend into the realm of morality (124/265).

To appreciate these movements we must understand that Kant is neither treating objects of sense nor limiting the force and power of the sublime to the side of nature. More specifically, we must appreciate how it is that the 'violence' felt by the imagination in such a judgment places the imagination on the threshold of a larger attunement of the intellect. As, for example, "our power of estimating the magnitude of things in the world of sense," the imagination faces the specter of its own "inadequacy," then translates the arousal of this reckoning back into "the feeling that we have within us a supersensible power" (106/250). The imagination, that is, is affected and effects an "emotional satisfaction" such that the magnitude of "crude nature" (109/252–53) discloses an inadequate apprehension on the one hand, and (since we are aware of this inadequacy) "a mental power that surpasses any standard of sense" on the other (111/254). Says Kant, "If the human mind is nonetheless to *be able even to think* the given infinite without contradiction, it must have within itself a power that is supersensible" (109/253). That the imagination makes such a necessity possible is not unlike its role in furnishing schemata in the first *Critique*—both uses consist in the imagination as a mode of estimation, though in a sublime judgment it is the "effort" of the imagination in view of its very 'inadequacy' that testifies to "a supersensible substrate (which underlies both nature and our ability to think), a substrate that is large beyond any standard of sense and hence makes us judge as *sublime* not so much the object as the mental attunement in which we find ourselves when we estimate the object" (112/255–56). As a measure of attunement, then, the imagination is also productive of a "supersensible vocation" within reason's 'respect' for law. In this more practical bearing, imagination's feeling of inadequacy to an idea denotes a striving *for* adequacy, and thereby "makes intuitable for us the superiority of the rational vocation of our cognitive powers over the greatest power of sensibility" (114–15/257–58). Displeasure over inadequacy moves the reflection toward the pleasure attached to the magnitude of ideas of reason. What is felt as contrapurposive signals an intrinsic capacity for the purposiveness of reason "as the source of ideas, i.e., as the source of . . . intellectual comprehension (117/260). Speaking from this movement of imagination, Kant explains that "the subject's own inability discloses in him the consciousness of an unlimited ability which is also his" (116/259). What is by necessity an aesthetic discovery yields, by way of the imagination, a larger attunement in the power of reason.

The same structure applies under the dynamically sublime, where it is the power of nature that arouses in us a vocation of "strength" by, specifically, elevating "our imagination [to] exhibit those cases where the mind can come to feel its own sublimity" (121/262). Accordingly, Kant notes that "the imagination strains to treat nature as a schema" (124/265) for reason and indeed in an aesthetic judgment such as this the feeling for the sublime is referred to reason and not the understanding (125/266). Though, as in the case of beauty, concepts are not the destination for the imagination's work, what the imagination constitutes in the sublime is a *relation* (more than a quality) by which we recognize how "the sensible [element] in the presentation of nature [is] suitable for a possible supersensible use" (126/266–67). Kant characterizes this as a "moral feeling" that, like the communicability of taste, "*obligates absolutely*" (126/267). He explains: "The judging strains the imagination because it is based on a feeling that the mind has a vocation that wholly transcends the domain of nature . . . and it is with regard to this feeling that we judge the presentation of the object as subjectively purposive" (128/268). In the imagination of the poet, for example, the purposiveness felt by a view of an ocean calmly "bounded only by the sky" or as "an abyss threatening to engulf everything" constitutes an aesthetic judgment that reflects back upon the lawful purposiveness of subjective freedom (130–32/270).

The free hand and the fundamental retrieval

My preceding discussions do not exhaust the question of the imagination in Kant's thought but the synopsis affords a necessary and adequate account of those touchstones in the problematic, together with the attending questions, which are essential to the way forward. Though mine is not a book on Kant, *per se*, without his recovery and redeployment of this mysterious faculty of the soul my investigation would exhibit a rather 'blurred sketch' of its subject matter, and there would be little imagination to speak of in the thought of Schelling or Heidegger. In view of the work ahead, and in keeping with my textual focus, I want now to say an introductory word regarding the pronounced way in which these thinkers found in Kant's treatment of the imagination not only a vital problematic, but also more importantly a point of possibility and orientation for their own distinct paths.

Imagination in the depth of intuition

Already in his *Philosophical Letters on Dogmatism and Criticism* and *Of the I as Principle of Philosophy* (1795) Schelling exhibits a decided focus on broadening the scope and centrality of both *intuition* and *imagination* as delimited by Kant. That is not to say Kant's more constructive hopes for carrying his system "of the *epigenisis* of pure reason" (CPR B168) forward under the disciplined ideal of pure reason or its practical employment are lost on Schelling, or that reason's canon of questions (*What can I know? What ought I do? What may I hope?*, A805/B833) and higher systematic hopes for the legislation of knowledge in its diverse modes (A832/B860) are beside the point. Rather, it is to acknowledge with Kant the then 'ruinous' state of the sciences and the forked road of dogmatism and skepticism (A852–56/B880–84), and yet to return through Kant to the unspent resources of the transcendental elements. Schelling says of intuition: "Kant started from this that the first in our knowledge is the intuition [*Anschauung*]. Very soon this gave rise to the proposition that the intuition is the lowest grade of knowledge. Yet it is the highest in the human mind [*Geist*], it is that from which all other knowledge borrows its worth and its reality" (UHK 145n.97/ SW1 355). And of the imagination: "It is to be hoped that time, the mother of all development, will also foster and eventually develop, unto completion of the whole science, those seeds of great disclosures about this wondrous faculty which Kant has sown in his immortal work" (LDC 190n/SW1 333).

But to understand the connection between this highest grade and this promising faculty, it is important to note that Schelling's thought at this time maintains with Fichte the primacy of an *unconditional* certainty—namely the certainty that *I am I*.[20] The Pantheism Controversy of the 1780s had resulted, in part, in focusing the reception of Kant's first *Critique* on this question of the unconditioned 'I' in the consciousness of the transcendental subject.[21] If the subject provides the ground for his own knowledge of 'nature' (Kant: '*natura materialiter spectata*', CPR B163), this suggests, for Fichte, that the subject is free in self-reflection and thus necessarily noumenal. Seen in this way, the question of the unconditioned (*das Unbedingte*), particularly for Schelling, becomes a matter not only in the order of knowing, but also for the order of being. Deeper than Kant's transcendental unity of apperception, and more concrete than his 'idea' of an unconditioned laying at the origin of a complete synthesis or beyond reason in the things themselves (cf. A416–17/B443–45), Schelling has in mind the manner in which the subject attains a free, nonsensuous intuition of the "eternal" on which the judgment that any being "is" a being, and not merely an appearance, depends. The basis for any relation between the subject and the objective world must, it seems, be grounded in a side of nature or being, which encompasses both; but taking the measure of such a unity would seem implausible to say the least. This necessity contributes to the aspirations of what is termed *intellectual intuition* (*intellektuelle Anschauung*), a form of knowledge drawn "from an immediate experience in the strictest sense, that is, from an experience produced by ourselves and independent of any objective causality" (LDC 180–81/SW1 318–19).[22]

It is not difficult to see how such an assertion turns the depth of Kantian intuition against the very criteria of critical philosophy. On the one hand, judgment is freed to recognize, without circumspection, the bearing of its determinacy on beings, not appearances. On the other, though it would be overly reductive to call Kant a thinker of 'objective causality,' the notion of an intuition lacking any sensible reference is untenable. Even the pure concepts of the understanding, though free in their employment from the limitations of sensible conditions, would be "empty" of "body and meaning" if void of sensible objects (CPR B148–49). The closest approximation available in Kant would be the subjective feeling for the supersensible substrate in the sublime judgment, though this requires a presentation of nature. Schelling's intellectual intuition would, nevertheless, seem to fail Kant's initial stricture that "it is not permissible to invent any new original powers, as, for instance, an understanding capable of intuiting its objects without the aid of senses" (CPR A770/B798). The question becomes whether or not the nonsensuous "eternal" qualifies as an 'object' of possible experience. I will not resolve the matter here, but will note that, insofar as intellectual intuition is an intuition of "the infinite" (LDC 186/SW1 327) in the self, Schelling understands it is a risky venture, and one that may well involve the imagination at its best or worst.

The risks and promise of intellectual intuition arise from the matter of *absolute identity* that moves in its depths.[23] Though detached from what we today may call the concrete world, such intuition is ultimately a profound matter of experience and existence. In a statement that sounds almost like a preparatory reference to Heidegger's being-in-the-world, Schelling asserts: "Even the most abstract concepts with which our cognition plays depend upon an experience of life and existence [*Dasein*]" (LDC 181/SW1 319–20). Intellectual intuition is an intensification of such experience, and its quality is not unlike Spinoza's 'self-intuition' (*Selbstanschauung*) (LDC 180/SW1 318). Though Schelling does not subscribe to Spinoza's view that immediate cognitions are intuitions of divine attributes, he does speak of the 'object' of such intuition as the 'eternal.' Adapting a language similar to that with which he describes the imagination, he observes:

> We all have a secret and wondrous capacity of withdrawing from temporal change into our innermost self, which we divest of every exterior accretion. There, in the form of immutability, we intuit the eternal in us. This intuition is the innermost and in the strictest sense our own experience, upon which depends everything we know and believe of the supersensuous world. It is this intuition which first convinces us that anything *is*, strictly speaking, while everything else merely *appears*, and *is* only inasmuch as we transfer the word *being* to it. This intuition is distinguished from every sensuous intuition by the fact that it is produced by freedom alone, and that it is foreign and unknown to any whose freedom, overcome by the invading power of the objects, is almost insufficient for the production of consciousness. (LDC 180/SW1 318)

The movement here described is inward not outward—from lived time to immutable eternity, and this by way of heightening experience, not diminishing it. What Schelling intuits is that depth of experience at the root of the sensuous consciousness and the supersensuous imagination, a depth wherein "time and duration vanish for us; it is not *we* who are in time, but time is *in us*; in fact it is not time but rather pure absolute eternity that is in ourselves. It is not we who are lost in the intuition of the objective world; it is the world that is lost in our intuition" (LDC 181/SW1 319). This language indicates that, at this stage in his development, Schelling stands midway between what Frederick Beiser calls the "subjective/formal" idealism of Kant and Fichte and the "objective/ absolute" idealism that Hölderlin, the early Hegel, and Schelling himself will adopt.[24] The depth of the intuition opens out upon an eternity that may well transcend the intuiting subject himself.[25] And the risk in this withdraw into the absolute identity 'of' the subject consists in an avoidance of the mystery it unfolds and thus a misdirection of its supersensuous element (LDC 187/SW1 328).

Schelling borrows a term from Kant to describe this mistake: *Schwärmerei* (enthusiasm, eccentric fantasy) (LDC 182/SW1 321).[26] It is an enthusiasm or swarming rapture for the 'the infinite' that, in the rush to command or delineate the discovery, forgets its location. Schelling explains: "Whenever such fantastication becomes a system, it arises from nothing but the objectified intuition, from the fact that one would take the intuition of oneself for an intuition of an object outside of oneself, the intuition of the inner intellectual world for an intuition of a supersensuous world outside of oneself" (LDC 182/SW1 321). This says that if what is intuited is the eternal, infinite absolute *in us*, then it can only be called a 'subject,' and yet it is so much the habit of consciousness to speak of intuited 'objects' that we imagine it thus and ascribe to it an otherworldly dimension. This is not merely a logical mistake. *Schwärmerei* has very good reasons, for the intellectual intuition is as much a story of strife as unconditional certainty. As I have begun to indicate, the specific consciousness of actuality (*Wirlichkeit*) it unfolds (the eternal, infinite) is utterly disorienting; it signals a potential vanishing of all objects, including the intuiting self. "I must grasp myself with might," says Schelling, "in order to save myself from the abyss of intuition" (LDC 185/SW1 325). The intuition thus comes at a considerable price, and 'enthusiasm' is phantasy's way of defraying the cost—though objectifying the absolute (as in dogmatism) will present its own abyss for the subject.

The task, then, in avoiding this risk and enduring this strife is for criticism (as Schelling understands it) to somehow balance its consciousness *of* actuality without imagining the intuited mystery (the absolute, the eternal) *as* actual and thus objective. At stake in this balance is the *freedom* of the imagination that, in Kant's *Critique of Judgment*, quickened the understanding beyond the limits of the conceptual. "The absolute," says Schelling, "if represented as realized (as existing), becomes objective; it becomes an object of *knowledge* and therewith ceases to be an object of *freedom*" (LDC 189/SW1 331–32).[27] Transcendental consciousness, by way of this radical intuition, is thus put in a position of having to arrest its own drive toward determinate knowledge (if criticism is to attend to the 'matter' in a more adequate way than dogmatism). The subject in whom the intuition unfolds is not to be confused with the 'subject/object' identity it intuits. Schelling finds Spinoza's confusion on this point rather telling, for Spinoza assumed "intellectual intuition was intuition of self . . . He believed himself identical with the absolute" and "lost in its nonfiniteness. Believing this, he deceived himself. It was not he who had vanished in the intuition of the absolute object. On the contrary, everything objective had vanished for him, in the intuition of himself" (LDC 181/SW1 319) Schelling is not yet able to pose an alternative, for neither criticism nor dogmatism offers an adequate approach to the 'actuality' of the intuited matter. However, he does entertain the possibilities of the imagination in navigating this impasse:

> And if criticism represents the ultimate goal as *realizable*, then, though it does not set up the absolute as an object of *knowledge* . . . it must leave a free hand to the faculty of imagination, which always anticipates actuality [*Wirklichkeit*], and which, standing halfway between the cognitive and the realizing faculty, takes a hand at the point where cognition ceases and realization has not yet begun. (LDC 190/SW1 333)

The Kantian structure of the imagination in both the first and third *Critiques* is evident. But, continuing, Schelling expresses doubts as to imagination's ability to avoid 'enthusiasm' (*Schwärmerei*)—would it not be all too inclined to represent the absolute as "realized" and not simply "realizable?" (LDC 190/SW1 333). There is an unresolved tension in his thought on this precise point. Attached to his hesitation over the imagination is a footnote in which he elaborates on the meaning of this 'faculty,' as though testing the worth of retrieving it out of its own depths. I have already quoted the closing word of hope earlier ('wondrous faculty'). The main body of the remark is as follows:

> Imagination [*Einbildungskraft*], as the connecting middle between the *theoretical* and the practical faculty, is analogous with theoretical reason inasmuch as this is dependent upon cognition of the *object*, and analogous with *practical* reason insofar as this produces its object, itself. Imagination *actively produces* an object by putting itself in complete dependence on that object, into full *passivity*. What the creature of imagination lacks in objectivity, imagination itself supplies by the passivity which, through an act of spontaneity, it voluntarily assumes toward the idea of that object. Thus imagination could be defined as the faculty of putting oneself into complete passivity by full self-activity. (LDC 190/SW1 333n)[28]

The emphasis on active passivity captures much of the confusion surrounding Kant's treatment of this power in the A and B Deductions. But to speak of "imagination itself" and its "act of spontaneity" without reference to understanding or combination is to thematize the faculty in a manner Kant would not or could not permit. How Schelling will come to adapt the Kantian imagination without inviting the misdirections of *Schwärmerei* remains to be seen. It is enough for now to note that the matter has appeared at the very heart of Schelling's early reflections on intellectual intuition. In this way, the imagination is of methodological and intuitive interest because the Absolute is of central interest. The depth of the intuition that signals the Absolute parallels the depth of imagination.

Imagination and interpretation in the depth of synthesis

Heidegger, like Schelling, locates both within and behind Kant's excavation of transcendental elements a critical itinerary far exceeding the mere delineation of epistemological faculties or the discipline of pure reason. If Schelling finds in Kant's breakthrough a possible means of securing passage to the Absolute, Heidegger finds a means of 'deducing' the turn of metaphysics to fundamental ontology. Both approaches, and their ensuing discourses, are shaped by larger tremors within the tradition—including Fichte's subjective idealism for Schelling, and Husserl's phenomenology for Heidegger[29]—but Heidegger, like Schelling, will uncover in Kant those elements that awaken philosophical possibility in a way that his era had not yet grasped. One clue to the nature of such possibility lies in the preface to the 1973 edition of his *Kant and the Problem of Metaphysics*. Heidegger remarks: "Kant's text became a refuge, as I sought in Kant an advocate for the question of Being which I posed" (KPM xv). The refuge was the manner in which Kant's *Critique* rendered metaphysics, the science "of beings as such in their totality," a problem for itself (xix). By placing reason before its own tribunal, Kant's project comprised a "laying of the ground" (*Grundlegung*) for metaphysics and thus an implicit reckoning with fundamental ontology as that which constitutes the very possibility of metaphysics (KPM 1/ GA3 1). That Heidegger's focus was on the first *Critique* and not on the third is evidently a result of this readiness to find in the question of *synthetic a priori knowledge* a point of dialogue with his own project in *Being and Time* (1927). His 1929 text is the first publication following *Being and Time*, and is itself based on a 1927–28 Marburg lecture course in which he proceeds section by section through Kant's Transcendental Doctrine of Elements to the chapter on the Schematism. Thus, at the precise moment of his revolutionary work in the 1920s, it stands to consider that Heidegger apprenticed himself to Kant's first *Critique*. What we want to ascertain in this brief section is how and why Heidegger will privilege the *power of imagination* in Kant's project as "not just the mid-point 'between' pure intuition and pure thinking, but rather the mid-point in the sense of center and *root*" (PIK 195/GA25 287).

What has the question of *synthetic a priori knowledge* to do with fundamental ontology? What has *Einbildungskraft* to do with *Dasein*? In lecture courses from this period, Heidegger holds that Kant's *Critique* "is the first attempt since Plato and Aristotle to really make ontology a philosophical problem" (MFL 150–51/GA26 191–92) and "[t]ranscendental philosophy denotes nothing but ontology" (BPP 128/ GA24 180). This problem is borne out in the question of a 'laying of the ground' for metaphysics, insofar as Kant's *elemental* direction exceeds the scope of mere logical relationships and begs the deeper question of what it as once 'pure' and 'finite.' For Heidegger, retrieving the problem of ground-laying in part means relinquishing the assumption that being as such will emerge as a 'what' under the auspices of a general metaphysics, and at the same time restoring the "problem of the finitude in human beings" to the realm of the *Seinsfrage* (KPM 151/GA3 214). Such a retrieval involves reconsidering the place of finitude and ground in the posing of the question. For Kant to delimit the soul's faculties, for example, quite apart from compiling a list of transcendentals, is to gain some headway in this regard—to capture what is intrinsic to finitude and to regard the *a priori* possibilities of consciousness in terms of both meaning and necessity. Transcendental inquiry, that is, is not at root a mere question of "seeking particular grounds *for* something," but, more deeply, a question of attaining "insight into that which ground as such means" (MFL 213/GA26 275–76). If then the *ground* to be laid is, for Kant, the possibility of experience (what Heidegger terms "transcendence"), it is for Heidegger not a "principle" in the traditional sense, but rather "the expression of the most original phenomenological knowledge of the innermost, unified structure of transcendence" (KPM 81/GA3 115). It is in this vein of the 'innermost' matter that Heidegger will contend that "going-back to the origin [*Ursprung*]" in the ground-laying depends most of all on "the freeing of pure synthesis and with that the interpretation of the power of imagination" which is "the root of both stems, sensibility and understanding" (KPM 92/GA3 128; 138/197).

These elements, we are now well aware, present rather slippery footholds in Kant's path of investigation. For Heidegger, however, the ontological, hermeneutical, and phenomenological shape of Kant's ground-laying depends precisely on regarding "the transcendental power of the imagination" as the phenomenon that "reveals itself as the ground for the inner possibility of ontological synthesis" (KPM 92-3/GA3 129). Indeed, Heidegger believes Kant's general orientation toward the unity of pure intuition and pure thinking must "lead out beyond itself" by way of a deepening of the 'matter' that is the imagination: "in this way the transcendental power of imagination reveals itself more and more as a structure of possibility, i.e., in its making possible of transcendence as the essence of the finite self" (94/131–32; 106–07/150). Such disclosure already suggests that transcendental 'truth' and "ontological knowledge" are synonymous, and that imagination functions to 'form' transcendence in the depths of ontological synthesis (84–5/119–20). Even the essential *spontaneity* and *freedom* of pure thinking in general and pure apperception in particular must "spring forth [*entspringen*]" from the imagination. If one endeavors to 'lead back' pure intuition and pure thinking, he will find that the imagination "loses not only the character of an empirical faculty of the soul which has been picked up, but also the restriction, hitherto in effect, of its essence to the root-Being [*Wurzelsein*] for the theoretical faculty as such" (106–07/151).

In both his lecture course and the ensuing text, Heidegger makes this case by contending that the power of imagination is otherwise rendered "dispensable," and "everything operates on the basis of intuition and thinking as the point of departure" (PIK 191/GA25 281) *if* one allows Kant to give "mastery back to the understanding" even though, by Kant's own account, synthesis itself, and its spontaneous activity "springs purely from the power of imagination" (KPM 166–67/GA3 237; PIK 190/ GA25 279). More specifically, to allow that the logical function of understanding "codetermines what the power of imagination builds in this formation [*Gebilde*]" of synthesis 'brought' to concept is to neglect how the "*content* of a concept, which Kant calls concept of understanding, is constituted by [the pure synthesis], i.e., *imaginatively unified time*" (PIK 190/GA25 280; 192/283). Kant's carelessness and evident reluctance with respect to this 'indispensable function of the soul' is not simply disappointing, but amounts to an inconsistency whereby Kant will, on the one hand, explicitly distinguish imagination from understanding, and yet proceed to allow the *unity* underwriting synthesis, concepts, and the larger logical function of judgment to fall under the determinacy of understanding (PIK 188–89/GA25 277).[30] Speaking from the context of CPR A79/B104f, Heidegger observes that "in all of Kant's subsequent discussions the power of imagination and understanding battle with each other for priority as the basic source of knowledge" (PIK 198/GA25 291–92). The imagination battles quietly from the margins, but remains strategic—sometimes evident in the confusion generated by its absence. This is the case in the Doctrine of the Schematism, a crucial discussion, which when viewed "in terms of the arrangement of the Kantian presentation . . . grounds the transcendental deduction." But when the categories are understood to "belong essentially to the original whole of the pure time-related imaginative synthesis," one understands the schematism as "a reference to the original sphere of the radical grounding of the possibility of ontological knowledge" (PIK 291–92/GA25 430–31). What these tensions reveal, for Heidegger, is that though Kant gives us reason to believe that transcendental imagination is at the center of the ontological ground-laying, he fails to follow this discovery to its proper and most penetrating conclusions.

That we today, with some exceptions, remain unaccustomed to reading the first *Critique* as an ontological treatise or phenomenological study bears retrospective witness to Kant's own reluctance in following the imagination to its radical end. There is a correspondence between our interpretive posture and Kant's analytic position. This means that Heidegger, more than simply protesting on behalf of the imagination, must undertake a new mode of interpretation. We have already begun to see this in play, but the issue requires more direct attention. Consider this clear description of the interpretive predicament from the 1927–28 course:

> When one reads the *Critique* under the pressure of tradition and so comes upon the power of imagination, this power appears at first as a suspicious faculty of the soul, i.e., fantasy [*Phantasie*]. Because one thinks that one has to purify Kant from psychology, one crosses out all these phenomena. Doing so, one is struck with the words and is blind to the dimension of human Dasein, into which Kant in fact looked, only to be scared away from it. If, on the other hand, we radically and without prejudice submit to the matters at stake and inquire into Dasein, then we shall see that it is completely erroneous to think that one must avoid as quickly as possible the power of imagination and the like. Whoever erases the power of imagination from the significant context of the problem of the *Critique* (as Kant himself was inclined to do), shall remove Kant from the abyss [*Abgrund*] on whose very edges every genuine philosophy must constantly move. We are for Kant against Kantianism. (PIK 189–90/GA25 279)

This says that what stands vulnerable under our reading—the imagination—is also a point of retreat for Kant, and yet what is nevertheless at the center of the first *Critique*. But this also suggests that 'genuine philosophy' is a matter of 'submission' to the 'matter' before it. At the end of this same lecture course, Heidegger remarks that in Kant "as in no other thinker one has the immediate certainty that he does not cheat" and indeed "the meaning of doing philosophy consists in awakening the need for this genuineness and in keeping it awake" (PIK 293/GA25 431). Kant does not cheat philosophy out of its necessary abyss, but to reawaken the 'genuine' philosophy he exemplifies, we must, as it were, remain with the very matter he could not sustain. For Schelling, we recall, intellectual intuition entertains its own abyss, and this position in turn leads Schelling to weigh the possibilities of the imagination. Heidegger's charge, in a similar manner, is to 'submit' to the abyss 'of' imagination in CPR by disclosing "the decisive content of this work and thereby to bring out what Kant 'had wanted to say'," so as to affect a "retrieval [*Wiederholung*]" of the ground-laying's more original possibility (KPM 137–38/GA3 195). The phenomenon of imagination requires a phenomenological mode of interpretation. To exhibit the ground-laying as an "occurrence [*Geschehen*]" through the shape of its "innermost drive" then, is an interpretive undertaking aimed at 'letting-be' the manner in which pure thinking is "rooted in the transcendental power of imagination" (KPM 146–47/GA3 209; 100/140).

Though the notion of saying what Kant 'wanted to say' is an easy bait for critics (Cassirer among them), Heidegger cautions that this is not "the wanting-to-know-better, but just the task of freeing the innermost drive of the ground-laying, and with it its ownmost problematic which guides all the efforts of the interpretation" (KPM 146–47/GA3 209). On the surface, 'submission' may lead to apparent 'violence'[31] against Kant's text, though it is in fact a means of 'liberating' his subject matter. For every mention of what *springs forth* in synthesis for the work of determination, Heidegger will insist on following the motion back to its subject, even when it means pointing "to connections which presumably are no longer explicitly in Kant's intentions, but still present themselves . . . " (PIK 194–95/GA25 286). Heidegger's *Auslegung* and *Fragestellung* carry the spirit of Husserl's '*Zu den Sachen selbst*' toward the disclosedness (*Erschlossenheit*) of the occurrence. If the hallmark of Kant's 'genuine' philosophy consisted in carrying out a critique "prescribed by the very nature of reason itself" (CPR Avii), a genuine *interpretation* of Kant's work consists in the parallel phenomenological necessity to attend to the 'matter' of the imagination in this work.

With these comments on the phenomenon and its interpretation in mind, we are in a better position to appreciate how the imagination sustains Kant's text as a genuine 'refuge' for Heidegger on the brink of the metaphysical 'abyss.' Within the text (the A Deduction especially) the ontological ground-laying discloses the imagination as the "primordial productivity of the 'subject'" (MFL 210/GA26 272).[32] This means the cognitive faculties—the "'creative' capacities of the finite human creature"—depend on the same creative, innermost ground of finitude, which contains the primordial understanding of Being.[33] Heidegger understands that this point would 'rattle' the metaphysical understanding of Being as that which enjoys a superlative universality, which, though indefinable, is thought to be conceptually self-evident on the basis of representational reflection.[34] When Kant 'shrinks back' from the imagination it is not because Hume is looking over his shoulder, but because he did not know to ground the powers of the soul in an "*antecedent fundamental ontology* of Dasein." Heidegger explains:

> Kant came upon the central function of the power of imagination. However, he did not come to terms with an interpretation of this power in terms of fundamental ontology; for this he was much too strongly tied to the traditional doctrine of the faculties of the soul and even more so to the division—still prevalent today—of the basic faculty of knowledge into intuition and thinking, which begins already in antiquity, with the distinction between αἴσθησις and νόησις.
>
> (PIK 190–91/GA25 280)

Had Kant acknowledged and heeded the ontological weight of the imagination, it would have required him to "raze his own building" (MFL 210/GA26 272). The transcendental subject would have to become the finite Dasein, for whom the imagination is fundamental to the possibility of any native understanding of Being.[35] Alas, "the question of the being of the Dasein as such is simply not raised" (BPP 153/GA24 218). But the first *Critique* is a refuge insofar as it affords a view back upon the ontological tradition, hovers in the mystery of a grounding synthesis, and points in every direction to the need for fundamental ontology. It is telling that, where Heidegger concluded his lecture course on a point of 'genuine' philosophy in Kant, he concludes *Kant and the Problem of Metaphysics* on the need to "befriend the essential, the simple, and the constant." The terrain of synthetic *a priori* knowledge enacted such a friendship (*philia*), sheltering the imagination in spite of itself, and so signals the genuine depth "from which the question concerning the concept of Being (*sophia*)—the grounding question of philosophy—arises" (KPM 168/GA3 239). What remains to be seen is the manner in which Heidegger's retrieval of the imagination remains an organizing principle or inner dynamic for his own elemental questioning, and to what extent it gives way or gives shape to other beginnings at the limit of metaphysics.

That the 'play' of the Kantian imagination is productive both *in* the powers of the soul and *for* the thought of Schelling and Heidegger is now evident. The pronounced, if ambiguous, contribution it affords to transcendental consciousness is paralleled by the force it brings to the itineraries of absolute idealism and fundamental ontology. Though the constellation of themes unfolding from Kant's recovery of the imagination may seem to affirm Hugo's exasperated pronouncement, "What floods ideas are! . . . and how rapidly they create frightful abysses!"[36] Schelling's interest in the depth of intuition and Heidegger's interest in the ontological ground of synthesis yield several elements that shall remain crucial in our study of the poetic imagination. These include the shape of imagination as a *spontaneous occurrence*, the position and meaning of imagination at the '*ground*' of finite being, its *motion* and reach beyond determinative concepts, its '*attunement*' in aesthetic production, and the larger means by which its presentative aspect signals a core *creative capacity* in the work of thought. To prepare the way for a 'poetic' turn in these elements we do well to recall the elusive 'flash' and 'happy impulse of the spirit' Kant observed in the imagination of the genius. Schelling speaks of "a certain profoundness of mind [*Tiefsinn*] of which one is not aware, and which one would try in vain to produce at will" (LDC 180/SW1 318). And Heidegger accounts for poetry's (*Dichtung*) singular privilege as bearing "the elementary emergence into words, the becoming-uncovered, of existence as being-in-the-world" (BPP 171–72/GA24 244). Such statements are uttered from the space wherein the architectonic concentration on the productive imagination opens out upon a broader terrain of *poiesis*, and thus evoke a sense of cautious possibility for cultivating Kant's 'root.'

Production and Artistry in Schelling's Philosophy of Identity

Having left Schelling at the borders of an intellectual intuition of the supersensuous and unconditional, and there extending a 'free hand' to the faculty of imagination, the aim of this chapter is to highlight the place of the imagination in the emergence of Schelling's philosophy of identity between 1797 and 1803.[1] We have noted the figurative and schematizing function of this power at the root of the possibility for synthetic judgments in Kant's first *Critique*, as well as its animated play and productivity in substantiating taste and furnishing aesthetic ideas in the *Critique of Judgment*. Never regarded in isolation, the imagination is indispensible to the treatment of representations and the reach of transcendental apperception in one sense, and integral to the quickening of the understanding and the supersensible stirrings of subjective freedom in the other. But what does a productive faculty, ostensibly limited to the realm of cognition, have to do with the larger odysseys of nature, history, and mind? By what necessities does this apparent 'root' of sensibility and understanding mature as both a matter of investigation and a mode of aesthetic, even philosophical, production?

The predicament is as practical as it is ambitious, especially for the thinker who believes philosophy "is itself the striving to participate in primordial knowledge [*Urwissen*]" (US 12/SW5 218). "Under the guise of Reason," says Maurice Merleau-Ponty in a lecture on Schelling, "is hidden an exercise of the arbitrary,"[2] and the task of manifesting and mirroring this exercise falls to a philosophy understood, in Schelling's terms, as a "science born of poetry" (STI 176/SW3 558–59). For the philosopher, Schelling appears to allow in 1797, "must possess just as much aesthetic power as the poet,"[3] and indeed (in 1802) "an artistic instinct is involved in philosophy no less than in poetry" (US 58/SW5 264). In a certain sense, the wager that there is a 'primordial' knowledge, together with our striving to 'participate' in it (and not merely apprehend it), is a claim that will be justified on the basis of showing what such a subject-matter does to reason when reason risks becoming an "aesthetic act."[4] This step, I believe, is precisely what Schelling ventures in a period of thought otherwise famous for his work on intellectual intuition and absolute identity. It is a period wherein Schelling speaks of the imagination as "the original activity *of the spirit*" (T 72/SW1 357) and contends that "'pure reason'" is not itself an "*absolute activity,*" but is "merely *imagination* enhanced (by practical reason)" (T 109/SW1 410, my emphasis). It is a period in which he likewise asserts that "what is commonly called theoretical reason is nothing else but *imagination* in the service of freedom" (STI 176/SW3 558–59), and that productive intuition, taken in its aesthetic aspect, is creative on the basis of the only capacity "whereby we are able to think and to couple together even what is contradictory—and its name is *imagination*" (STI 230–31/SW3 626–27).[5] Indeed, in the Jena lectures of 1802, Schelling holds that "reason and imagination . . . are one and the same" when understood in terms of the "inner esense of the absolute" (US 61–2/SW5 267). Such remarks begin to suggest an ascending labor of the 'free hand' from the spade work of *a priori* synthesis to the keystone by which the arches of theoretical and practical reason, the ideal and the real, are joined.

Even so, the temptation in writing on Schelling's thought in this period is to reduce it to a system of idealism centered on what, by 1801, he calls *the absolute* and its intuition in reason, and thereby work backwards and forwards through an apparent series of false starts, hesitations, and protean developments. There is no question 'the absolute' (from root *absolvere*, what is absolved from dependence on externality) emerges as the most definite article in his confederacy of identity, and that it comes to constitute the preeminent and primordial axis on which all that is real and ideal, phenomenal and pure, temporal and eternal, and natural and archetypical turn. It is all too easy, however, to take this matter as a gilded concept or synonym for 'God' and thereby blind oneself to the underlying adventure in which it arises. It is to miss the simple fact that Schelling is not interested in furnishing a "universally valid philosophy,"[6] but rather in exhibiting the necessary and possible "resolution of the real in the ideal" (US 9/SW5 215); and it is to forget that his every ascent to what is highest, purest, or metaphysically totalizing is in fact a strenuous recovery of what is already most original. We may begin to repair the glosses of the 'developmental' approach if we recall that Schelling is, with acute consistency, a thinker of unity by way of opposition, of a primordial 'whole' abiding behind the many differences or cleavages (*Entzweiung*) that subsist in the field of experience and the practice of knowing.[7] This is the dialectical pressure weighing on his larger discourse, and the very prospect of productive resolution is inspired specifically by the mediating activity of the creative faculty—what he calls the "true imagination," (as opposed to "the disorderly reproduction of sensory images"), the "poetry [*Poesie*] of philosophy" that "can be developed, enhanced, and its resources multiplied ad infinitum" (US 61–2/SW5 267–68). We soon discover, as well, that Schelling's is a philosophy of the absolute only because Schelling himself is a thinker of *standpoints*, and a thinker for whom, says James Dodd, philosophical reflection is "a striving for the elucidation of a hidden principle."[8] It is in his self-assigned task of thinking through and from a sequence of standpoints that, I hope to show, he tightens his grip on the imagination—both as a vital matter of investigation as well as a conscious partner in the exercises of intuition, production, and abstraction. Schelling, after all, will not hesitate to speak of the "creative imagination" as the site wherein "everything is free and moves about in the same realm without crowding or chafing, for each is within itself equal of the whole" (ART 37/SW5 393). To attribute this quality of concerted individuation and unity is for Schelling, as we shall see, the highest praise.

In the sections to come we will follow his passage through mere consciousness to self-consciousness, identity, and indifference. In so doing, I will specify his early attention to the necessary elements of mediation between poles of intuiting and producing, finitude and will, and consciousness and unconsciousness, as well as his remarkable treatment of aesthetic intuition and the status of the symbolic in works of artistic genius. I will argue that the power of imagination is afforded an increasingly poetic horizon—a work and life of imagination conducive of his arising interests in the unconscious, artistic productivity, and the deeper question of ground. The poetic horizon will be framed by Schelling's initial post-Kantian interest in *Einbildungskraft* and the problem of absolute identity, as well as his later, increasingly resolute post-Fichtean interest in *Ineinsbildung* and the problem of absolute reason. If, as I will indicate, Schelling's focus on intuition in its *productive* aspect is the blueprint by which he will reposition Kant's cognitive elements, the power of imagination provides the traction and stability required by the system he aims to ground. My primary focus will be on his 1797 "Treatise Explicatory of the Idealism in the *Science of Knowledge*," his 1800 *System of Transcendental Idealism*, and his 1802–1803 *Lectures on Art*; though I will also refer to his 1801–1802 *Presentations*, his 1802–1803 lectures at Jena entitled *On University Studies*, and his 1802 dialogue, *Bruno*. With these destinations and texts in view we now ask: In what framework and by virtue of which philosophical necessities does Schelling come to infuse the elemental imagination with the life of *creative production* and *poetic consciousness*?

The ideal receptivity for the real

Schelling's 1797 "Treatise Explicatory of the Idealism in the *Science of Knowledge*" is a revealing propaedeutic to his systematic ambitions at a time in which the integrity of the Kantian project remains in question and the promise Fichte's subjective idealism is at once compelling and myopic. He anchors his discussion in a reading of Kant's first *Critique* meant to defend Kant from readers who misconstrue his philosophy as speculative. Short of any apology for the letter of Kant's cognitive architecture, Schelling echoes Fichte in offering an exposition of the spirit of the elemental terrain that celebrates the transcendental turn while also insisting on its need for a grounding, unconditional principle. As this objective unfolds, one learns that the principle is crucial to the operations of philosophical *inquiry* on the one hand, and to the integrity of human *consciousness* and the systemic essence of *spirit* on the other. He will in fact characterize the *unity* of these elements such that the Fichtean notion of a grounding determination (*Bestimmung*) is, with the aid of the imagination in at least two manifestations, pressed beyond the transcendental logic and formal identity to encompass spirit, reason, nature, and history in a concerted genesis of the *real*. Its title notwithstanding, the text is not a précis of Fichte's *Wissenschaftslehre*. While highlighting the Kantian emphasis on production in intuition, and embracing the priority Fichte affords the imagination, Schelling will follow the Fichtean path toward intellectual intuition and systemization yet escape the enclosure of the subjective ego by pressing the issue of synthetic identity. One finds in the *Treatise* an emerging conception of an ideal/real synthesis, the intuition of absolute identity expressive of such, and a focus on the power of imagination that prepares the way for his decisive appeal to the *mediating imagination* and *aesthetic production* in the *System*.

Schelling begins the *Treatise* by insisting that the true mettle of the philosophic spirit is measured by the intractable necessities which compel a thinker to demand of inquiry an answer to the question made central in Descartes and Hume, and bequeathed in a more revolutionary way by Kant: "What, then, is ultimately the reality that inheres in our representations?" (T 69/SW1 352–53).[9] Such a question foists itself upon empiricist tedium and dogmatic speculation with a stubborn drive toward the "higher principles" and "guiding ideas" that lie at the origin of knowledge, and evidences a marked dissatisfaction with the confusion engendered by the "chimera" of things in themselves (T 69/SW1 352–53, 72/357). Schelling's *System* will open on a similar note, insisting that the "*highest* task of transcendental philosophy" is to answer the question: "*How can we think both of presentations as conforming to objects, and objects as conforming to presentations?*" (STI 11/SW3 347–48). In this later formulation Schelling is direct in stating that the answer will entail a "*predetermined harmony*" between the ideal and the real, and still later, an "absolute indifference" of the two (P 370n.37/SW4 144). In the earlier formulation the qualification is more exploratory, as though the conception of such a harmony is still underway and shall be unfolded through an incremental procedure, ultimately resulting in his 1802 assertion that what is "purely ideal and thereby purely real" is in fact rooted in the archetypal nature of knowledge itself (US 10/SW5 216). In advance of this, he says in 1797 that the temper of the question demands two conditions in the thinker: "a primordial tendency toward the real [*zum Realen*], on the one hand, and a capacity to elevate oneself above reality [*das Wirkliche*]." What is meant by this apparent misdirection? Schelling explains that "without the former *such* a question will entangle us all too easily in idealistic speculations, and . . . without the latter the senses, rendered dull by the individual object, retain *no receptivity whatsoever* for the real" (T 69/SW1 352–53). Playing both on the meaning of 'reality' and on the trademark 'receptivity' of the sensible faculty, this says that the path of the primordial is a path of elevation, and that it is the privilege of sensibility to escape enthusiasm and the illusions of *das Wirkliche*. This attempt to hold together the real and ideal in a reciprocal, productive balance for inquiry is important because it mirrors the unity of activity Schelling will disclose within the cognitive faculties in general, and within intuition most importantly. Though his *System* will right away declare "absolute identity" to be the "ground of harmony between the subjective and the objective in action" (STI 4/SW3 333–34), and though his 1801 "Presentation of My System of Philosophy" will detail the absolute identity of subject and object, being and cognizing, *idealiter* and *realiter* in the propositional form of identity (A=A), the *Treatise* reveals the discovery of this necessity in a performative way.

Before tracing Schelling's initial development of these matters through the interior *activity* of intuition to spirit's own *striving* for self-determination, several points of orientation merit a more formal positioning. *First*, the very posing of the preceding question indicates that the theoretical interest in identifying the reality attached to representations, and thus the origin of cognitive knowledge, is (as Fichte held) already practical. As the question of an unconditional grounding determination develops into the question of absolute identity, it will always have an adjoining interest in explaining, beyond Kant, how and why "theoretical philosophy already presupposes practical philosophy in its very first principles" (T 101/SW1 399).[10] As is so often the case in Schelling, what is intimated through the power of suggestion nevertheless requires, and already anticipates, an intuition capable of catching such unity, as it were, in the act. *Second*, the Kantian preoccupation with respecting the unapproachable singularity of the noumenal substrate (things in themselves) is a useful clue to the *supersensuous* nature of the desired grounding principle, but amounts to a misleading boundary against this principle's attainment.[11] Schelling believes the very ability to draw the limitation, 'things in themselves,' already points to an intrinsic *act* of self-determination (namely the autonomy of the *will* in Kant's practical philosophy) on which the ability to distinguish between the "*real world of appearances*" and the "ideal *world of things in themselves*" depends (T 106–07/SW1 406–07). Schelling, at this time, is also more invested in the possibilities arising from a philosophy of nature than he is concerned with the elusiveness of the noumena. In 1796 he remarks: "While the Kantians . . . are grappling with figments of their imagination, their 'things-in-themselves,' men of truly philosophical spirit are quietly making discoveries in natural science, which healthy philosophy will soon put to use."[12] If his own *Philosophy of Nature* (1797) is any indication, he is *en route* to announcing, as he does in 1801, that the "standpoint of reason" consists in "a knowing of things as they are in themselves" and that "[t]he power that bursts forth in the stuff of nature is the same in essence as that which displays itself in the world of mind" (P 349/SW4 115, 358/128). The interweaving of points one and two in Schelling's thought will thus lead him to the central principle of the *will* in and behind all practical and theoretical activity, and to pitting the shared domain of the real and ideal (the "self-contained absolute world") against the phenomenal world belonging to the standpoint of "finite discursive reason" (US 14/SW5 220). The problems attending a dualism of the phenomenal and noumenal will be overcome by virtue of being absorbed into a higher standpoint.

The *third*, and related, point of orientation is implicit in the leading question and its conditional criteria: though Kant's edifice claims for its supports external and unknowable things in themselves and an internal transcendental unity of apperception, these theoretical principles are inadequate to the task of grounding a *system*. Something more is needed in order to bridge the gap between the genesis of the 'real' and the so-called 'reality' of our knowledge. "As long as we are merely concerned with setting up a philosophical *edifice*," says Schelling, "we may content ourselves with such a foundation, just as we are satisfied when the house we are building stands on firm ground. Yet when speaking of a *system*, we must ask on what the ground itself rests, and on what that second ground [rests], and so for ad infinitum" (T 101/SW1 399–400). A system, that is, must look within itself for its support and not to some "external ground for its movements and its coherence" (T 101–02/SW1 400).[13] Schelling is not yet in a position of asserting, as he will in 1802, that: "The original purpose of all philosophy is precisely to go beyond the facts of consciousness and to arrive at something absolute in itself" (US 63/SW5 269). The reason, however, is not reducible to a difference between subjective and objective idealism, but is better understood as a development by which the unconditional ground for a system is entertained as a necessity, then enacted as a standpoint, then understood more rigorously as both. The immediate task will be to observe how and where the distinction between edifice and system moves Schelling's investigation and shapes his accelerating interest in the question of a preconceptual ground. In so doing, we will see how Schelling deflects worries over "how the representations of this world could have entered *into* our consciousness" (T 77/SW1 364) so as to concentrate, rather, on the grounding 'for-itself' nature of *spirit* and the singular *freedom* underwriting intuition's intrinsic activity—both of which are evident, if undervalued, in the constructive work of Kant's productive imagination.

Finally, there is in the very question of the reality inhering in representations, and indeed in the presumption to inquire after the origin of knowledge of possible experience, a hermeneutical wager not lost on Schelling. To work at such is to risk an *analysis*—a parsing apart—of what is in consciousness spontaneous and "previously combined by necessity" (T 70/SW1 354). For example, Schelling will speak of the cognitive faculties in their own individual right, but he will at the same time wonder in dismay at philosophers "who to this very day charge Kant with 'an utter separation of the understanding and sensibility'" (73/359). A minimum of speculative partitioning is required, but the needs of inquiry must not occlude the 'whole' they purport to serve. Though Kant, "had to *dissect* human knowledge and concepts into their individual components . . . he left it to his heirs to delineate with one stroke the great, remarkable *whole* of our nature that is composed of these parts" (74/360, my emphases). Schelling likewise speaks of a "talent to *separate* what has never been separated, and to divide into thoughts what is *united* everywhere within nature," and also demands that such analysis (strict sense) be "conjoined with the *philosophical* [talent] that reunites what has been separated" (73–4/359–60, my emphases). Evidently, then, the methodological caution is itself meant to signal the larger emphasis on the overarching, systemic unity that Schelling will substantiate in terms of *activity* and *spirit*—the elemental markers of principled movement and relation of which perhaps even 'analysis' itself may be an expression.[14]

With these points of orientation aligned with Schelling's preparatory question, it is evident that the issue of *what reality inheres in representations* is simply the immediate and strategic opening upon a much deeper subject matter. How and why such an inquiry "belongs properly to *aesthetics*" (T 103/SW1 402) is not yet clear, though it will suffice for now to note that the spiraling motion is instigated from within Kant's own transcendental aesthetic, and it is to this discussion that we now turn.

The imagination and the genesis of activity

If the larger ambition of Schelling's *System* is "to enlarge transcendental idealism into what it really should be, namely a system of all knowledge" (STI 1/SW3 329–30), and if the domain of such expansion is the subjective, then "the sole organ of this mode of philosophizing is therefore *inner sense*," (13/349–50) meaning intuition. This root of the "subjective element in knowledge," then, will comprise the "nonconscious activity" which brings forth nature and anticipates the "conscious activity expressed in willing" (17/355–57, 12/348–49). In the *Treatise* Schelling elects to pursue this endeavor by explaining that within *intuition* there is an assemblage of moving parts that constitute a whole of activity. Kant "said that intuition had to be preceded by an affection of our sensible faculty, although he left the question concerning the origin of this faculty altogether undecided" (T 70/SW1 355). To mend this lacuna, Schelling begins by seeking this 'origin' *in* subjectivity—namely in intuition's most basic constitutive activity. The productive imagination is his clue: "If Kant spoke of a synthesis by the imagination in intuition, then surely this synthesis was an *activity* of our subjectivity and, consequently, space and time as forms of this synthesis [are] *modes of activity* of our subject" (71/355). It is one thing to treat the pure aesthetic forms of intuition (space and time) as "conditions for intuition," but the formal or general consideration of their nature forgets that they are "two absolutely opposing activities" that "can serve as a principle according to which the *material* of the original modes of activity of the subject can be determined in intuition" (71–2/356–57). The 'oppositional' nature of space and time consists in the pull of time toward object form, and the pull of space toward object extension; the purity of both works positively, while the need for determination and delimitation works negatively. This means intuition is a site in which "two activities, originally and by their very *nature* opposed, must be united . . . must convene, determine, and limit one another reciprocally" (72/357). To say that sensibility is 'receptive' is thus to say that it is comprised by a dialectical motion even at the level of its purest constituents. The formal motion of *opposition* then reflects back as a principle on the material *activity* of intuition more broadly, and this in turn marks the genesis of a consciousness of objects.

The significance of tracing the story of sensibility back through receptivity and affectivity to this interior, productive motion is this: the essential material activity of intuition is, for Schelling, analogous to "the entire system of the human spirit" (T 71/SW1 355). Within the focus on intuition, then, there is the Fichtean attention to the "imagination [as] the creator [*Schöpferin*] of consciousness"[15] and yet the momentum toward a system of spirit suggests that Schelling is poised to look beyond the anthropological depth of Fichte's self-positing 'I' to a larger domain of sensuous activity.[16] Schelling understands Kant's synthesis by the imagination as a "hint" (ibid) that the positive side of synthesis is "the original activity *of the spirit*" (72/357). In any given intuition, the 'object' is "strictly the product of the original, spontaneous activity of the spirit which creates and produces from opposing activities a third, communal one (*koinon* in Plato)" (72/357). Before treating the systemic level of spirit, then, we have a clear connection between the *activity of spirit* and the *activity of the productive imagination*; only the imagination is a faculty "capable of comprising and exhibiting in one communal product the negative and positive activities" (ibid). But what, exactly, is the meaning of *Geist* in this regard? Is it not tautological to speak of the intuiting self and the activity of spirit?

One must understand that Schelling's use of 'spirit' (*Geist*) in 1797 reflects his devotion to what Pfau calls the "domain of *intuition*" as opposed to the instruments of "a priori *concepts*" or the theoretical domain of the Fichtean 'ego.'[17] Spirit is indicative of a framework within which Schelling "is concerned with rethinking 'Being' (*Seyn*) in such a way as to preserve its material and historical autonomy as Being (*das Seyende*), albeit an autonomy that proves strictly relative (to Man)."[18] Just as intuition's focus concerns instances of underlying, preconceptual identity, *Geist* and *Seyn* denote an archetypal activity that results, among other things, in nature, matter, and self-consciousness. *Geist*, then, is an element regarded in terms of *constitution*—of consciousness and the identity enabling any consciousness of objects across historical genesis.[19] The tension, for Schelling, is that *Geist* is not a strict determinable entity (or substrate), but is nevertheless an entity that reflects "the unconditional identity of the absolute" and constitutes the "ground of unity for consciousness."[20] It is, as we will note, "that which is only its own object" and "can only be apprehended in its activity" (T 78–9/ SW1 366–67), as well as that which is manifest—as forms—in history, nature, and finite consciousness. Because of Schelling's interest in self-consciousness (cir. 1797–1800) he often speaks of the 'human spirit,' though there is a sense in which finite consciousness belongs to an anterior spiritual activity and not the reverse. Transcendental cognition, or even *reinen Vernunft*, is by no means equivalent to spirit. Rather, spirit is closer to the Scholastic conception of God as *nous* and *logos*, the active, creative divine mind at work in history.[21] Spirit names an agency that is before the synthetic power of the faculties and is manifest as "an *eternal becoming*" (79/367).[22] Whether or not Schelling 'can' in fact make discursive use of spirit, describe its tendencies, and so on, without objectifying it is not my concern. What interests me, rather, is that the world of activity constituting transcendental cognition and, more specifically, productive intuition, is not simply the performance of the human mind but of this and (and on account of) a larger system of spirit. What is ascribed on the side 'of' intuition is at the same time already ascribed on the side 'of' this anterior spiritual movement.

Returning to this connection between spirit's original activity and the productive motion of imagination, we may note that Schelling's emphasis on spirit's purchase within intuition begins to redirect anxieties about Kant's noumenal substrate toward the more positive possibility that the enactments of the productive imagination lay a genuine claim on the province of the 'real.' What the imagination performs with respect to *opposition*, for example, will be paralleled by spirit's larger productive *conflict*, for "the very essence of the spirit involves an original conflict in self-consciousness resulting in the creation of a real world outside the spirit through intuition (a creation *ex nihilo*)" (T 73/SW1 358). What is localized in the passive/active, positive/negative negotiations of intuitive synthesis bears broader witness to spirit's intrinsic production of the knowable. The parallel affords Schelling's *System* its crucial point of departure: the subjective (self, intelligence, the presentative) and the objective (nature, the presented) are found to be "mutually opposed" yet concurrent in knowing (STI 5/ SW3 339). In short, the larger aim of procuring a 'harmony' of the real and ideal, and a 'congruence' of the objective and subjective, is precipitated by the situation of imagination within primordial intuition. The situation is an elemental schematic for the larger story of conflict, production, and mediation. It is also the literal explanation of the 1797 belief that "[t]he philosophy of the spirit is an aesthetic philosophy."[23]

The imagination in the service of reason

Although the necessity of a harmonizing principle for the real and ideal has insinuated itself as a possibility *in* the concentration on primordial activity and imaginative production, we do not yet have an experience of this principle or a standpoint for grasping it. And though it is one thing to speak of the fundamental work of transcendental synthesis in furnishing the possibility for any knowledge of the 'real,' what may be said of the *understanding* and *judgment*, pure concepts and schematism? Schelling allows that "intuition alone does not suffice" for a knowledge of objects 'outside' myself (T 73/SW1 358). But having established 'activity' as his guiding heuristic for the cognitive elements, his account of the faculties returns time and again to the primacy of intuition, to the unique function of the imagination, and to the determinate production of spirit it expresses. The limitation placed on intuition is pragmatic and is in no way a deference to understanding or judgment's authority over the 'real' (which "subsists only in intuition" (73/359)).[24] For speculation and analysis (that is, *knowing*) to attain any traction on the level of conscious experience, 'independent' objects are required. Within subjective intuition, the "synthesis of the imagination" creates the object, but it would be absurd to ask of the same intuition that it affords the object a "reality and an autonomous existence independent of the subject" (73/358). One cannot halt intuitive activity and then treat its products empirically. It is thus up to the understanding, as it were, to objectify the object: "Only after the creative faculty has completed [its activity], does the faculty of understanding enter the picture, according to Kant—an ancillary faculty that merely apprehends, *comprehends* [and] arrests what has been furnished by another faculty" (73/358–59). Schelling justifies this apparent demotion by retelling the story of *a priori* mediation and reducing Kant's B Deduction emphasis on intellectual synthesis and combination to a mode of *imitation*: understanding can "only *imitate*, only *repeat* that original act of intuition wherein the object first existed" (73/359). The statement is descriptive, not evaluative, for such imitation/repetition does hold considerable promise.[25] For the moment, however, we may deem the understanding a 'secondary' activity within the primordial matrix from which consciousness arises. And understanding's accomplishment, most importantly, depends on the *imagination* to mediate the faculties by way of *schema*.

We have then two modalities of the imagination: its *material* production in intuition cannot be repeated (since that would mean a circle of syntheses), but its *formal* aspect can perform a delineation of "the contour of an object hovering in time and space in general" (T 73/SW1 359). The 'contour', then, is what Kant means by 'schema', and this is the larger activity of imagination as the power of mediation. Such figuration on the basis of what cognition requires, however, is not identical to the work of imagination in 'creating' the real. Kant's schema "possesses no intrinsic reality," and "[a] concept without sensibilization by the imagination is a word without sense, a sound without meaning" (73/359). To commit the productive imagination to mere mediation, as it were, is to satisfy the legitimate needs of cognition, but this allowance must not obfuscate spirit's deeper, active genesis of the real. A similar lesson is learned in the case of *judgment*. Schelling endorses Kant's contention that this faculty is rooted in "an art hidden in the depth of the human soul" (97/393), and is critical to the apprehension of any given object. But the challenge in judgment is to allow representation and 'object' to refer to one another without, however, conflating concept and object. The imagination navigates this tension by overseeing the action 'upon' concepts, much like it does in Kant's judgments of the sublime.

To summarize, this reconstruction of Kant's transcendental aesthetic, emphasizing the *primacy of intuition* and the ongoing *work of imagination* within cognition, reveals several elements that will prove formative in the treatment and accomplishment of *identity*. First, the productive imagination balances the positive/negative play of *oppositional* activities between the pure forms of intuition, thereby winning for intuition the 'communal product' Schelling must have in mind when he speaks of the object's original belonging to intuition. Second, he has likewise endorsed Kant's characterization of the imagination as capable of both activity and passivity, and he has aligned its work in this regard with the 'original activity of the spirit.' Finally, he has rendered the understanding's own activity in attaining consciousness of a given object indebted to the mediating or schematizing labor of the imagination. This places the imagination in a position whereby it constitutes the repetition of its own initial effort, and where, in its formal figuration, it must necessarily have a native or elemental 'sense' of the link between the 'real' and the ensuing 'objective.' When reason begins to exercise itself by way of analysis and separation, one finds these three elements standing in reserve for the task of treating the central predicament of *identity*.[26] Schelling will turn this predicament into a possibility by naming it *absolute identity*, and it is in the realization of this possibility that knowing will have its unconditional ground. Since, however, a transcendental or logical 'identity' is thought to be synonymous with 'immediacy,' it may appear as a state unattenuated by any mediation and therefore in no need of the Kantian imagination. However, if the immediacy of identity is regarded as an 'activity' brimming with the balanced play of opposites, of the real and the ideal, and even of theoretical and practical reason, then we have a predicament that the imagination, so to speak, knows well. Remaining with Schelling's *Treatise*, we now turn to this matter of identity and the way in which production, self-consciousness, and imagination are, as interlocking themes, constitutive of the problem's resolution.

From the standpoint of consciousness, for the standpoint of identity

Identity names the problem reason faces after having performed its speculative works of separation. That philosophers persist in the anxiety of considering "knowledge *real* only to the extent that it corresponds with its object" speaks to the specific way in which the correspondence model of truth has handicapped the ability to reason from within that horizon of spirit's productive activity in which there is an "absolute coinherence" (T 77/SW1 365) of object and representation, being and cognition.[27] Analysis attempts to reunite the terms by way of conceptual mediation (such as "regarding the object as the *cause* and the representation as its *effect*"),[28] and yet the identity remains elusive, even though "the common understanding has always presupposed it in each of its predications" (77–8/365). How are we to bring such an identity to the level of possible experience? Schelling's answer sets a difficult course: "It is readily apparent that it would be possible only under *one* condition, [namely,] if there existed a being capable of an intuition of itself, that is, simultaneously representing and represented or intuiting and intuited" (78/365–66). This quality of simultaneity is more than a criterion, for it resonates with the nature of spirit in its essential activity, and thereby calls for intuition to indwell its productive principle more fully.

The path of turning the predicament into a possibility in the *Treatise* consists in attaching identity to the activity constitutive of self-consciousness. At this early stage, Schelling is not yet working by what he will reconstrue as 'deduction,' but rather by running together the matter of identity at the level of the 'I' of consciousness as well as the 'subject' that is spirit.[29] Since we know that he believes the active/passive quality of imagination in synthesis to be a clue to the larger system of spirit, this discursive proximity is not as surprising as it may seem. If he can establish a connection between the *for-itself* nature of spirit and the *for-myself* nature of self-consciousness then the identity of representation and object will be manifest as something beyond the pale of predication. It is a matter of subtraction—removing predication and recovering essential identity on the basis of original activity. When spirit is the subject of Schelling's remarks he will argue on the basis of necessity, using a language of what must be 'already assumed' and 'ought to be possible,' and then express the consequences of this necessity in terms of 'our knowledge.' For example:

> The identity of representation and object . . . exists only in the intuition-of-self [*Selbstanschauung*] of the spirit. Hence, to demonstrate this absolute correspondence of representation and object, which is the sole ground for the reality of our *entire* knowledge, it ought to be possible to *prove* that the spirit, by having any intuition of *whatever* object, merely intuits itself. If this can be demonstrated, the reality of our knowledge will have been ascertained. (T 78/ SW1 366)

This says that the security of knowledge depends on an intuition belonging to spirit, where spirit means "that which is only *its own* object" (T 78/SW1 367). Absolute identity is the potential privilege of spirit on the basis of spirit's unique comportment to its own activity, and such immediacy collapses the need to speak of representation as belonging to an outside object. To use a language common today, such an assertion discloses a 'benchmark' for that which the thinking subject's self-consciousness wants to attain. However, to attain and secure this "standpoint where subject and object or the intuiting and intuited poles form an identity *within us*" (78/366, my emphasis) requires something different from analysis or transcendental reflection. It requires that inquiry, like intuition, be *productive*—so attuned to the essential manner of *activity* constitutive of finite consciousness that the identity principle surfaces as a matter of genetic necessity.

Disclosing activity

Schelling deploys two measures that will ultimately allow him to place the accent of 'identity' on what he has called self-consciousness. Both are expansive reformulations of the aforementioned connection between spirit's activity and imagination's productivity—the notion that the definitive features of *spirit* are already inscribed within preconscious *intuition*. *First*, he demonstrates that intuitive activity is born through a union of infinity and finitude, activity and passivity, in spirit's own essential character.[30] The signature 'activity' of spirit is that it "exists only in *becoming* or, rather, it is nothing but an *eternal becoming*;" spirit "becomes an object only *through itself*, that is, by means of its *own activity*" (T 79/SW1 367). This juncture of becoming and self-objectification denotes a play of the *infinite* and *finite* in spirit's very character. To apprehend itself—to avoid remaining an empty concept ('for-itself')—spirit must objectify itself in terms of that (finite) being that is already encompassed within spirit's activity. Only the intuiting subject fits the profile: "Finitude and infinity . . . are *originally united* only in the *Being* of a spirited nature. This absolute *simultaneity* of the infinite and the finite, then, contains the essence of an *individual* nature (of selfhood)" (79/368).[31] What is necessary from the genetic view of spirit's essential activity is then affirmed by the primordial view of our intuitive activity: "Those two activities [the infinite and finite] are originally united within me; however, that this is so I merely know because I comprise both in one activity. This activity we call *intuition*" (80/368). In short, the primordial makeup of intuition mirrors the essential nature of spirit. The back-story to intuition consists in spirit's necessary and productive progression toward self-consciousness and self-determination. This argumentation alone proves neither that identity *is* the unconditional ground for the idealist system nor yet professes a discrete intuition *of* identity. But it is an initial exercise in presenting the history of self-consciousness—one that follows the lessons 'hinted' at in Schelling's early attention to imaginative activity, and replaces the habits of predication with what we may call an ontology of activity.

Since drawing together the character of productive intuition and spiritual individuation does not explain *how* the individuated spirit (the self) can come to apprehend itself in its unifying activity—to grasp itself as the identity of two poles *and* as the finite display of spirit's primordial active/passive unity—Schelling must borrow a *second* element from spirit's primordial character, namely *freedom*. Here we find a considerable leap from arguing by way of primordial necessity to abstracting from the basis of spirit's essential freedom. If intuition is offspring of the infinite becoming of the spiritual *for-itself*, then in the immediacy of intuition there is already a nexus of free activity, something like a transcendental reflex that knows nothing of the divide between the theoretical and practical.[32] Presumably, then, the standpoint of identity (now understood as spirit's unity) already happens as a "free act" (T 78/SW1 366) in every intuitive production. The trick is to grasp it in the act. By Schelling's account, the intentional, material attainment of identity thus turns on a free act of abstraction "from the product of our intuition" (81/370). The structure of free abstraction is a 'repetition' similar to the secondary operation of imagination in schematizing its own intuitive product for the 'ancillary' purpose of conceptual delimitation; the task is to render the *product* of intuitive activity an *object*.[33] In this case, the repeated matter is not simply the formal figuration of imagination, but the "original mode of activity (of the spirit)" (81/370). Consciousness apprehends the object as the product of intuitive activity, and discovers *itself* as this unified nexus of activity.[34] If the first of our elements (intuition as a result of spirit's individuation) prepared the approach to identity by way of primordial activity, this second element (primordial freedom) fortifies the requisite methodology of abstraction with a 'real-time' readiness to intuit in an 'object' the abiding expression of identity. The intuition of absolute identity will dovetail with a self-intuition of the primordial self—"that of which we have and *can* have original and true knowledge" (83/373).

These two elements are preparatory for the intellectual intuition of absolute identity. I have mentioned them so as to show how Schelling's ascent toward the disclosure of identity unfolds along a course that is marked, on the one hand, by the central tenets of his desired unconditional ground for knowing, and which, on the other, follows the path of the productive imagination in closing the distance between the intuiting subject and spirit in the mode of individuation. To summarize, Schelling believes that "the reliability of all our knowledge is grounded in the *immediacy* of intuition," and to recover this ground we require an intuition of the "original identity of the object and the representation" (T 85–6/376–78). Toward this end, he has undertaken a renewed appraisal of 'abstraction,' an account of the genesis of consciousness from within a matrix of freedom and opposition, and an elucidation of spirit's movement toward individuation in the self. Self-consciousness names the expanded version of the desired subject/object identity, and it is by way of spirit's essential 'for-itself' drive toward this end (88–9/380–82) that such identity becomes manifestly 'absolute.' I have suggested how these associations were already glimpsed in the essentially 'spiritual' activity of the productive imagination. The pattern of the imagination's material production and formal repetition—in the basic constitution of an object for consciousness—serves as a specified schema for the objectification of spirit's essential nature in and through the constitution of pure self-consciousness. This means that a self-consciousness 'of identity' in and through the subject is, so to speak, a living and active 'objectification' of spirit's primordial identity. When Schelling speaks of the "superior perspective" these elucidations seek, he means that fully formed self-consciousness that ascertains the harmony of the ideal/real, representation/object (82/372).

Striving and willing

One wonders, however, why the path toward such a perspective must be so difficult. Is not the task simply to recover that which was already signaled in the specific power of the productive imagination—in the 'clue' that linked intuitive activity with the system of spirit—and to secure it consciously within the compass of freedom? If Schelling were holding to a strictly Fichtean line on the matter, he could claim the intuition of identity as an accomplishment of the imagination understood as "figural productivity," the "creator of consciousness," and the "grounding faculty of the Self."[35] However, since his own account of self-consciousness has turned on an account of spirit as anterior to selfhood (in the order of priority, thought not succession *per se*) Schelling has begun to surpass the locus of the phenomenal self (as freedom), and located the condition for the possibility of identity in what is, suffice it to say, a greater whole. That is not to suggest that Fichte understood the self as a 'thing' or 'subject,' and that Schelling sought a simply 'broader' point of departure, but rather that, inspired by the trajectory of Fichte's I = I, Schelling nevertheless seeks in the freedom of nature (*natura naturans*) a still more promising point of departure. In addition, we begin to see how Schelling's discussion itself exhibits the movement of his subject matter. The treatment of one question gives way to another, then returns to itself weighted all the more bounding and broadening in a steady march of necessity reluctant to resolve itself. Since inferential and/or reflective discourse is not adequate to assuming the full standpoint of intuition, Schelling means to discipline thought to accompany spirit—to follow it "from representation to representation, from product to product, up to the point where for the first time it rends itself in its pure activity and subsequently will form an intuition of *itself* only in its absolute activity" (T 90/SW1 383). In so doing, he prepares his discourse for a perceptual attunement that will enact, and not simply posit, the standpoint of identity. This brings us to a pivotal *third* element: a proper 'submission' to the matter of identity entails an immersion in the *striving* of spirit toward this very end. What is the nature of this striving such that it is not only a discursive 'theme' but also a modality of thinking?

Striving is a qualitative and decisive addition to the free for-itself 'becoming' by which Schelling understands the 'activity' of spirit at this time. Its emergence marks the moment in which the philosophy of spirit begins to become "aesthetic" and "sensuous" in its performance, though its relationship to the imagination is not yet clear.[36] Striving denotes the primordial self-determination of spirit, on the basis of its being "simultaneously active and passive" (T 99/SW1 395–96), to overcome opposition, pass through finitude and objectification, and carry forward its essential 'becoming' to attain a full intuition of itself as absolute identity. Schelling speaks of a *thrust* [*Schwung*] of "primordial energy" inherently disposed to rendering "the universal equilibrium of forces" (98/394, 96/392, 101–02/400) coherent and organized on a basis solely its own. And in human spirit, this same orientation consists in a striving "toward the system, that is, toward absolute purposiveness" (92/386). Schelling could well have paired this purposiveness with the constitutive work of imagination between sensible affectation and consciousness, but in the *Treatise* he does not. Instead, he moves decidedly outward from the elemental terrain of the subject, contending that it is on account of this purposive drive that the structure and motion of history are constituted as the systemic framework for self-consciousness. "Hence, the history of the human spirit," he explains, "will prove none other than the history of the different *stages* in passing through which the spirit progressively attains an intuition of itself, [which is] *pure* self-consciousness" (90/383).

Moreover, Schelling characterizes striving as a mode of spirit's free *willing*—an act that occurs unconditionally. The reach of this willing is absolute, enveloping the necessary stage of finite objectification such that "spirit becomes immediately conscious of its activity only as a *will*, and the act of *will* is generally the *supreme condition of self-consciousness*" (T 98/SW1 395). Here then we have a primordial autonomy that qualifies as the absolute standpoint of identity we have sought. The seemingly 'ad infinitum' question of system's ground and the seemingly indefinite flux of representations within consciousness and history, together with the point of unity for all theoretical and practical philosophy, are thus resolved in the disclosure of will beneath and before all striving. Accordingly, Schelling remarks:

> The source of all self-consciousness is the *will*. However, in the *absolute will* the spirit becomes aware of itself immediately, that is, it has an *intellectual intuition of itself*. We call this an *intuition* because it [is] *unmediated* [and] *intellectual*, because it has for its object an *activity* that goes far beyond anything empirical and thus can never be reached by *concepts*. (T 102/SW1 401)

Though this intuition of absolute identity is rightly attributed to spirit, Schelling has not lost sight of the horizon of self-consciousness and what there began as a practical need for subject/object identity. He has freed consciousness from all conceptual habituation in addressing the matter, and has redeemed abstraction for the purposes of an intuition, which, like Kant's judgment of taste, is universal and communicable:

> Here, then, we have an *intuition* whose object is a *primordial act*, namely, an intuition that we must not merely attempt to *awaken* in others by means of *concepts*, but which we are *entitled to postulate* for everyone, because without this act the *moral law* itself—i.e., a postulate directed *absolutely* and *unconditionally* at every human being by virtue of its humanity—would prove completely unintelligible. (T 116/SW1 420)

It is not difficult to see in these remarks an amalgamation of several components of Kant's critical project, though at a level of spirit Kant did not explore. The intellectual intuition of absolute identity amounts to an 'abstraction' not unlike the imagination's abstraction of 'form' from the artistic object in the judgment of taste. The feeling of purposiveness in such a judgment is also echoed in the intrinsic striving of spirit for this intuition. The supersensible principle of autonomy, central to Kant's practical philosophy, is now the unconditional principle for all activity—theoretical and practical. Finally, Kant's closest approximation to an unconditional ground in the first *Critique*—the transcendental unity of apperception—at last receives the deeper support it required. As Schelling notes: "It is this continuous intuition *of ourselves* in our pure activity that alone renders possible the *objective* unity of apperception and the correlate of all apperception, the *I think*" (T 103/SW1 401). The answer to the question of what/ how reality inheres in representations is this: "spirit *wills*" (99/396). Spirit's absolute act discloses the will as the grounding element of all intuitive activity. The deepest ground internal to human spirit and constitutive of the larger historical motion of spirit is won by an abstracting, intellectual intuition of the self—an act of will that reveals the will at and as the origins of self-consciousness.

Insofar as our chief interest concerns the place of the imagination in this initial formulation of identity, we leave the *Treatise* on a note of tension as well as possibility. Subtracting nothing from the singular importance of this principle of volition, I have sought to disclose how the structure and mode of its attainment is anticipated by Schelling's interpretation of the primordial imagination. In the imagination he finds a hallmark of the activity of spirit that mediates production, abstraction, and intuition through a string of dialectical pairs: the active and passive, real and ideal, theoretical and practical. The productive and mediating imagination is, so to speak, the genetic code of pure self-consciousness. With the issue of striving we have emphasized the aesthetic bearing of Schelling's discourse, and yet we must admit that Schelling does not call upon the imagination in the act of intellectual intuition. Is striving creative in the same way the imaginative power is productive? Is the event of intellectual intuition, along with the feeling of identity, somehow aesthetic in the artistic (and not just affective) sense?

It is worth noting that Schelling concludes his *Treatise* by defending the account of absolute identity from imagination's dubious double: *enthusiasm*. He understands that enthusiasm would be a transgression of the limits of reason. But insofar as these limits are now understood as what spirit "establishes for itself," it is "truly ridiculous to suspect of enthusiasm precisely *that* which renders enthusiasm impossible forever" (T 103/SW1 402). Since the productive imagination bears witness to spirit's underlying activity, may we allow that imagination is itself, then, an agent of warding off enthusiasm? The imagination is productive by virtue of being active and passive, and it mirrors spirit's essential 'becoming' by figuring finite objects yet "creating *ideas* of what freedom is to realize in such a manner that these ideas are capable of infinite expansion." The imagination thus sustains the productivity demanded of will, and in so doing, it "remains within the limits of moral postulates." In this way the imagination serves practical reason as the "*faculty of ideas,*" a designation that in turn also renders it "*theoretical* reason" (123–24/431–32). At the same time, the larger inquiry is called 'aesthetic' because it is from start to finish a story of affectivity—initially *disclosed* in the heart of sensibility, then *enacted* in an intuition of/for the self, then finally *felt* in the phenomenon of identity.

We are left, however, with an uncertain constellation of what have become principal interpretive themes. Though the power of the *imagination*, the primordial force of *striving*, and the increasingly *aesthetic* nature of thought have each, in their own right, facilitated the recovery of identity through self-consciousness, the full concerted work of these elements is not yet evident. If Schelling is to furnish a true system of knowledge, and not an edifice, then these elements will have to converge in a unified production that bears witness to the whole of the absolute standpoint. It is with this necessity in mind that we now turn to his *System of Transcendental Idealism* and the 'poetic consciousness' there disclosed.

Reimagining harmonious production

On the basis of Schelling's decisive interest in the productive imagination, together with his appeal to the larger primordial activity of spirit, it should be evident that his inquiry in the *Treatise*, and the shape of its intellectual intuition in particular, is by no means reducible to a Fichtean sphere of subjective consciousness, which the *System* alone would then surmount by expanding the story of production in a historical–spiritual direction. The revelation of 'will' at the heart of the identity principle resembles the Fichtean emphasis on subjective freedom, but Schelling's 'will' is a pretheoretical, primordial drive, and his 'identity' transcends the subject-object pairing Fichte's ego holds in strict subjective balance. Discursively, Schelling's movement between standpoints was realized by converting a logic of necessity into a motion of possibility, a turn made possible by the status of 'activity' in intuition, abstraction, and in spirit's essential striving. Dialectically, the power of imagination disclosed the productive balancing of apparent opposites (infinite/finite, real/ideal, practical/theoretical, becoming/object) in the genesis of consciousness and in the purposiveness of spirit, thereby raising the volitional nature of activity to the surface of the inquiry in an immediate way. Schelling's self-consciousness, as well, expresses the immediacy of self and spirit though without situating intuition's productive drive and spirit's activity within the plane of the merely theoretical or subjective. Schelling speaks rather of a "productive force" that "inheres in all external things," constituting them as "*creatures* [or] *productions of a spirit*" (Treatise 93/SW1 387). There is a "system of the world . . . a kind of organization that has developed from a common center" (92–3/387), which, though most manifest in self-consciousness, is also constitutive of natural organisms and of history, and hence more archetypal and synthetic than even the most subjectively idealistic of egos.[37]

It is true, however, that a chief objective of the *System* is to sharpen and improve these distinctions by way of engaging thought, as Richard Velkley observes, "in watching ordinary consciousness gradually disclose its own essence, and thus also its ultimate identity with the principle of nature."[38] In so doing, the principle of absolute identity will undergo several advances in the *System*, among them the formative irrationality of the *unconscious* in the constitution of self, nature, and history, as well as the *indifference* at the root of self-consciousness, and the turn toward aesthetic or *artistic production* as a disclosure of conscious and nonconscious identity. We cannot account for these matters in full. However, I will examine their operation so as to highlight how the imagination structures the ongoing movement of self-intuition, and the affiliated disclosure of the ground for subject/object harmony in intuition. I will contend that the *System*'s rigor lies in the fact that Schelling will allow the problem of mediation and grounding—in the self and revealed through intuition—to become even more difficult so as to anticipate a more exhaustive and indeed imaginative resolution.

When, early in the *System*, Schelling speaks of self-consciousness as a "*primary knowledge*" and as "the lamp for the whole system of knowledge" (STI 16–18/SW3 355–58), he is announcing the conclusion won by the *Treatise*. As we have seen, the twin emphases on activity and productivity intrinsic to the self and to spirit drew forth an intellectual intuition of a grounding freedom that is 'felt' in a supra-empirical manner. The intuition's 'object' is subjective activity—be it in the eternal becoming of spirit or in the infinite producing of the self—and it is, as the *System* reminds us, irreducible to conceptualization or actualization. It is not a 'being' but rather the essential 'how' of all knowing (cf. 17/355–57), the pure self as a "*producing that becomes an object to itself*" (28/370). Now, as if to refurbish the 'lamp,' Schelling's goal remains one of illuminating self-consciousness with an intuition of that grounding principle, which is constitutive of self-determination yet inseparable from the immediacy of knowing. The difference between the two projects, owing largely to advances in Schelling's philosophy of nature (1797–1799), is one of degree. Identity now concerns not only the "coincidence or agreement between subject and object" but also, more broadly, between "intelligence and nature."[39] To reconstitute the principle of absolute identity "in action" through an aggressive "knowing of knowing" (4/33–4, 9/345) is to account for the historical genesis of self-consciousness (and indeed the very system of spirit governing the realms of nature, history, and knowing) without yielding to ontic or empirical expressions that would subtract from its freedom. This project effectively raises the mediational stakes underwriting self-consciousness and intellectual intuition alike. The self, for Schelling, is "*being-itself*" (32/376)—that entity which carries the principle of identity in the same way that something like flight carries the laws of physics or a variable carries its coefficient. The concern of the

System is not to 'actualize' the principle of grounding unity more effectively than the *Treatise*, but to draw a larger formula—to write the history of self-consciousness in terms of "the parallelism of nature with intelligence" (2/331), and thereby magnify the mediating motion between coefficient and variable.

The mediating factor

The leading problem is thus a familiar one: On what *mediating* basis is the intuiting self able to apprehend its intrinsic producing activity? How does free production 'know' itself without losing the self in the ideal realm of willing? If in philosophy "one is not simply the object of contemplation, but always at the same time the subject," and if intuition is an "act of *construction*" (STI 13/SW3 350–51), then the 'proof' that the absolute standpoint is already written in the pure activity that is the self will require a further disclosure 'of' productive intuition 'by' the power of intuition. Schelling frames the issue as a task of unveiling that which mediates production and intuition—the "*universally mediating factor in our knowledge*" (15/353). We must appreciate this production–intuition tension in two ways. First, *production* is now the summary term for that striving drive manifest in the essential activity of spirit, which is generative of self, nature, and history; *intuition* (itself productive) names the work of creative thought to enact an immediate grasp of this drive though without reducing it to 'objective' knowledge. Second, and in a related vein, to attain a mediation of production and intuition is to signal the overcoming of a philosophical standpoint of reflection, and to assume a standpoint in which 'reason' is no longer subjective or objective but is, as he will later summarize, "the true *in-itself* . . . located precisely in the indifference-point of the subjective and the objective" (P 349/SW4 115, cf. 345/109).

Together, this means that the *System* formalizes the two-tiered motion of inquiry in the *Treatise*: as 'matters' of identity, production, and intuition are invested in mediation, and it is up to an ongoing revolution in thought itself to work out and work from this mediation. Both movements, then, require an intrinsic creativity.[40] Mediation, as well, is not a question of joining two unrelated terms. It is more a question of allowing the variable to catch hold of its coefficient without ever sundering the two. Schelling announces early in the *System* that the elusive mediating factor will be attained via an "*aesthetic act* of the imagination" (STI 13/SW3 351). On the surface, this says that he means to continue the aesthetic mode of inquiry introduced in the *Treatise*, and that he will do so having no residual compunctions about 'enthusiasm.' More deeply, the phrasing intimates that the imagination, as a power of elemental activity and mediation within intuition and for understanding, still has much to offer an inquiry itself bent on disclosing mediation. If, as I have indicated, one feature of 'aesthetic inquiry' is that it reenacts the enactments proper to its subject matter, we do well to expect that Schelling will further aestheticize the mediation of production and intuition, and appeal to an *aesthetic intuition*—an artistic imagination—for the purposes of uncovering this mediation.

The first way in which the question of mediation underscores an aesthetic turn lies in the meaning of *harmony* attributed to knowledge, history, and nature.[41]

If knowledge is a "primordial whole," the endeavor of Schelling's 'history' is to exercise a "free imitation" that will outline the "various epochs" through which "that one absolute synthesis is successively put together" (STI 15/SW3 353, 49/397, 50/399). The case for a "predetermined harmony" (11/348) between the ideal and the real likewise turns on the markers of mediated unity imprinted in nature's production; for "the same powers of intuition which reside in the self can also be exhibited up to a certain point in nature" (3/331). Schelling speaks of a productive activity in which the ideal world and the real world arise in concert, something overseeing the synthesis of the "*nonconscious activity* that has brought forth nature, and the *conscious activity* expressed in willing" (12/348–49, my emphases). This emphasis on nature's nonconscious productivity amounts to a decisive lens laid upon the central standpoint of self-consciousness. Nature now *names* the absolute identity of subject and object, and self-consciousness is said to be "its highest potentiality" (17/355–57).[42] Nature is not a sum of appearances, but rather an ally in the productive history of self-consciousness and in the 'bringing-forth' (28/371, from *hervorbringen*) of this history for the self. Nature is party to spirit's striving; nature "in its purposive forms speaks figuratively" (215/608). Nature and self thus share a history of productive, purposive, becoming, and the aim of duplicating their harmony through philosophical construction is neither to "make an intelligence out of nature [nature philosophy], or a nature out of intelligence [transcendental philosophy]," but to appreciate their "parallelism" as a means for intuiting a reflection of the ideal world in the self (7/342–43, 2/331, 232/628–29).

What is most interesting is how Schelling elects to disclose the nonconscious, originating source of such harmonies. A singular species of consciousness is required to reveal the mediated harmony of an activity that is "simultaneously conscious and nonconscious," a *poietic* activity that brings forth nature and self-consciousness alike (STI 12/SW3 348). Everything depends on making manifest this seed of harmony at the root of indifference. But this is not the first time Schelling must maneuver the philosophical standpoint through such a difficulty. The status of the all-encompassing nonconscious or irrational drive, and the attendant issue of mediation, is a rather pronounced extension of the problem of immediacy and spontaneity seen in the primordial investigations of the *Treatise*. It echoes the production in intuition, which the conscious philosopher wants to know by means of abstracting an 'object' from the 'product,' and is an expanded form of the same concealed artistry of synthesis and spirit that furnished the genesis of our mere consciousness of an individual object, an irrational artistry of the presentative that is necessarily concurrent with the conscious objectivity of the presented (5/349). But the expansion of this nonconscious element in the *System* renders the discursive challenge still more pronounced. By submitting to this matter of the nonconscious in the larger story of nature and history, Schelling creates a more deliberate schema for navigating the double activity of producing and intuiting (13/351). What we now want to appreciate is how the kind of intuition required for making manifest the mediating element (what I have called the coefficient) will be one in which the irrational and conscious sides of production reflect their own generative and otherwise concealed activity (the 'for-itself'). The lamp of self-consciousness is, so to speak, lit by a dark charge.

It is a poetry best captured in a poetic production. As Tilliette observes, "if it is true that philosophy alone penetrates to the secret of the work of art, inversely Art, poetic and plastic at once, illumines the meaning of the history of consciousness."[43]

The artistry of intuition and the striving of imagination

Schelling has this puzzle of production in mind when he speaks of nature as "a poem lying pent in a mysterious and wonderful script," and of the need to exhibit an appearance of the self that is "at once conscious and unconscious *for itself*" (STI 232/ SW3 628, 217–18/610). "Conscious and unconscious activities," he explains, "are to be absolutely one in the product, just as they also are in the organic product, but they are to be one in a different manner; the two are to be one *for the self itself*" (220/613–14). This means the self must become conscious of the conscious and unconscious sides of production, allowing them their necessary opposition for the sake of production, yet also manifesting their identity for the self. The immediate awareness of such identity—via self-intuition—obtains, much as in the *Treatise*, in the form of a *feeling*, in this case "of infinite tranquility" (221/614). Tranquility implies the attainment of an end, a surmounting of conflict. It is a feeling evoked by the passage of free oppositional activity into unity. Schelling explains:

> This unknown . . . whereby the objective and the conscious activities are here brought into unexpected harmony, is none other than the absolute which contains the common ground of the preestablished harmony between the conscious and the unconscious. Hence, if this absolute is reflected from out of the product, it will appear to the intelligence as something lying above the latter, and which, in contrast to freedom, brings an element of the unintended to that which was begun with consciousness and intention. (STI 221–22/SW3 615)

In the very bearing of the unconscious, then, and in the very conflict that carries production, lies a harmonizing force. But a unique product is required if such a reconciling production is to be exhibited. What is such a product, and where is this productive intuition to be found?

It is in view of this distillation of mediation in terms of the conscious and unconscious sides of production that Schelling makes his provocative turn to *aesthetic*, or artistic, production and intuition. Within this specific turn we will be able to repair the apparent divide (left standing in the *Treatise*) between the *power of imagination* and the free *striving of spirit*. Schelling asks: "how are *we* to explain transcendentally *to ourselves* an intuition such as this, in which the unconscious activity operates as it were, through the conscious, to the point of attaining complete identity therewith?" (STI 219/SW3 612). His answer consists in extending and privileging the "*aesthetic* sense" (14/351) of philosophizing, on the one hand, and elucidating the *aesthetic activity* constitutive of works of art on the other. This is not a case of invoking artistic production as an 'analogy' or 'surrogate' for intellectual intuition or an 'example' of the double activity of producing and intuiting. Rather, it is a turn of attention in his subject matter and a parallel turn of inquiry itself—artistic and philosophical production alike are to be carried by "an *aesthetic act* of the imagination" (13/351). The virtue of treating artistic activity is that the production proper renders the doubling more visible. In and through artistic creation, the "ideal world of art and the real world of objects are . . . products of one and the same activity; the concurrence of the two (the conscious and the nonconscious) *without* consciousness yields the real, and *with* consciousness the aesthetic world" (12/349). If, that is, transcendental inquiry can attain an aesthetic attunement, then it will see in artistic production (aesthetic intuition) the harmonizing concurrence or mediation underway.

The light of genius

When, in the *Treatise*, Schelling explained the genesis of consciousness of an individual object, he first formulated the tension between a 'product' belonging to the primordial work of intuition and the inevitable 'objectivization' of this product under the imitative work of abstraction. This formulation was itself patterned on the *material* work of imagination in a fundamental sense, and the *formal* figurative work of the imagination in the service of understanding and judgment. Schelling now finds a point of entry into the active principle of identity without having to run the risk of analysis or separation; artistic production mirrors intuitive production, but is a process that is as concrete as the 'product' it creates. To say that "the philosophy of art is the true organon of philosophy" (STI 14/SW3 351) is to suggest that the aesthetic orientation of a reflection on art reveals a concentrated form of the proximity possible between an intuitive inquiry and the productive intuition afoot in its subject matter. To the artist belongs an intuition that is "conscious in respect of production, unconscious in regard to the product" (219/613). Such a double orientation mirrors the tension in freedom between infinite willing and finite operation, while also recalling the unconscious purposiveness of nature (176/558–59, 214/606) and the harmonizing intentions of the absolute. The genius is that productive self in whom the mediation of nature and freedom, and of the unconscious and conscious, the ideal and the real, happens. A work of art is won from a process of limitation and opposition, a process of conflict welcomed and required by an involuntary drive, an "irresistible urge" in the artist's own nature and a "feeling of inner contradiction" (222/614).[44] The contradiction is an inspired production, a mediation that results in the *event* of absolute identity: art is "the one everlasting revelation which yields that concurrence, and the marvel which, had it existed but once only, would necessarily have convinced us of the absolute reality of that supreme event" (223/618).

But apart from the testimony of the artist, how is this disclosure manifest for the philosopher? The answer has everything to do with the artistic 'product,' provided it is sheltered from the objectifying tendencies of abstraction. Schelling adopts a language of illumination when speaking of such a product, as though it magnifies the 'lamp' of self-consciousness all the more. He explains:

> This unchanging identity, which can never attain to consciousness, and merely
> radiates back from the product, is for the producer precisely what destiny is for the
> agent, namely a dark unknown force which supplies the element of completeness

or objectivity to the piecework of freedom; and as that power is called destiny, which through our free action realizes, without our knowledge and even against our will, goals *that we did not envisage*, so likewise that incomprehensible agency which supplies objectivity to the conscious, without the cooperation of freedom, and to some extent in opposition to freedom (wherein is eternally dispersed what in this production is united), is denominated by means of the obscure concept of *genius*. (STI 222/SW3 616)

Schelling defines the act of genius as "an unexpected concurrence of the unconscious with the conscious activity" (STI 228/SW3 624). The language of destiny in the preceding remarks connects the work of genius to the work of thought (to the 'talent' for thinking, and the 'superior perspective' noted earlier), and denotes the infusion of the absolute's harmonizing necessity in and through the conflict of production. What for Kant was a gift of nature manifest as a *human* genius is here, for Schelling's artist, a distinct capacity to manifest *nature's* ontological genius in and through the progression of aesthetic intuition; the artistic imagination, in this regard, allows the philosopher to intuit the genius of nature.[45] A radiation issues from the product, reflecting back the modality of its creation such that the purposiveness of an 'unknown' and 'incomprehensible' agency is revealed. Artistic productivity, understood as an outgrowth of aesthetic intuition, is a manifest case of spirit's striving and a visible rendering of the internal identity between the subjective and objective, conscious and unconscious. "The idea of genius," Tilliette explains, "does not count among the acts of evolutionary syntheses, it is rather that this entire theoretical–practical organism is subsumed by aesthetic intuition."[46] Schelling continues:

> The work of art merely *reflects* to me what is otherwise not reflected by anything, namely that absolutely identical which has already divided itself even in the self. Hence, that which the philosopher allows to be divided even in the primary act of consciousness, and which would otherwise be inaccessible to any intuition, comes, through the miracle [*Wunder*] of art, to be *radiated* back from the products thereof. (STI 230/SW3 625, my emphases)

Let us be clear about this 'miracle.' Schelling describes the unconscious factor in aesthetic production as "the element of *poetry* in art," and characterizes this *felt* contradiction as that freedom that precisely sets in motion the "whole of man" and "strikes at *the ultimate in him*, the root of his whole being" (STI 224/SW3 618, 222/614). May we say that the imagination sustains this striving 'drive,' this 'poetry' so interior to the artist? This would suggest that the creative imagination is a power of accomplishing harmony by means of conflict and contradiction. Is this reference to the 'root' in man not an echo of that same way in which Kant first spoke of the imagination in its mediating work in cognition? Without question there is a functional and qualitative parallel between the productive imagination as Schelling understood it in his reading of Kant's transcendental aesthetic (a primordial and productive unity in opposition), and the creative imagination as he now understands it in the artistic drive. Where the imagination was a 'clue' in resolving the issue of the 'real' in representations and an activity of spirit in the genesis of consciousness, it is now a more active and concrete disclosure of the larger problem of harmony and mediation. The affiliation of the productive imagination with spirit's essential *activity* is mirrored by the affiliation of the creative imagination with the absolute's essential *unity*. "Every genuine work of art," says Schelling, "created by the imagination, is a unity of the same opposites as those unified in the Ideas." The *creative imagination* brings forth the "inner essence of the absolute . . . the eternal unity [*ewige In-Eins-Bildung*] of the universal and the particular," the very same matter that is felt in the immediacy of *intellectual intuition* (US 61–2/SW5 267).[47]

The common root

Though it is true that aesthetic and intellectual intuition enjoy different "conditions of . . . emergence" (STI 231/SW3 626), settling the question of mediation at the heart of absolute identity clearly depends on evoking the poetic root shared by both forms of production. They have in common an 'internal' conflict at the core of production, and aesthetic intuition is characterized by the same dichotomy of activities that intellectual intuition intuits but struggles to resolve into an intelligible object. Schelling says as much when he contends that the power of productive intuition in philosophy is "the same whereby art also achieves the impossible, namely to resolve an infinite opposition in a finite product" (230/626). The difference is not one of analogy, but also one of standpoint; in aesthetic production the 'unconscious' side of opposition is more accessible, and thus reflects back from its product a heightened awareness of the primordial root of all intuition. In this way, art bears witness to the integrity of intellectual intuition. Schelling goes so far as to ask: "How . . . can it be established beyond doubt, that such an [intellectual] intuition does not rest upon a purely subjective deception, if it possesses no objectivity that is universal and acknowledged by all men?" And he answers: "This universally acknowledged and altogether incontestable objectivity of intellectual intuition is art itself. For the aesthetic intuition simply is the intellectual intuition become objective" (229/625). This defense is also indicative of a deeper point. Just as the 'product' of art reflects back on the conflict inherent in the creative drive, the fact of this 'resolution' is meant to reflect back on a deeper understanding of the 'productive power' at the root of self-consciousness. The element of 'poetry' in art is also in thought. Schelling explains:

> It is the poetic gift, which in its primary potentiality constitutes the primordial intuition, and conversely. [W]hat we speak of as the poetic gift is merely productive intuition, reiterated to its highest power. It is one and the same capacity that is active in both, the only one whereby we are able to think and to couple together even what is contradictory—and its name is imagination [*Einbildungskraft*]. (STI 230/SW3 626)

Aesthetic intuition, in other words, unveils the more primordial productivity at the heart of intellectual intuition that mediating power that is the hidden aspect of theoretical and practical reason: the imagination.

Here we do well to recall a simple lesson from the *Treatise*—that spirit tends toward an intuition of itself (T 88/SW1 380), a tendency that is the basis for all activity constitutive of consciousness and knowing. The artistic imagination brings this unconscious tendency to the surface of a specific production, and, in so doing, particularizes the same purposive striving from which self-consciousness arises. Artistry mediates formal purposiveness with material limitation, and the traces of these constituents are borne on the surface of the 'work'—a 'product' of the creative imagination and an 'image' of the identity stowed in the immediacy of intellectual intuition. In the relationship between aesthetic production and intellectual intuition we have then a repetition of the structure in the *Treatise* concerning philosophical abstraction (which needs an object) and intuitive production (cf. STI 222/SW3 613–14). The difference consists in the fact that, now in the *System*, where we are working from the standpoint of pure self-consciousness and conscious volition, we are able to treat the aesthetic and intellectual intuitions as phenomenal events issuing from one same absolute emanation unfolding through history and in nature. Both are 'real' events having an 'ideal' meaning. By definition, visual (or in the case of Goethe's poetry, for example, oral), the product of genius is a work of creative imagination that *shows* (or sounds) the work of intellectual intuition. The imagination is once again a 'clue' to the disclosure of identity. In rather soaring language, Schelling explains:

> If aesthetic intuition is merely intellectual intuition become objective, it is self-evident that art is at once the only true and eternal organ and document of philosophy, which ever and again continues to speak to us of what philosophy cannot depict in external form, namely the unconscious element in acting and producing, and its original identity with the conscious. Art is paramount to the philosopher, precisely because it opens to him, as it were, the holy of holies, where burns in eternal and original unity, as if in a single flame, that which in nature and history is rent asunder, and in life and action, no less than in thought, must forever fly apart. . . . Each splendid painting owes, as it were, its genesis to a removal of the invisible barrier dividing the real from the ideal world, and is no more than the gateway, through which come forth completely the shapes and scenes of that world of fantasy [*Phantasiewelt*] which gleams but imperfectly through the real. (STI 231–32/SW3 628)

The import of the discovery is such that even artistic 'fantasy' is reinstated and attached to the horizon of the ideal. Schelling is so assured of the aesthetic disclosure that he gives fodder to the charges of 'enthusiasm.' He embraces this risk because the turn toward art has proved a fitting match for the poetic life of the absolute itself (as it navigates the nonconscious and conscious, the ideal and real), and, in so doing, he has accounted for the standpoint of self-consciousness and 'made the philosopher sensuous' along the way.[48] He continues:

> The ultimate ground of all harmony between subjective and objective could be exhibited in its original identity only through intellectual intuition; and it is precisely this ground which, by means of the work of art, has been brought forth [*herausgebracht*] entirely from the subjective, and rendered wholly objective, in such wise, that we have gradually led our object, the self itself, up to the very point where we ourselves were standing when we began to philosophize . . . Philosophy

was born and nourished by poetry in the infancy of knowledge, and with it all those sciences it has guided toward perfection; we may thus expect them, on completion, to flow back like so many individual streams into the universal ocean of poetry from which they took their source. (STI 232/SW3 628)[49]

Whether or not Schelling and his absolute ground remain within such a poetic flow is a question that reflects on the ultimate status of the poetic imagination in his identity period. In the following section we will navigate these currents by examining several of his works between 1801 and 1802—works in which his regard for *aesthetic production* and his ambitions for *absolute reason* present the reader with tensions that may be resolved only by a proper appreciation for the advance from *Einbildungskraft* to *Ineinsbildung*.

The art of creation and the absolute standpoint

Earlier in this chapter I described Schelling's initial interest in the question of subject/object identity as a practical one. A system of knowledge requires a grounding principle that assures the reality inhering in representations, and recovers the harmony subsisting beneath and beyond the cleavages (*Entzweiungen*) of speculative and scientific thought. On the basis of this need Schelling established the workshop in which his system of identity would emerge—an apprenticeship that began under Fichte, reassigned itself to the larger striving of spirit in consciousness, nature, and history, then wed itself to the studio of the artistic genius and the poetic, harmonizing force of the absolute. The *Treatise* and *System* comprise a sustained and expansive movement toward the disclosure of the absolute as the essential identity of the ideal and real, the "supreme presupposition of all knowledge" (US 10/SW5 216). The imagination has served as both traction and accelerant for this movement. And the work of disclosing the absolute has involved a striving of inquiry suited to catch and join the striving of spirit—a *poiesis* of the grounding principle, that is, by turns intellectual and aesthetic, intuitive and productive. Art exhibits a *real* harmony of the real and ideal, and philosophy, thanks to the reflection and radiance of the artistic product, is understood to exhibit an *ideal* harmony of the same. The two, says Schelling, "meet at the summit [*Gipfel*], and because both are absolute, each can be the archetype of the other" (US 147/SW5 348). The lesson to be won from this disclosure is not one of an Archimedian authority of self-consciousness nor a template for a resolved departure from the phenomenal domain, but rather the invitation to explore how the creative imagination is invested in manifesting and recovering that "truly absolute identity" (US 67/SW5 273), which transcends the logic and fate of all antitheses. The early system of identity is, ultimately, an exercise in rendering thought a work that is productive and poetic in the deepest, most 'spiritual' and 'primordial' sense of the terms. Identity began as a 'problem,' matured as a possibility, and now, on the heels of the *System*, names an ambition to indwell the absolution from all limited standpoints.

But any reading of Schelling's lectures and texts between 1801 and 1803 (and recent scholarship devoted to them) leaves one wondering if the productive and aesthetic bearing of the *System* remains decisive in a more rigorously deductive and constructive formulation of what it means to think from the horizon of indifference. Two questions capture the pertinence of this tension to our present interests: (1) Does the rigor of absolute *reason* (its treatment and apparent performance) 1801–1803 indeed jettison the artistic production that seemed of great consequence in years prior? (2) Does the increasingly formal account of absolute *identity* suggest that Schelling has surmounted his own appeal to, and employment of, the productive imagination in the standpoint of intellectual intuition? To answer these questions we must first establish the terms of the tension more clearly. A brief account of two texts— *Presentation of My System of Philosophy* (1801) and his lectures on *The Philosophy of Art* (1802–1803)—will suffice.

Deduction in the domain of *Ineinsbildung*

In his *Presentation of My System of Philosophy* Schelling situates his thought in the grounding principle and demonstrates that the indifference-point of absolute identity and that of *absolute reason* are one and the same.[50] He explains that "[t]he standpoint of philosophy is the standpoint of reason; its kind of knowing is a knowing of things as they are in themselves, i.e., as they are in reason" (P 349/ SW4 115). And if, as he argues, "*it belongs to the essence of absolute identity to be,*" then the principle of identity is also already an ontological totalizing of the absolute such that "*Each individual being is as such a determined form of the being of absolute identity*" (351/118, 361/131, 351/118).[51] Schelling elucidates this point through a series of deductions from the law of identity (the proposition A=A).[52] A distinction between essence and being (*Seyn*) accounts for the place of differentiation, finitude, and potency (as A=B) within the indifference of A=A, but from the standpoint of *production* (as opposed to that of *reflection*, "idealism in the objective sense" 345/109) absolute identity remains analogous to an indivisible line.[53] In this way, Schelling's *Presentation* is an enactment and further justification of the kind of cognizing one enjoys after having followed the direction of intellectual intuition to absolute identity and totality, and having taken up the site of absolute reason; it is the *Erkennen*, as opposed to *Wissen*, that happens at the indifference-point between transcendental philosophy and philosophy of nature.[54]

Schelling indeed believes he has substantiated the means for converting the phenomenal/ideal and necessity/freedom divide into two expressions of the same absolute totality. The accomplishment ultimately amounts to a renewed grounding for reason and its sciences. In his comments before a Jena audience in 1802 he charges that man, freshly equipped with a standing in absolute reason, is the being destined "to supplement the phenomenal world" (US 12/SW5 218). But is a vocation of supplementation necessarily reducible to a triumph of essence over image, reason over imagination, or *Vernunftanschauung* over *aesthetic intuition*. In a subtle way, Schelling's hopes for absolute reason echo the imaging and reflection of harmony he found in the work of genius: "man," he explains, "is meant to express the image [*Bild*] of the same divine nature as it is in itself, i.e., in its ideal aspect" (12/218). In these same lectures he remarks that art "is a direct and necessary expression of the absolute" and the "philosopher who sees in art the inner essence of his own science as in a magic and symbolic mirror will inevitably make the philosophy of art one of his goals" (144/345, 150/351).[55] Is such language indicative of a continued interest in the aesthetic shape of intuition and reason?

The organizing theme of the lectures compiled as *The Philosophy of Art* (1802–1803) is *creation*. It is an extension and religious specification of the thought of production and the 'miracle' of art so central to the *System*'s culmination. As a concurrence of the divine and human, creation carries that sense of striving we have charted in the purposiveness of spirit and the artistic imagination. "Art," says Schelling, is the objective representation of "divine creation," an aesthetic manifestation of the "informing of infinite ideality into the real" (ART 31–2/SW5 386). Such informing echoes the *System*'s movement through opposition and contradiction to a synthesis of the real and ideal, the necessary and free, and thus specifies the conversion underway between the realm of the phenomenal/temporal and that of the absolute. Although the creative imagination (particularly in the poetic world of Greek mythology) is treated principally on the side of the divine or absolute, artistic objects are not simply ontic effects of a divine cause; the unconscious drive of the genius observed in the *System* remains in effect, but is characterized afresh in terms of the 'unity' so decisive to Schelling's *Presentation*. One sees this difference on the level of operative terms: *Ineinsbildung* ("mutual informing into unity") places a pronounced accent upon *Einbildungskraft* while also subtracting the subjectivist orientation denoted by Kant's '*kraft*.'[56] The terms advance a simultaneity of unity and individuation—the former assured by the divine informing, the latter accomplished by the artist who intuits their accord. As a result, Schelling's affiliated treatments of fantasy, the symbolic, and the sublime situate us in the ground of the absolute totality in a more daunting and compelling way than the deductive presentation of 1801 may have suggested.[57]

The status of *Ineinsbildung* in these lectures indicates that Schelling's concern is not to prove absolute identity as a grounding principle nor substantiate the claims of intellectual intuition, but rather to report on the imaginative life of the absolute. Artistic production presents the most poignant intersection with this life, a poetic proximity that requires us to pause before simply converting, on Schelling's behalf, absolute identity into absolute reason. The human imagination, including "fantasy," can apprehend and carry absolute unity's movement in and through finite limitation. Says Schelling, "according to this law [of unity] life flows out into the world from the absolute as from that which is without qualification *one*. According to the same law the universe forms and molds itself within the reflex of human creative imagination into a world of fantasy whose consistent and pervading law is absoluteness in limitation" (ART 37/SW5 393).[58] He thus characterizes the connection between absolute and world, between divine freedom and life, by a mode of formation moving between the divine imagination and human fantasy. The implication is that fantasy, of all things, enjoys a privilege that philosophical abstraction, deduction, and construction would do well to absorb. Moreover, where this imaginative reflex obtains there is also a prescient awareness of "the initial ground of existence," an eternal "region of darkness and formlessness" (37/394). Art, then, consists in a generation of form from chaos, much like the dialectic of the nonconscious and conscious in the *System*, and even the material and formal figurations of the productive imagination before it. Paralleling the generative work of what has been called 'spirit' and 'the absolute,' form is generated via a play of the universal and the particular. This generation is manifest in what Schelling calls 'schematism' (to reinscribe an old term), 'allegory,' and most importantly, the 'symbolic,' for it is the symbolic that "constitutes the absolute form" (46/407). In the symbolism of the sublime, for example, the limits of concrete intuition create a situation in which "the truly infinite appears for which the merely concretely infinite is the symbol" (86/462–63).[59] The appearance, moreover, depends on that disposition in the *subject* to intuit the finite *as* a symbol of the infinite. The reflexive imagination of the beholder, as it were, is hermeneutically equipped to symbolize the freedom of the absolute—to grasp the sublime disclosure of unboundedness. Schelling calls this event an "aesthetic intuition" and goes so far as to contend that it, like the intellectual intuition, "is the poesy that any human being can practice" (86–7/463; cf. T 116/SW1 420).[60] The emphasis is on the possibility, for the poesy of symbolism 'supplements' the phenomenal realm. The artistic imagination, ever tethered to the finite, steps beyond the finite standpoint.

What is significant is this connection established between an aesthetic intuition that must exceed the mere sensible, and the incomprehensible "primal chaos" that marks the "inner essence of the absolute" (ART 88/SW5 465). The intuitions (intellectual and aesthetic) of the *System* anticipated this connection, and the *Presentation* provided a logical outline for the life of unity in and through the law of identity, but here, under the guise of a philosophy of art, Schelling has provided a model for the conversion of reason's working standpoint. The intuition of, and reasoning from, absolute identity remains decisive, but an intuition of incomprehensibility, says Schelling, "appears to be the first step toward philosophy, or at least toward an aesthetic view of the world" (88/465). But such a statement returns us to the tension introduced in our two questions earlier. Is art an illustration of what the conversion to the absolute standpoint (from that of consciousness) entails, or is it a way of disciplining thought to become more aesthetic? Even with the specification of aesthetic intuition and the artistic/affective imaginations in Schelling's philosophy of art, many scholars argue that Schelling's post-*System* period chiefly consists in a correlation of philosophical reason and absolute identity that jettisons the interest in aesthetic intuition specifically, and any poetic conception of thought more generally. Insofar as Schelling is, says Vater, "guided by the idea of an absolute principle neither internal to knowing nor external to it" and rigorously committed to deductive and constructive presentations of absolute indifference, absolute reason effectively overtakes all forms of transcendental reflection and the appeal to imaginative production, intuition, and mediation is at best secondary.[61] Such a view is too rigid. I have no interest in challenging the obvious centrality of absolute reason for Schelling circa 1802, but I am reluctant to embrace a developmental typology that fails to understand and appreciate how, without his steadfast attention to the artistry of imagination, Schelling's absolute reason and intended *wissenschaft* of intellectual intuition have no standing. I will demonstrate this point by briefly treating the two texts often cited for the opposite case: *Bruno* and *Further Presentations*.

The possessive imagination

The conversation in *Bruno* develops the matter of absolute unity by exploring the unconditional identity of truth and beauty (B 120/SW3 218). In so doing, the dialogue compares the efficacy of philosophy and poetry in apprehending this unity, though both strive for it. Schelling's Anselm observes that although artists may lack a conscious possession of the idea of identity, "they are possessed by it" (131–32/231). The statement locates the text's discussion in the immediate aftermath of Schelling's *System* remarks concerning aesthetic intuition and production. The case of the philosopher, Anselm continues, is similar though more conscious—he "employs, but in an inward way, the same God-given faculty that the artist uses externally and unknowingly" (132/231). The task then is to characterize the philosopher's intentional employment of the faculty, which grasps and exercises the absolute principle with respect to not only the identity of truth and beauty, but also the identity of all things natural and divine—a principle indicative of what Schelling has elsewhere called absolute totality. Such identity, as Bruno puts it, likewise encompasses the magnetism by which the numerous metaphysical and productive poles enjoy a disclosure of unity surpassing all difference: the ground of the ideal and real, the unity of thought and intuition, the particular and universal, difference and indifference, possibility and actuality, being and knowing. To enact a philosophical inwardness rooted in such identity is, like the grounding self-consciousness of reasoning based in identity, to outstrip the "finite cognition, which keeps object and concept, particular and universal distinct from one another" (141/241).

No doubt this program for inwardness appears to subsume the privileges ascribed to aesthetic intuition in years prior. And yet, the very contours of inwardness are presented on the bases of a conception of philosophical production manifestly shaped by an artistic parallel. *Bruno*'s ensuing attempts to determine the formal domain of the absolute—*as* and *by* reason and not finite cognition or reflection— are performed according to an artistic and imaginative hermeneutic apparatus. Philosophical inwardness is not just analogous to artistic or poetic production, but happens according to their very terms. Explicating the meaning of absolute identity and reason in terms of beauty and truth's identity, for example, is no mere romantic flourish. Schelling treats nature and its entities in terms of a "living artistry [*lebendigen Kunst*]" of the archetypal (*Urbild*) (B 125/SW3 223–24, cf. 178/282). He explains the principle of indifference, moreover, and the play of opposition within it, in terms of a mirror imaging of object and copy—a harmonious relation Bruno leverages to illustrate how "philosophy should be a true copy of the universe" (137/237). The very mark of comparison between finite understanding and the "supreme idea" of absolute identity, Bruno continues, is the ability to ascertain how it is that "the beautiful is what absolutely identifies the universal and the particular"—an ontological quality otherwise cognized as though "reflected in a pool of water" (143–44/243–44). Recalling the problem of 'immediacy' in the *Treatise*, identity here consists in "the *immediate image* of the idea itself" (162/262). Such imagery is not delimited by the Platonic suspicion of derivation and removal, but rather one that has the quality of animation and 'ensouling' (cf. 167/267–68, 178/280–81)—the *formative* rescue effort of a world of appearances and mechanistic nature, restoring them as entities that image the *essential* unity of thought and being (cf. 198–99/301–03).

What these connections suggest is that the scope and manner of philosophical inwardness (and its best expression, absolute reason) is established as an attunement of the imagination. The qualitative nature of identity demands a poeticization of thought. We have already observed the operation of *Ineinsbildung* with respect to identity's motion toward the symbolic, and it now appears as though a similar structure of 'forming into unity' is the very thing Schelling requires between aesthetic intuition and the intuition of reason. All elements pertaining to the manner in which "the finite inheres in the infinite"—the image world's intrinsic communion or fellowship with the absolute—and one's ability to recognize *spirit* as "the unity of all things" (B 150–51/SW3 251–52, cf. 187/289), are, for Schelling's Bruno, captured by a metaphorical and artistic refrain reducible to this: "the thing carries within itself the stamp of the eternal, an image of eternity, as it were [*ein Abbild des Ewigen*]" (160/260; cf. 187/289, 194/297).[62] An eternal image indeed trumps a phenomenal image, but this does not imply that absolute reason rids itself of aesthetic figuration or poetic imagination. Though the field of philosophical *inwardness* means Bruno's specific task is "the deduction of consciousness from the idea of the eternal itself and from its internal identity" (179/282), and though this alters the path of deduction from one of nature and history in the *System*, and even the logical law of identity in the *Darstellung*, the very ability to say that phenomenal images do not display "perfect indifference" and that absolute cognition "includes both thought and being itself, already absolutely united within it" (198/301, 216/323), depends from the start on a decision to *reason* through *images*—to catch the eternal as it informs the real with the beauty of truth. The more the philosophical inwardness accelerates as a standpoint to be won, the more *Bruno* imbues its components with the 'springing forth' and striving we have found native to nature and to the artistic genius. To say, then, that "It is reason alone that knows everything divine, for in knowing itself, it universally establishes its native indifference as the matter and form of all things" (198/301) does not mean aesthetic intuition, artistic productivity, or the philosophy of art in general are now revised as remote or provisional interests for Schelling. It says, rather, that the advantage reason now enjoys over understanding (196–97/299–300) consists in the same advantage the striving genius and his work (if even unconsciously) enjoyed over finite reflection and separation.

We may test this view by turning to Schelling's *Further Presentations*. What is peculiar about this text is not that it concerns the same unity of thought and being in absolute cognition so central to *Bruno*[63] but that it is a no-frills display of philosophical 'construction' (the systematicity that overtakes reflection) *and* is as indebted to the poetic imagination as *Bruno*, if not more so. Let us observe how such construction unfolds. Just as *Bruno* characterized philosophical inwardness as the ability to comprehend "the fact that everything is contained in everything . . . the abundance of the whole universe is stored in individual beings" (B 188/SW3 291),[64] Schelling now argues that one must grasp "how everything is contained in everything, and how what is expressed on the one side of being, and on the other in thought, reflects the whole organism of reason" (FP 378/SW4 363–64). Reason is, as it were, alive—having a life in which "the absolute itself and knowledge of the absolute" share (381/368). This convergence means, as we have come to expect, that to speak of a knowledge 'of' the absolute is to speak from both directions of the genitive—to incarnate a knowledge beyond reflection, Criticism, and finite cognition such that one carries a "reason-intuition" (382/368–69) that identifies thought and being as one and is itself an expression of this essential unity. The philosopher invested in and by such knowledge practices an absolute science "of *the eternal, in its very self*" (382n.6/369). We have then a clearly delimited account of an "absolute mode of cognition" (383/370) that by all appearances enjoys a mastery exceeding the glimmer of identity found in aesthetic intuition—for the cognition issues from an identity point in which absolute knowledge and the absolute itself are equal (383n.8/390; cf. 384n.11/391). But we also have an assertion that reason, and not just the entity, is stamped with an image of eternity. Indwardness again becomes a story of *Ineinsbildung*. The absolute itself, says Schelling, "is *informed in us* as the idea and the essence of our soul" (383n.8/390). He returns to *Bruno*'s language of creative imaging, for example, in stating that the "innermost mystery of creation" is "the divine identification (imaging) of original and copy that is the true root of every being" (386/394). *Ineinsbildung* again denotes the unifying movement, and we may now understand it as the larger creation narrative in which the current chapter of *identification* is told. It is the eternal, all enveloping action of *Einbildungskraft* that gives reason (as absolute cognition) its life. So doing, it accounts for and expands on the notions of 'living artistry' and 'stamp' of identification noted in *Bruno*. The absolute reason attained via philosophical inwardness thus arises as an exercise that is party to (and parcel of) a more divine and original *schematism*—a divine *in-forming* that eliminates all differences between possibility and actuality (387/394–95).

That here, in the heart of what many consider to be the highpoint of his identity system, Schelling would return once again to the apparatus of the productive imagination, is nothing short of remarkable. To be sure, Schelling's concern in this discussion is not the formative activity of the human artist, but a construction of the unity by which the absolute subsists and of which every entity (plant, organism, being, etc.) partakes. A divine artistry—the very movement of absolute knowing and being—supplants the world taken as a field of appearances with a standpoint by which every entity is regarded as a unity "under which the whole is minted" (FP 386/SW4 394), a figuration of the absolute essence in a manifest form. Philosophical construction attunes one's gaze to the living fruit of this artistry, there disclosing "one being in all the original schematisms of world intuition" (387/394). The philosophy of nature and the philosophy of art are thus drawn together under the rubric of this divine in-forming—what we may call the poetic imagination of the absolute. Entities, from a more general standpoint, *strive* to comprehend "the universal in their particularity and the particular in their universality" (387–88/396–97), for every 'particular' consists in its own individual schematism yet subsists under the schematizing life of *Ineinsbildung*. Schelling explains this point by conjoining the Epicurean language of the Apostle Paul with the Kantian language of the productive faculty: "Everything lives and moves because of this twofold striving, and this striving springs from the first forming-into-one {identification} or from the fact that the undivided essence of the absolute is stamped identically upon the real and the ideal, and that substance *is* only in this way" (387–88/395–96). As the keystone of the identity system, *Ineinsbildung* wins for Schelling not only a construction of absolute unity, but also a legend for working out the totality of philosophy. The chief instrument of thought is that absolute form which "discloses essence and . . . universally mediates between knowing and the absolute" (391/403). Philosophical thought, that is, works on and according to the path of mediation hewn by the absolute imagination. The identification "of form with essence in intellectual intuition" constitutes absolute idealism as such—a path of thinking equivalent to the path of being—and the root rigor of identification is constituted by the living artistry of *Ineinsbildung* that constitutes essential identity as "the one-in-all and all-in-one" (392/404, 397/411).

Here we may rebound from the preeminence of this element to our original point of departure and reprise briefly the decisive place of imagination in the identity philosophy. Intent on furnishing a system of knowledge anchored in an unconditional principle, Schelling's focus on the productive capacities of intuition and the activity of spirit led him to establish a connection between the for-itself nature of spirit and the for-myself nature of self-consciousness. So doing, the proximity between ontological genesis and intuitive production disclosed the possibility for absolute identity, namely an intellectual intuition of the harmony intrinsic to spiritual volition. Self-consciousness came to name the standpoint from which every intuitive act echoed the striving of spirit, and this entailed the sensuous experience of mediation and production in a way necessarily alert to identity. What made this deduction of identity possible was a sustained elaboration of the power of imagination in a discourse of ontological, not merely logical or metaphysical, proportions. At the same time, inquiry itself turned a profound aesthetic corner, taking on the sensuous, kinetic cast shared by spirit and imagination alike. The work of productive imagination in the *Treatise* was followed by the decisive work of creative imagination in the *System*. As the account of generative unity and mediation broadened to include not just subject and object, but also nature and intelligence, intuition and production, the sought for standpoint of identity came to encompass history, nature, and knowledge. Identity bore the accent of a higher harmony and the assumption of such identity in the self bore the necessity of bringing forth knowledge of the conscious and unconscious in harmony. Schelling, here again, recalled philosophy to its aesthetic sense while investing it in the activity of the artistic imagination. The essential unity of the absolute was disclosed through an appeal to creative imagination broadly, and the production of the genius specifically. The precise kinship between philosophy and poetry, accordingly, was evident insofar as imagination now named the primordial potentiality at work in intuition. Indeed, in the *Darstellung* and *Philosophy of Art* Schelling underscored the artistic inner essence of philosophy and broached the imaginative life of the absolute as a movement of *Ineinsbildung* commensurate with the telling production of *Einbildung* in intuition. *Bruno* and the *Fernere Darstellung* translated the inwardness of intuition and inquiry into the fellowship of divine creation, essentially inviting the philosopher to follow the genius by reasoning through images in accordance with the harmony of the finite and infinite.

If pressed to classify this system of the absolute, we do best to regard it as an ontology of imagination according to which the absolute standpoint of reason is as sensuous and aesthetic as the harmony it intuits. In short, Schelling's philosophy of identity is in each progressive articulation a philosophy of the imagination. The system of the absolute names the work wrought by philosophy whereby thought itself belongs to the movement of imagination and is exercised along an aesthetic, indeed poetic, course.

Imagination and Ground in Schelling's *Freiheitsschrift*

We ended the last chapter by highlighting the character of *Ineinsbildung* in Schelling's conception of absolute identity and absolute cognition. By virtue of this informative movement of "the one-in-all and all-in-one" (FP 397/SW4 411), the philosophy of identity attained a point of connection between the unifying essence of the absolute and the constructive essence of philosophical inwardness. Stamped with an image of eternity, reason is minted in the press of a divine schematism and thus capacitated to share in the artistry of the absolute. To say that Schelling's more rigorous and logical deductions of identity effectively jettison the intellectual and aesthetic intuitions in favor of sheer 'absolute reason' in the period of the Darstellungs is to oversimplify his conception of standpoint and overlook the central poeticization of identity. On the basis of his lectures on *The Philosophy of Art*, his constructions in the *Further Presentations*, and his dialogical studies in *Bruno*, Schelling's system ambitions in this post *System* (1800) period do indeed assume a philosophical *Erkennen* rooted in the indifference standpoint of absolute reason, but the quality and performance of this knowing are shaped by an increasing appeal to the imaginative, creative life of the absolute. The law of unity, though exhibited logically in the proposition A=A, is thought in terms of the productive potency and differentiation within the determinative life of absolute being and primordial knowledge. Nothing is settled by assuming the standpoint of indifference or absolute reason. Even the aesthetic attunement of intuition (in play at least since the *System*, 1800) echoes in the attunement of reason to the eternal *Ineinsbildung*, and the ambition of the system is to attain "an aesthetic view of the world" (ART 88/SW5 465), a conversion of reason into what Schelling will in 1809 call an 'inspired' (from *Begeisterung*) and 'productive' (*erzeugenden*) dialectical science helmed by a 'word' of 'measure' (*Maß*) befitting the whole (F 75–6/SW7 415–16).

The purpose of the present chapter is to elucidate the weight and work of the imagination, together with the increasingly aesthetic bearing of philosophical reason, in a moment whereby Schelling's system faces its most strenuous self-assigned task. Our primary text is Schelling's *Philosophical Investigations into the Essence of Human Freedom and Matters Connected Therewith* (1809). Taking his 1807 address, *Concerning the Relation of the Plastic Arts to Nature*, as a point of departure, we will clarify the meaning of an 'essential' investigation and underscore the significance of nature, genesis, and whole for Schelling in the years leading up to 1809. We will then trace the singular importance of the divine imagination in the *Freedom Essay*'s account of God's self-revelation, the *poietic* framework for Schelling's ground/existence distinction in this account, and the priority of the 'word' in sustaining the inspired unity of the 'whole.' With the theme of *Ineinsbildung* abiding in the background to these elements, we will track how the question of freedom provokes in Schelling a reorientation *in inquiry* from intuition and abstraction to dialectic and *poiesis*, a reappraisal *in system* of the meaning of identity and ground, and yet a profound renewal of the creative, productive, and poetic imagination in the life of the absolute and in the reason it inspires.

Essence and connected matters

Read commonly as a *theodicy* in the traditional sense of the term, or as a "theodicy *of reason*" in a more penetrating sense,[1] Schelling's *Freedom Essay* pits the gathering force of his identity philosophy against a harrowing problem: the supposed contradiction between the very notion of system and the feeling or fact of human freedom.[2] Two comments by Schelling's contemporaries illustrate the elementary reach of this problem on the heels of the famous *Pantheismusstreit* of the 1780s. In 1789 Friedrich Heinrich Jacobi, observes: "Among living beings we know only man to be endowed with that degree of consciousness of his self-activity, which carries within itself the calling and impetus toward *free acts*."[3] In 1807 Franz Xavier von Baader remarks that "there is nonetheless evil—an evil spirit—in man, the recognition of which is independent of all theories and histories: How did this evil spirit come into man or arise in him?"[4] How, in other words, is a theoretical and practical system of the absolute—a system undergirded by a conception of absolute necessity—commensurate with the evident experience of freedom and evil? The question is shaped by Jacobi's intensified polarity between reason and immanence on one side, and revelation and transcendence on the other. But this context is best understood as a touchstone for Schelling's more ambitious integration of his system with the "deeper disclosures" required of a "complete, finished . . . whole" (F 4–5/SW7 333–34). The touchstone is a catalyst for this larger disclosure because its critical force centers on the authority accredited to an opposition. Parrying the implicit charge of a Spinozistic rationalism and atheism is one thing, but enabling "the higher, or rather, the genuine opposition [to] emerge, that of necessity and freedom, with which the innermost centerpoint of philosophy first comes into consideration" (4/333) is the aporetic heart of the matter. The language of 'centerpoint' is a shibboleth for the discourse of 'indifference' and the underlying motion of *Ineinsbildung* we have noted. But to recover and reveal this centerpoint in its full aporetic light Schelling must do more than reason from the immediacy of intuition, the stages of spirit, and the deductive and constructive elaborations of abstraction. He must, as his title indicates, undertake an investigation of 'essence' (*Wesen*).[5]

What is the sense of *Wesen* in this context, and is it a question Schelling's identity philosophy has anticipated? In his *Presentation* (1801) Schelling characterized absolute identity as an ontological necessity in which each individual being is "*a determined form of the being of absolute identity*" (P 361/SW4 131). He not only likened this identity to a line representing the *essential* indifference of A=A on the one hand, but also the differentiation and potency of A=B on the other. Questions of essence were thus answered through accentuating the standpoint one takes on identity as a fusion of essence and form, real and ideal. In his *Further Presentations* what is essential amid the differentiation of beings and the streams of cognition was likewise folded back on the absolute totality as the essential unity of absolute knowing and reason-intuition. Divisions of form and essence, though necessary for nature and cognition, were embedded in a larger comprehension of particularity and universality, a comprehension of the *informing* artistry of *Ineinsbildung* that intellectual intuition could apprehend as the creative identification of form with essence. The essence of absolute identity 'to be,' as it were, was the consideration in which all other matters of philosophical inwardness would find their assurance. When, at the outset of the *Freedom Essay*, Schelling maintains that the "unwavering, the diligent and the inner are again being sought" (F 5/SW7 334) we have no cause to believe he has withdrawn from the earlier standpoint on identity. Absolute identity remains a line through which form and essence are woven.

However, to investigate the *essence* of human freedom by disclosing a terrific 'opposition' is to entertain a place in the line's determinative course that would appear to splinter in multiple directions. It is to allow that there is another dimension in which the line (absolute identity) must be viewed, indeed tested, by a standpoint in which a particular essence of a particular being may well contaminate the fusion of essence and form in the informing life of identity. It is in this light that we must understand the stakes of the *Freedom Essay*, not simply as a resolution of the freedom-necessity contradiction, but rather an investigation of 'essence' oriented toward what Bernard Freydberg calls a moral and aesthetical "unfolding of the whole."[6] Furthermore, the difference between the 'line' and the 'whole' has everything to do with the 'matters connected' to the question of essence—matters irreducible to A=A or A=B 'formulations, but which nevertheless stand as the very *Sachen* intrinsic to revealing the meaning of the 'whole' in the *arkhe* and *logos* of the divine life and creation. The matters of ground, existence, and word, in particular, are connected to the question of essence in what we will call an originary and ontological way, not as subsequent argumentative considerations. Only by grasping this connection may one understand the work of the investigation as ultimately "the articulation of freedom" as "the articulation of system," and how this will require a "radical transformation of the understanding of the whole."[7] The quality of belonging attained under the motion of *Ineinsbildung* is to be 'said' from the ground up, imbued in a word of *Wesen* that is irreducible to *ratio* or cause. Distinct from the philosophical constructions of reason-intuition and from a logical–mathematical outline of absolute identity, we must anticipate how Schelling will present these connections by way of a mode of explanation (*Erklärung*) appropriate to disclosing the living and positive 'word' of divine yearning and personality, and to deriving 'one being' for all opposites.[8] But such anticipation is fraught with difficulties. In the least, it requires one to understand how to question the 'essence' (*Wesen*) of human freedom is to perform a work of thought oriented to the essential and not merely the conceptual. What ought one expect from an investigation of essence?

An aesthetic prolegomenon

Schelling's address, *Concerning the Relation of the Plastic Arts to Nature* is not concerned directly with the problem of necessity and freedom but is nevertheless a telling rehearsal of a philosophical investigation into 'essence'. Under the auspices of a commentary on theories of art and the historical stages of artistic development, it displays the orchestrated elements of his philosophy of nature, his conceptions of eternal ideas and creative force, and his view of the person in light of the whole. Specifically, Schelling's remarks exhibit a prognosis of the failure to think the theme of artistic production from the standpoint of a "living centre" (PA 324/SW3 392). He will raise a similar concern in the *Freedom Essay* when he cites the failure to think themes of freedom and immanence from the standpoint of the "ruling centerpoints" of a "living ground [*lebendigen Grund*]" (F 9/SW7 336, 27/356). In 1807 the summary obstacle to 'essence' is an overreliance on 'form', and in 1809, the leading obstacle will be an overreliance on abstract conceptualization; both are, we shall observe, failures of the imagination. By virtue of its subject matter, the *Plastic Arts* address also reveals the aesthetic accents moving at the root of Schelling's philosophies of nature and creation—elements crucial to the *Freedom Essay* yet introduced obscurely. We will consider briefly just a few of these distinctions before returning to the question of essence, ground, and imagination in 1809.

Ascertaining the essence of art depends first of all on understanding a relationship and its governing necessity. Artists, theories of art, and most of all nature are party to this relationship: "The whole of this treatise demonstrates that the foundations of art, and hence of beauty as well, lie in the vitality of nature" (PA 361n.7).[9] To speak of foundations is to position the question of essence within a field of necessity—"to make the inter-relationship of the whole structure of art manifest in the light of a higher necessity" (325/393). In so doing, one must disclose the origin or ground of a relational whole as primal and forceful. Schelling employs an array of organic metaphors such as art's "wellsprings," "fountainhead [*Urquelle*]," and "fundament [*Grund*]" (324/392, 347/416) to solicit this disclosure. Most artists, however, "seldom achieve a conception of what nature's essence is," and thus stand detached from "the world's holy, eternally creating primal energy, which engenders and actively brings forth [*hervorbringt*] all things out of itself" (324–25/392–93). Philosophers have obscured this fundamental relationship by maligning nature as "a dumb . . . dead image, to which even inwardly no living word was innate" (325/393).[10] Art's essence will show itself only to a proper pupil of nature. Plastic art and poetry, he explains, occupy "the position of an active link between the soul and nature" (324/392). To honor this link, an "inspired investigator" is needed, a "spiritual eye that penetrates [the] husk" of artworks "and feels the force at work within them" (325/393, 327/395). The criterion is not rhetorical but is rather imperative to a sensuous communication of essence beyond the privilege of mere form: "If we do not look at things in terms of their inner essence, but only in terms of their empty, abstracted form, they in turn say nothing to our inner being" (326/394).[11] That is not to discount all formal appraisals of works of art or philosophical problems, but rather to correct a problem of the direction taken by the inquiring standpoint.[12] To 'intensify the relative' and cloak essence beneath an enthusiasm for form is to remain adrift from "the absolute," and "the spirit" that is "essential and ultimate" (328/396).

How does one know when the 'inner essence' of a work of art speaks to his 'inner being'? Here Schelling does not appeal to intuition, feeling, or reflection, but rather speaks of attunement, imagination, and beauty. To apprehend essence *in* form is to derive a "spiritual" unity through an attunement to the science of nature's 'wellsprings.' One will grasp a unity of idea and deed, a unity "conducted by a super-powerful spirit" (PA 330/SW3 399) and most evident in man. In its creative motion, nature's science expresses the designs of an eternal, divine program. "Everything," Schelling explains, "is ministered over by an eternal idea, designed in the infinite intelligence" and delivered into reality through the "creative science" of the artist (331/400). One is on the path of the essential when he is attuned to the infinite and creative. In the case of Greek art, the path is delivered through "profound convulsions of the imagination [*Erschütterung der Phantasie*]" (337/406). Specifically, the imagination hosts an eruption wherein an apprehension of nonsensuous *beauty* is brought to sensuous representation as an "unfalsified natural force of creation" (331/400). 'Convulsions' in this case conveys a sense of the imagination being overwhelmed by a higher, albeit natural, force. In keeping with his earlier conception of aesthetic production, Schelling explains that the highest art often results from a "unanimity and mutual interpenetration" of unconscious force and conscious activity, a collaboration of nature's potency with man's creativity. Instead of appealing to his own philosophy of symbolism (presumably because symbolism would not capture the full force of nature), Schelling emphasizes the necessary and magical movement of "the living idea" that runs like a thread from the eternal idea, through the unconscious force and conscious activity, into the work, and then back to nature (332/401). His language is that of an expansive spiritual *mimesis*, not 'intuition'; the artist is to "emulate this spirit of nature, which is at work in the core of things," and artistic beauty "is essence, the universal, the vision and expression of the indwelling spirit of nature" (332/401).

Schelling no doubt assumes that infinite intelligence and eternal ideas arise as portions of a whole that, considered *as* a whole, must be beautiful. Beauty is also won from a field of striving and strife; the artist, like nature, must wrestle with form, and must fashion "into a world of its own, a genus, an eternal prototype [*ewigen Urbild*]" so that the work might "emerge consummate and beautiful in the whole" (PA 335–36/ SW3 404–05). Beauty is an event in a work that conveys what is essential in nature and also stands for "full and complete existence" (332/402). It is not an isolated errand of a whimsical deity, but a living typology of the whole, a creative cooperation with the energy of nature's spirit such that one finds "a certain fullness of beauty . . . the whole choral melody of beauty at once" (335/404). In the works of Raphael and Leonardo, for example, and in Homer's *Illiad*, beauty emerges from its essential "roots" and "come[s] into being" by masters who understand how to "bring forth [*hervorzubringen*] living beauty" (338/307, 341/409).

The appearance of *hervorbringen* is specific, but accentuates a broader conception of *poiesis*, a revelatory work of the "creative spirit [*schaffende Geist*]" wherein the "spirit of nature" realizes a "kinship with the soul" (PA 342/SW3 410). Opposition and antitheses are vital components of this bringing forth; essence must negotiate form, sculpture must perform a "complete corporeal expression of the spiritual," artists such as Correggio will show the fusion of light (soul) and dark (matter) principles as they elevate the corporeal "to the level of the spirit" (348/416, 351/419). And the highest works, to be sure, show the essence of art by virtue of their speaking a "bond of . . . divine love" together with an image of "eternal necessity" (351/420). Anticipating a pivotal theme of the *Freedom Essay*, Schelling adds that such *poiesis* is not limited to artistic production or beauty, but is emblematic as well of "the primal energy of thought" (343/412). The force of Schelling's discussion is in fact most profound when he announces the unity of phantasy and spirit, philosophy and poetry, in the person of Raphael:

> The flower of life at its most cultivated and the fragrance of phantasy, together with the savour of the spirit, breathe in unison from his works. He is no longer a painter, he is a philosopher, a poet at the same time. Beside the power of his spirit stands wisdom, and as he portrays things, so they are ordered in eternal necessity. In him art has reached its goal, and because the pure equipoise of divine and human can hardly exist at more than one point, the seal [*Siegel*] of uniqueness is set upon his works. (PA 351/SW3 420)

The answer to the question of the essence of art, one could say, lies in the poetic imagination of Raphael. Recalling Kant's sense of genius as a gift bestowed by nature, "this spiritual generative power" is vested by nature in man, and "like every spiritual worker, the artist can only obey the law which God and nature have inscribed in his heart, and no other" (PA 353/SW3 422, 355–56/427).

The *Plastic Arts* address has clarified the meaning and manner of an investigation into essence in several ways. First, a consideration of essence requires that the "vitality of nature" (PA 361n.7) and not the abstraction of form constitute the primary attunement for inquiry. Nature is the spring-like source of creative power, and ascertaining art's essence requires 'inspiration' in philosophy much the same as high art requires the striving inspiration of natural, creative force in the artist. Second, essence is to be disclosed under the living rubric of the 'whole' and governed by an 'eternal idea' for which a communication between the 'inner essence' of a work and the 'inner being' of a person is vital. An essential work, one could say, speaks a creative bond between the eternal spirit and intelligence of nature and the human imagination, a bond revealed through beauty to be good and loving. Third, whereas the productive force in nature and the energy of the artist consist in a moving, sensuous negotiation in matter and soul, the essence of art lies in a *poietic* bringing-forth that figures the 'extraordinary' through opposition, the "transfigured [*sich verklärt*]" (353/422) through limitation (language recalling the *informative* motion of *Ineinsbildung*). Finally, what is essential is so on account of a spiritual generative power whose point of consummation rests in a divine–human balance, a balance manifested concretely by the fusion of dark with light and body with soul.

The mechanizing imagination and the being of the copula

To follow a lecture on the essence of fine art with a treatise on the essence of human freedom is not *per se* to exchange one matter for another. It is to raise a more difficult question, but one that will require a wager of inspired investigation adopting and refining the elements deployed in the first study. To investigate the essence of human freedom is to discipline thought toward a standpoint of the whole, to work in terms of that necessity that subsists in the system's center or living ground. In the art address Schelling did this by tracing the passage of natural, primal necessity through art to beauty and the consummate bond of phantasy with spirit, human with divine, the work of the imagination with the work of nature. He steered the investigation of essence through the philosophy of nature, overlaying the discourse of vitality and creative force with one of infinite intelligence, eternal ideas, and spiritual work.[13] In the *Freedom Essay* the rendering of the whole in terms of necessity is more taxing, for the instrumental necessity itself appears to problematize the notion of human freedom. As in the artistic correspondence between idea and deed, design and execution (see PA 330/SW3 399), the essence of freedom will consist in the unity of act with inner necessity: free, says Schelling, "is what acts only in accord with the laws of its own being and is determined by nothing else" (F 50/SW7 385).[14] And though freedom is irreducible to causal connectedness just as artistry is irreducible to form, to say that "inner necessity is itself freedom" (49–50/383–85) is to color the creative force of the person (and of God) in more penetrating hues. Where the wrestling with form and limitation is fundamental to artistic production and unity, the wresting of "actuality from potency" (54/390) in the human will is a seed of potential discord and imbalance. To disclose the essence of human freedom, then, is also a matter of tracing the possibility for disharmony and sin in the very ground of human being. This play of disclosure and possibility is a preliminary indication of the two levels of 'bringing-forth' operative in this study: the *investigation* must bring forth a standpoint capable of seeing necessity and freedom as *Ein Wesen* (50/385), and the *matter* under investigation 'is' itself somehow an originary bringing-forth.

Toward these ends, Schelling advances the elements of his philosophy of nature toward God and, more specifically, nature in God. The discourse of nature's wellsprings, productive force, primal energy, and infinite intelligence will be located in God, reconfiguring the metaphysical God of conceptual determinism into the primal being of will, personality, ground, and existence. The sense of nature as the fountainhead of creative, spiritual striving will be transposed into the sense of God as primal yearning and divine imagination. The bond of the whole and the governance of inner necessity shall remain paradigms for these advances, but the very life of necessity will become more creative and the 'word' of the bond more active so as to account for the positive risks essential to freedom. Since our chief interest lies with the status of the poetic imagination in this work we will focus on Schelling's disclosure of 'essence' by way of the articulation and imaging he reveals within the life and motion of the 'connected matters.' Especially, we will account for the "creative" unity he inscribes in the law of identity (F 17/SW7 345) and the imaginative production brought forth from what he calls the primal will (*Urwille*) of/as the primal Being (*Ursein, Urwesen*) (23/352, 21/350). The question of human freedom's 'essence', we shall learn, has everything to do with the *poiesis* of what he terms the "divine" or "true" imagination—a force of imagination engaged in the procession (*Folge*) of beings from God, the immanent "differentiation [*Spezifikation*] of beings in the world," and the yearning and unity of "the Word" as the "bond of living forces" in nature and spirit (18/347, 29–30/359, 34/366).

Difference in identity

While the discussion of art's essence required an initial critique of the overreliance on *form*, the discussion of freedom's essence requires an initial critique of conceptual abstractions, specifically "the mechanistic kind of representation [*Vorstellungsart*]" (F 4/SW7 333) prevalent in inquiries of nature and essence. Misguided abstractions result from the errant habits of the inquiring imagination. As *form* had to be properly situated in the outworking of eternal ideas through beauty, *concepts* must be corrected in terms of the "driving force of all striving for knowledge," and, we shall discover, the beauty intended by "representations [*Repräsentationen*] of the divinity" (10/338, 18/347). Failing to understand this work of critique and restoration handicaps any effort to understand Schelling's appraisal of the human imagination, as well as his deeper sense of the creative, inspired task bestowed upon philosophy itself. Why is the spirit of abstraction a problem for Schelling? It is a problem because it substantiates a misguided view of necessity, dependence, and becoming—elements central to any system associated with immanence. To simply assume an incompatibility between freedom and system, for example, is to presume the clarity of conceptual judgment in lieu of arguments "drawn from the essence of reason and knowledge" (10/338). Schelling attributes to such an assumption "a level of dialectical immaturity" (14/343) inclined to treat the relationship of things to God as one of consequence to ground, and to assume that dependence abolishes independence. Hence, abstraction and mechanistic representation are logical and speculative instruments ill-disposed toward an ontological subject matter. An essential investigation, by contrast, will be interested in the very *Wesen* of the copula ('is') in the creative nature of the ground, in what a distinction between being and becoming brings to the question of dependency, and in the self-revelation of the living God (17–18/345–47). To understand these imperative points of difference we must account for a discussion that was pertinent to the plastic arts address but not treated in detail: Schelling's renewed appraisal of the law of identity.

The being and meaning of the copula ('is') is the pivot on which the relationship between necessity and freedom, system and person, turns. The meaning of the copula is of course central to any logical judgment and is the critical, if unreflective, touchstone for those (like Jacobi) who hear in all Spinozism, pantheism, and immanence a system of absolute identity that "abolishes all individuality" (F 15/SW7 343). Thanks to a "complete ignorance regarding the nature of the copula," Schelling explains, identity has been misconstrued as sameness (*Einerleiheit*) (13/341–42), when in fact it is grounded on a preservation of difference (*Differenz*). The 'is' in the statement "the body is blue," for example, obviously does not mean the body is blue and only blue, and that blue is body and only body. By the same token to say that the individual 'is' in God or that knowledge is knowledge 'of' the absolute (genitival meaning) need not imply a wholesale mechanistic subsumption of all entities and all knowing into a lifeless absolute. The copula, to be clear, "does not express a unity which, turning itself in the circle of seamless sameness, would not be progressive and, thus, insensate or lifeless" (17/345). But this misunderstanding is one reason why idealism (generally understood) fails to think freedom in an essential way. Thinking the meaning of the copula as sameness leads only to a "general" and "formal" concept of freedom, whereas thinking the being of the copula as difference and unity in concert will point toward "the real and vital concept . . . that freedom is the capacity for good and evil" (23/352).

This connection between the being of identity and the positive capacity intrinsic to freedom marks a vital step in Schelling's deepening conceptions of both system and necessity. The immediate result of animating the identity principle is a recapturing of the dependency issue from abstract representations. Identity may no longer be used to buttress a view of dependency that privileges the logical relationship of consequent to ground, predicate to subject. But there is a further, more radical result. Schelling remarks that "the law of the ground" is a "creative" domain that is "just as original" as that of the copula (F 17/SW7 345–46). One could well say that he is pressing the coin of logic into the currency of ontology, even raising the value. Under this new economy, the task is to think this semblance of *identity* and *ground* both in terms of the 'difference' that will capacitate human freedom and in the progressive, life-giving 'unity' of the whole, which governs being and becoming. The task is to raise anew the question of dependency in terms of "the divine being itself" and the "procession" [*Folge*] of creatures from this being. The being, of course, is God—not a mechanistic or causal deity, but rather the divine in its precise mode of "self-revelation" (18/347). To enact this task Schelling must further translate dependency into *becoming* and inflect the issue of necessity into that of *divine freedom*. The radical retrieval of identity and ground has prepared this development, but moving *into* the terrain of self-revelation will involve more daunting maneuvers from within the very limits of German Idealism.

To begin, Schelling speaks of the course of necessity flowing forth from the primal will (F 23/SW7 352). It is important to note that his statement, "Will is primal Being [*Ursein*]" (21/350), is a point of departure in the *Freedom Essay*, and not a point of discovery. The ontological primacy of the will marks idealism's "first complete concept of formal freedom" (21/351), but even a positive concept is, as the case of identity has shown, not adequate; Fichte's "in-itself," for example, attains a "completed system for itself," but for such a system and such a concept to again become "real" in a deeper sense it must show that "everything real (nature, the world of things) has activity, life and freedom as its ground" (22/351). Thus attuned to the corroboration of the 'real' with the 'ground,' Schelling sets in motion the primacy of the will so as to transpose the generative force of nature into the becoming of God. The intimacy of God and nature was assumed in the arts address, though left unspecified. Now, the very ability of system to account for necessity and freedom turns on a descent into the essence of divine freedom made manifest in the creative force of divine self-revelation.[15]

Schelling sounds this radical note when he explains that the "point of view which is fully adequate to the task to be undertaken here can only be developed from the fundamental principles of a true philosophy of nature" (26–7/356) then cites mystics as models of this undertaking.

But why gather generative nature in divine becoming by way of the *Ursein* that is Will? In simple terms 'will' denotes freedom and act, and in ontological terms 'primacy' of the will denotes necessity.[16] Together, these qualities suggest that the 'contradiction' between freedom and necessity is always already a productive opposition even as it disarms the authority of blanket conceptual formulations. Schelling believes that God, as a God of "the living" (F 18/SW7 347) (and not blind necessity), emerges by way of an internal, natal necessity—a birth from the matrix of originary activity in which opposition is enabling, not debilitating. Idealist generalities, says Schelling, have abstracted God as *actus purissumus*, effectively removing God from nature, limiting him to a moral world order, and indeed detaching nature itself from a "living ground" (26/356).[17] Whether or not primal will is in fact also a lingering abstraction is a question we shall revisit with Heidegger. For the moment we allow that Schelling's deity is not yet itself, properly or absolutely speaking. It is not manifest as a magisterial or authoritative subject predicated of through the traditional array of divine superlatives (omnipotence, omnipresence, omniscience). It is not even an agent spirit 'hovering over the waters' (Genesis 1:2) on the brink of its commanding word. This is the divine before the 'beginning,' the eternal productive impulse bereft of any complete *logos*. Primal will names the ambiguous freedom from which the divine is born.

The divine imagination and the being of two mysteries

Schelling's remarks concerning the principles of identity and ground, the nature of dependency and becoming, the difference between a formal and a capacitating view of freedom, and the more living conception of God have accomplished two things. First, they dispel the charge that immanence opposes freedom. Second, they comprise a course of conceptual correction through which Schelling prepares the grounds for his investigation into essence. Recalling our earlier point about the *poiesis* of inquiry, each element serves to attune the standpoint or point of view (F 26/SW7 353) required for carrying the discoveries of his natural philosophy into the site where the roots of a system of the absolute and the birth of divine existence itself share in the same original, generative motion. But the real challenge of Schelling's study now comes to the fore: To speak of an "essential dependence" or of any basic "connection between God and beings" (23/355) in terms of a real disclosure of the primal will is to invite the challenge of explaining the reality of evil without destroying the integrity of the divine. If human freedom is to consist in a capacity for good and evil, and if beings become *in* the becoming of God, then God's self-revelation seems itself poised on the rim of an estranging abyss. Two decisive themes arise through this puzzle. *First*, since God, born of primal willing, is capacitating but not evil in nature, Schelling deduces that freedom "must have a root [*Wurzel*] independent of God" (24/355). This point stands as an early insinuation of *difference* in the being of divine self-revelation, one that complicates any recourse to standard conceptions of emanation (25/354, see 18/347), and it points toward Schelling's central distinction between ground and existence 'in' God.[18] *Second*, to understand the relationship between capacity and self-revelation Schelling posits the *poietic* cornerstone of his inquiry: *the divine imagination*. Unlike the human imagination which "grants merely ideal reality to created beings," the "representations [*Repräsentationen*] of the divinity" are necessarily independent beings, "things in themselves" (18/347). In this way, the divine imagination performs the noted *differentiation* of beings. The distinction is not a dismissal of that human or artistic imagination, which Schelling has long privileged, but a means of hastening the inquiring standpoint to that generative side of the divine ground, which is as obscure in origins as it is unheralded in philosophy.[19] The act of divine self-revelation will in fact unfold through the divine imagination as a genealogy of the real (*reell*). The reformulation of dependency will be accomplished by recovering the sense of God's "look" (*Repräsentation*) at things in themselves as a creative, capacitating look. We will examine these elements of ground and existence and divine imagination in concert since the text offers no means of detaching them.

Imagination and ground

Tracing the generative agency of the divine imagination in the course of self-revelation depends disclosing the primal potency of nature *in* God. Schelling's positive argumentation toward the essence of freedom begins in the following statement:

> Since nothing is prior to, or outside of, God, he must have the ground of his existence in himself. All philosophies say this; but they speak of this ground as of a mere concept without making it into something real [*reell*] and actual [*wirklich*]. This ground of his existence, which God has in himself, is not God considered absolutely, that is, in so far as he exists; for it is only the ground of his existence. It [the ground] is *nature*—in God, a being indeed inseparable, yet still distinct, from him. (F 27/SW7 358)

The passage contains a statement of standpoint and a specification of task. The *standpoint* will concern the generative nature in God and not God regarded in the full consciousness and unity of his absolute existence. The decision for this standpoint is justified on the basis of what has been said regarding dependency as 'becoming,' though here the standpoint faces an immediate puzzle. Human beings are beings "for whose Being there is no ground other than God but who are as God is" (F 18/SW7 347), yet the individuated being of all things depends on a division from God—beings "must become [*werden*] in a ground different from God" (38/371). Since, Schelling reasons, "nothing indeed can be outside of God, this contradiction can only be resolved by things having their ground in that which in God himself is not *He Himself*, that is, in that which is the ground of his existence" (28/359). A similar necessity bears upon God. If we allow that God (considered absolutely) is a creator of creatures who bear his likeness, receive his revelation, and yet remain free, then we must allow, with Schelling: "God himself requires a ground so that he can exist; but only a ground that is not outside but inside him and has in itself a *nature* which, although belonging to him, is yet also different from him" (42/375).

The *task* is to make this ground 'real' and 'actual'; a decision, as well, to embrace the disorienting danger the early Schelling attributed to *Wirlichkeit* at the abyssal limits of intuition.[20] *Das Wirkliche*, from *wirken*, denotes actuality in the sense of "to have an effect," as opposed to, for example, *Abgeschlossenheit* ("something that is finished, completed").[21] The task is, in other words, to disclose in God the same creative difference and unity ascribed to the laws of identity and ground (see preceding text), and thereby present the act of divine self-revelation in accordance with the same primal potency and striving manifest in nature. Doing so, moreover, will establish the parameters for thinking "the severability of the principles" (F 33/SW7 363)—the capacitating root for the possibility of evil, and thus the comparison of divine and human selfhood through which the essence of human freedom will be understood. One is hard-pressed to imagine a more difficult route of inquiry. However, it is by honoring this difficulty that the *poiesis* of inquiry comes to comport with the *poiesis* of its matter. The means of elucidating the distinction between ground and existence (which is not a "heuristic aid" but is in fact "very real" (69–71/408–09)) consists in a play of ontological necessity and divine affectivity informing both the standpoint and the task.[22] The status of identity presents one example: we must understand the statement, "God is," to mean both "the yearning [*Sehnsucht*] the eternal One feels to give birth to itself" (28/359) and the grounding movement by which beings become.[23] Let us consider how this collaboration between necessity and affectivity unfolds as a work of imagination.

Schelling likens the relation in God between the being of his concealed ground and the being of his absolute existence to the relation between gravity and light. The point is more than an illustration: as the eternal "dark ground" of light, gravity is not itself actual (*actu*), but it is "absolute identity" manifest in the position of "potency [*Potenz*]" (F 27–8/SW7 359). Potency applies to the ground in God in the same way—gravity and ground take eternal precedence over existence and light, but not in the causal or temporal sense of priority. The eternal potency always already accompanies the full existence of God, as eternal act that (like gravity) is never finished or set aside, and through which existence (like light) becomes itself. Freydberg rightly observes that ground and existence are equiprimordial without being equivalent, for "there is excess in the ground that has no counterpart on the side of existence."[24] But what of this natal quality of 'yearning' and the events of differentiation stowed within potency and excess? As in the case of gravity, with yearning Schelling assimilates an analogy into the matter itself; we must appreciate his doing so as an exercise against the false representations of the abstract imagination, an exercise that will allow a discourse necessarily tethered to an exhausted metaphysical lexicon to nevertheless proceed.[25] Schelling describes his own point as a treatment of "the essence of yearning" (29/359), stripping it of any illustrative distance. The feeling of yearning is ascribed to the existent God in the mode of *prius*, but the yearning itself lives and moves as "will" in the dark ground (28/359). This will is not the complete will—the will with "understanding"—but is "a divining will" that belongs to the understanding in the same way that "anarchy" belongs to the form that orders it (28–9/359–60). Such yearning is the very ground of self-revelation and therefore creaturely becoming, the "indivisible remainder" that precedes the bond and order of understanding but "remains eternally in the ground" (29/360) (like potency's excess). Yearning bears witness to the side of the primordial will, which craves understanding and completion in the way darkness craves light. One could say that the yearning is a desire for the birth of that authority captured in the dynamic unity of the copula. But could one also say that it resembles that "irresistible urge" in the nature of the artistic genius who, though "unconscious in regard to product," nevertheless intuits the design by which the harmony of the subjective and objective are "rendered wholly objective" (STI 222/SW3 614, 14/351, 232/629)?

In a certain sense, the combination of darkness with yearning (*Sehnsucht*) in an "irrational principle" (F 41/SW7 374) echoes a theme Schelling has been plying for some time. In his *System* (1800), for example, there was the formative irrationality of "nonconscious activity" in the constitution of self, nature, and history (STI 12/SW3 348, 14/351–52). In his lectures on the *Philosophy of Art* he spoke of the birthplace of the artistic imagination as an eternal "region of darkness and formlessness" and of the "primal chaos" that marks the "inner essence of the absolute" (ART 37/SW5 394, 88/465). In the address of 1807 he alluded to the darkness of matter brought to inspired fusion with the light of soul and the striving of art to attain consummation with the eternal prototypes of beauty (PA 351/SW3 419–20, 364n.8). Discursive contexts no doubt distinguish these allusions. But if our interpretations in prior chapters are correct, we are justified in expecting of 'darkness' and 'yearning' a similar association with the work of the imagination that was found in our accounts of the 'unconscious' and 'striving.'[26] This expectation is verified by a consideration of the creative work of *divine representation* in yearning and the resulting emergence of *understanding* and *man*.

God's look

The productive ascent of the 'divining will' in yearning begins as "the first stirring of divine existence" (F 29–30/SW7 359). This stirring is manifest, remarkably, as a movement of *representation*: "an inner, reflexive representation is generated in God himself through which, since it can have no other object but God, God sees himself in an exact image of himself" (29–30/360–61). In a 1941 course Heidegger will speak of this motion as "the essential God completely in his ground, elevated into image;" the phrase he employs is "*Einen Anblick seiner selbst sich geben– »Bild«*" [*Giving to himself a view of himself—*"Image"] (GA49 125). The unfolding of divine self-revelation thus depends from the start on a figuration, a representation. But what is reflexive has no traction in the realm of the conscious or the ordered, for these elements have not yet appeared. The imaging obtains from within the darkness, the "anarchy of the ground"—the remainder Schelling famously describes as "the incomprehensible base of reality in things" (F 29/SW7 359–60)—*der nie aufgehende Rest*.[27] To recognize understanding in anarchy and will in yearning, the divine imagination exercises its creative capacity through a willfulness not yet fully formed. Representation, as it were, marks the delivery of *logos* and not the other way around. God does not calculate the merits of a creative project, but rather in his very self-imaging already enacts a word and will of loving formation; such self-imaging marks, at once, God's coming into existence with the creation of the world. Creation, in this sense, is, as Heidegger will observe, "not as a making but rather as allowing-to-become [*Werden-lassen*]" (GA49 125–26).[28] Will, as primordial *being*, obtains in this longing. God's reflexive representation

> is at the same time the understanding—the Word—of this yearning and the eternal spirit which, perceiving the word within itself and at the same time the infinite yearning, and impelled by the love that it itself is, proclaims the word so that the understanding and yearning together now become a freely creating and all-powerful will and build in the initial anarchy of nature as in its own element or instrument. (F 29–30/SW7 360)

Darkness moves toward light, anarchy toward word, by way of a unifying "impression" (*Ein-bildung*), an "awakening," an "idea" (F 31/SW7 361), yet without sundering the remainder through a figurative abstraction: "The understanding is born in the genuine sense from that which is without understanding. Without this preceding darkness creatures have no reality; darkness is their necessary inheritance" (29/360). The becoming of the understanding and will of God *in* God is thus not a tale of reason's evolution, but of the formless longing for form, the reflexive longing for image, the imagination longing to be creative, and, ultimately, the loving word of formation. (In the next chapter we will explore, with Heidegger, the questions resulting from this pairing of *das Sein der Schöpfung* with the "*becoming-image* as 'work of the understanding' [*Ein-bildung* als »Wirken des Verstandes«]" (GA49 125–26) and thus the primacy of a willful *logos* in Schelling's constellation of *Werden-lassen*.)

A similar activity of imagination is found in the account of man's emergence in this eternal act of divine self-revelation and from this dark ground. In this account, the tension between that which brings forth and that which "rises up [*sträubt sich*]" (man's arrogance) (F 29/SW7 360) is a more pronounced event within the play of dark and light, and with a view toward the necessary severability of principles. Schelling's attention to necessity and affectation remains in his disclosure of the ground in God as the ground for man's becoming. By way of reflexive impulse, the emergent soul is brought forth not simply as a likeness of the absolute deity, but through a "division of forces"—darkness (yearning, anarchy) and light (understanding, unity)—which take root as a "a dual principle in itself" (30–31/361–62) *in* the human being. But we must be careful not to speak too quickly of an individuated human will; the principal player in this birth remains yearning—yearning at the productive threshold between ground and existence. With and as the soul's emergence, yearning turns covetous. An *image* of unity emerges in the dark yearning, a "resplendent glimpse of life in the darkness of the depths" (30/361), and this proves intoxicating for the yearning.[29] Aroused by the figure of unity and light, yearning holds fast to the ground as though tugging on the side of the remainder against the force of existence. The tension is necessary to the division of forces and the act of individuation, but it ultimately means the emergence of the "soul" as "something inner out of the ground" is stamped as an emergence of something "independent of the original understanding" (31/362).

The ensuing tension is this: understanding's division effects a "genuine impression [*Ein-Bildung*], since that which arises in nature is impressed [*hineingebildet*] into her," but with this there arises the soul as "a particular and self-sufficient being" (31/362). Though the proclamation of the word (of existence and unity) is a "transfiguration of the initial principle of darkness into light," creatures have their 'inheritance' as well as their delivery; there is the self-will of the dark principle and the universal will of the light principle (31–2/362). The principles are not *per se* reducible to moral counterparts; they are two sides of one act of self-revelation that persists necessarily *in man*, an oscillation between the act of *impression* and separation and the act of *transfiguration* (cf. PA 353/SW3 425) and unity. Schelling explains:

> This raising of the deepest *centrum* into light occurs in none of the creatures visible to us other than man. In man there is the whole power of the dark principle and at the same time the whole strength of the light. In him there is the deepest abyss and loftiest sky or both *centra*. The human will is the seed—hidden in eternal yearning—of the God who is present still in the ground only; it is the divine panorama of life, locked up within the depths, which God beheld when he fashioned the will to nature. In him (in man) alone God loved the world, and precisely this likeness of God was possessed by yearning in the *centrum* as it came into opposition with the light. Because he emerges from the Ground (is creaturely), man has in relation to God a relatively independent principle in himself; but because precisely this principle—without it ceasing for that reason to be dark in accordance with its ground—is transfigured into light, there arises in him something higher, *spirit*. For the eternal spirit proclaims unity or the word into nature. (F 32/SW7 362)[30]

Notice that Schelling overlays the organic ('seed') and the figurative ('panorama') when speaking of the human will. The allusions carry forward the conception of man's independence and the principles' separability in God, and yet also stand situated in a larger bringing-forth—transfiguration as the spiritual word of unity. Schelling is reminding us that the broader life of identity between God and nature (the revelation of God's spirit through principles which are distinct yet "indissoluble" in God (as existing *actu*) (F 32–3/SW7 362–63)) is a story of moving through image to word, representation to proclamation; we must not think of this motion as something sequential, but as a genesis of fullness or completion transcending ontic time.[31] At the same time, the 'whole' in man also entails the severability of the principles in the human will as the possibility of a selfish (*selbstisch*) (33/363) personality in man, and therein the capacitating possibility of evil at the heart of the essence of human freedom.

These steps in Schelling's discussion echo the account of necessity and motion found in the Plastic Arts address, though the organic metaphors and aesthetic dynamism of this primordial register accompany a more focused movement of the imagination on several levels. To summarize: first, the representations (*Vorstellungen*) of the inquiring imagination stand bracketed beneath a more essential course of conceptual correction; second, the divine imagination stands distinct from the human imagination by virtue of having *Repräsentationen* that arouse real existence (*reell*) through *Spezifikation*, not just ideality; third, the operation of divine self-revelation (and all becoming therein) in and through the motion of ground and existence stands specified as a *Folge* rooted in figuration, impression and ongoing transfiguration before any determinative decisions of the understanding. Modal qualities of potency, reflexivity, and yearning, moreover, stand attached to these events of imagination in an original and originating way. The primal act and formation of will, in God and in man, is likewise inexplicable apart from instantiations of image, illumination, and word. Short of commenting on Schelling's discussion in full, we now want to explore how the appearance of evil in man, the decision of man at the summit of creation, and the larger sense of the 'whole' in this system of freedom are indicative of an elemental operation of imagination and a vocation of *poietic* measurement bestowed upon man and his reason.

The measuring imagination and the word of man

To appreciate the capacity for freedom as a capacity for evil we must anticipate a further tension between the divine and human imaginations, a tension in many ways more constitutive of the essence of human freedom than a doctrinal or dualistic moral discord. Schelling will treat the problematic activity of *human representations* on the primordial plane of principled movement and becoming, yet encompass this with the work of the divine imagination in passing from representation to word, from the life-giving *genesis* of images to the life-giving *measure* of *logos*. On the side of genesis, we already know that ground and existence (dark and light principles), though never separate in God, stand opposed in a way that is necessary for the unfolding of divine self-revelation. In this dialectical matrix real unity depends on severing, real love on discord (F 41/SW7 373–74). To say that human will is a 'seed' and 'panorama' of divine life is to tether human being's emergence to the emergence of God *actu*, and to allow that the human soul is 'of' the same nature in God. Measure (in the sense of a 'rule') belongs to genesis in the form of the intended proclamation of the 'word' of unity—as akin to a band—over the whole, but the fate of measure has everything to do with the path of the principles in human will. Crucial to understanding Schelling on the possibility and actuality of evil, we will see, is elucidating the divine imagination's wager on the imagination of man.

Letting-be and its counter-measures

The work of the divine imagination in divine self-revelation is a work that aspires to "divine measure and balance" (F 34/SW7 365). The proclamation of the word over the division of forces is to maintain this measuring unity of dark and light principles. Evil, however, is primordially capacitated from the "elevation of self-will" and "collapse" (*Zerrüttung*) of understanding's bond of unity (34/365). The failure to sustain the measure is not the fault of "finitude" or creaturely "deprivation," but of the volition of selfhood in raising itself to spirit by imprinting a "false unity" over the division of forces (38/370, 36/368, 38/371). Owing to the aforementioned covetousness of yearning, man's soul arises in the same motion as the will of the ground rises up. Thus, man's situation in the larger account of becoming is as follows:

> Man is placed on that summit [*Gipfel*] where he has in himself the source of self-movement toward good or evil in equal portions: the bond of principles in him is not a necessary but rather a free one. Man stands on the threshold; whatever he chooses, it will be his act: but he cannot remain undecided because God must necessarily reveal himself and because nothing at all can remain ambiguous in creation. (F 41/SW7 374)

The dark and light principles must be in man; whether they remain bonded or dissolved is a matter of human freedom—a matter of whether the will of the self preserves the harmony native to divine *poiesis*. Man's incumbent decisiveness will no doubt have a moral outcome, but the site of this summit and the life of this bond owe their origins to a positive "letting the ground be active" of the divine will, and to the "arousal of the irrational or dark principle in creatures" required by the essential will to revelation (F 42/SW7 374, 45/378, 43/375). Schelling thus speaks of "a *general* evil" (47/381), a capacity for evil that is necessary for disclosing the capacity for good. The site of the summit is thus attained, in part, *by* the positive capacity for evil, but since there is already in the ground a desire to master the glimpse of unity in the will's darkness (see 44/377, 47/381) it may appear as though man stands disposed to evil. The pivotal dilemma is whether or not the 'letting-be' of the ground will remain productive of real unity or compliant with yearning's covetous mastery over the image of unity. Though Schelling insists that the ground does not "make evil as such," for "evil remains always an individual's own choice," he means existent evil, evil's "appearance in man" (48/381, 54/389). The manifestation of *sin* in fact appears as a counter-measure: "sin strives to break the word, touch the ground of creation, and profane the mystery" (55/391).[32]

To sin, in this sense, is something different from an utterly volitional revolt. Sin is manifest through the will's uprising, but this happens on the basis of what Schelling, following the Platonic expression, calls "the false imagination [*falsche Imagination*] (*logismōi nothōi*), which is sin itself" (54–5/390).[33] The structure of this matter is the same as the dark ground's covetousness of the image of unity. The dark principle *in* man's selfhood, aroused to actuality in the unfolding of God's self-revelation, catches sight of actuality amid potency, and tries to wrest it from the intended loving bond of forces. The imagination then "borrows the appearance of Being from true being" and "strives by means of mirrorlike images" and "the radiant glimpse of life in the depths" to raise self-will to selfhood (55–6/390–91). The peril of sin is thus instigated by a collusion of the dark principle and the creaturely imagination. The consequence is a contamination of the whole gathering of ground and existence. "Thus is the beginning of sin," says Schelling, "that man transgresses from authentic Being into non-being [*Nichtseiende*], from truth into lies, from light into darkness, in order to become a self-creating ground and, with the power of the *centrum* which he has within himself, to rule over all things" (55/390). It would not be at all amiss to say that *transgression* is an offense against *transfiguration*, in which case it attenuates the course of *Ineinsbildung* as well. To speak of a Fall from grace is to speak first of a fall from harmony into discord, Being into nonbeing. It is not simply to break a word of command, but to break the word of the bonded whole, the "bond of creaturely existence" (55/391). The integrity of the word as measure of the whole thus depends on the use or misuse of imagination, a fact further evidenced by what the opposition in sin nevertheless reveals: "the most inner bond of the dependence of things and the being of God" (55/391).

Restorative measures

Though the human will is disposed toward evil in a general sense, and the human imagination prepares the choice for actual evil, Schelling doubles the initial and eternal procession between ground and existence with an equiprimodial and *salvific* restoration of the measure.[34] He does so in terms familiar to his long-standing interest in the artistic imagination. To understand this possibility in full we must navigate a passage from the striving of the false imagination to the striving of the measuring imagination; we must grasp the movement from representation to word. The practical site of concern here is the being of the summit—man—and, though Schelling does not use the term, it is advisable to think this summit as the site wherein *Ineinsbildung* is to be measured out in accordance with the ligaments of divine love. For the life of the summit to begin anew from eternity the "relation of the ground to God" must be reestablished, or indeed, 'let-be' such that the "ligature of the dark principle (selfhood)" is restored "into the light" (F 46/SW7 380). There is a "true good" belonging to the divine bond, and a "divine magic" (56/391) intent on combating discord. The realization of salvation also bears specifically on language—a "living word" is to reign over the chaos of Babel (46/380). But what of man's activity in this site? Schelling speaks of a conscientiousness (*Gewissenhaftigkeit*) enacted as a "resoluteness" superior to any "enthusiasm" in the negative sense (57/392). Man is to be "an enduring being" who grounds his portion of yearning in the "bright consciousness" of spirit (70/408). In this way, man's life under the bond of unity and love requires something much like divine artistry, in one sense, and artistic resoluteness in another. To speak of "a supreme clarity of moral life [arising] in grace and divine beauty" (58/394) is to transpose the essential experience of artistic consummation in 1807 into the redemption of human freedom and the recovery of harmony between the principles. It is to envision the standing of man at the intersection between will's beginning in yearning and becoming and will's more complete beginning in love. To be resolute in this standing is to turn from yearning's contamination of unity and measure toward the unity sheltered in the divine personality.

To disclose such standing in view of these restorative possibilities is to further the *poietic* bearing of the investigation's subject-matter. As we have noted, Schelling often joins to such moments of concentration a corresponding caution against the representational habits of philosophical inquiry. In this case the disclosure of God's self-determining personality (*Persönlichkeit*) as "a living unity of forces" requires a renewed disavowal of God as "a merely logical abstraction" (F 59/SW7 394–95). If the *Gewissenhaftigkeit* of man's standing in the summit is precisely at issue, and if the human imagination is misleading on the level of representational inquiry and false on the level of original becoming, then it stands to reason that Schelling is addressing the possibility of measure and word both as an ontological matter as well as a matter of philosophical standpoint. He cannot mollify the appearance of evil in men, but he can reorient the philosophical imagination toward the full standpoint of divine imagination and proclamation, resulting in a further disclosure of that life of the word meant to redeem and shape the philosophical task. And to attune the inquiring standpoint to the personhood (*Personalität*) of God is to draw closer to the eternal and salvific life of the bond in which yearning and understanding, ground and existence subsist.

These *poietic* possibilities are evident in the standpoint won for man by reflection on the will of love. In basic terms, the will of love in the second, salvific, beginning serves to free the will of the ground, and in so doing, to rescue the appetite of man from the vulnerabilities of his *false imagination* and reinstate him in the life of the *word*. The possibility of evil, we recall, arose in the primal ground (*Urgrund*) of existence "as" the striving of this ground "toward actuality in created beings," a reaction of the ground to the image of unity and a desire to own this unity in its own dark will (F 44/SW7 378, 47/380–81). Conversely, to envision God as personality is to pair the anarchy of the ground with the "archetype [*Urtypus*]" (62/398) accompanying the *Ursein* but hitherto concealed beneath the exercises of the false imagination—the archetypal beauty, goodness, and love.[35] The manifestation of evil in man at his summit position "looks" like a result of a ground that is "the originator of evil" (63/399), but this view is at least as inadequate as the image of unity coveted by yearning, and the creative assertions of the false imagination. This point of view, one could say, is like examining a work of art's detail yet neglecting the work's whole. Man's resoluteness at the summit requires a glimpse of his essential image in the personhood of God, a glimpse whereby one sees that "[t]he same thing that becomes evil through the will of the creature (if it tears itself completely free in order to be for itself), is in itself good as long as it remains wrapped up in the good and in the ground" (63/400). Whether man will enjoy and sustain the panoramic measure of goodness, beauty, and love is a question of whether he will opt for non-Being and unreality or the "bright consciousness" (67/404–05, 70/408) of a bonding word. Man's ontological inheritance and moral opportunity alike are rooted in the *poietic* fecundity of the divine imagination, a force of production and proclamation in which image and word conspire to inspire the life of the whole. Essential works of art, we recall, must 'speak' to our 'inner being'; formation 'is' a saying. To grasp a bonding measure in a figuration of archetypal beauty and grace is to hear the word of unity over the whole:

> Solely because God brought order to the disorderly offspring of chaos and proclaimed [*ausgesprochen*] his eternal unity into nature, he opposed darkness and posited the word as a constant *centrum* and eternal beacon against the anarchical movement of the principle bereft of understanding . . . (F 65/SW7 402)

Curiously, at the very point at which one would expect Schelling to extend this standpoint of the summit to the more practical function of man's essential freedom in sustaining this word of measure, he tasks himself with an ontological descent into a matter that is before all divine creation and imagination: "a being before all ground," an original "*non-ground* [*Ungrund*]" (F 68/SW7 406). Presumably, this move toward the "absolute *indifference* [*Indifferenz*]," which "precedes all opposites" (68/406, cf. 73/412), is an attempt to reckon with that deeper capacitating force that may necessarily lie beneath the absolute identity of the whole, beneath the "one being [*Ein Wesen*] for all oppositions, an absolute identity of light and darkness, good and evil," that is, "the one being [that] divides itself in two sorts of being in its two ways of acting" (68/406, 71/409). Is this a final conceptual correction of the absolute? A reconfiguration of the primal will in view of personality? A figuration of the impetus for his eternal beginnings that is avowedly noncausal? Or, more plainly, is it a final homage to any system's need for an original principle? (Here we arrive at what will be a crucial matter of criticism for Heidegger, but for the sake of consistency in our reading we will refrain from absorbing his problematic until the next chapter). If we begin by appreciating Schelling's task on this score as itself a *resolute* entry into what is most 'inner' (as opposed to external) to a system of freedom then we will better understand the culmination of his treatise as at once an appeal to the life of the whole *and* to the measuring imagination of man.

The artistry of antecedent *Indifferenz*

First, it is important to regard the full span of difficulty associated with questioning the origin of the being that informs ground and existence in God. As Freydberg observes, it "requires apprehending the origin before all unification as well as before all duality."[36] A system, he continues, requires an origin, but "How indeed can one designate this peculiar indifference, which itself has no predicates but which allows of non-antithetical predication?"[37] How can any *logos* approach that which precedes all ground and is manifest, if manifest at all, in a mode of withdrawal? The difficulty is exacerbated by the fact that this *Indifferenz* is of a different character than the *indifference-point* treated in the *Presentation* (1801)—which, in spite of its representing the absolute identity of essence and being (transcendental philosophy and philosophy of nature) in the form of an indivisible line, was not yet a full question of origin. Niether is *Indifferenz* equivalent to the *primal will* (which Schelling does not mention in these remarks), but rather appears to 'be' the origin of even this originary act.[38] In the present case, moreover, Schelling offers no figurative correction to abstract concepts, but simply speaks of the non-ground as the "the inner core" (*das Innere*) of system and "indeed the only possible concept of the absolute" (F 73/SW7 411–12). Echoing his own characterization of 'spirit' circa. 1797, he calls the non-ground "the absolute considered merely in itself" (70/408)—that which overrides all the inadequacies of a rational system. The non-ground is thus rendered on the basis of what it enables and affects. It is before "the identity of opposites" yet exceeds mere neutrality, it is the original division of the two eternal beginnings, and it is the condition of possibility for "life and love and personal existence" (68/406, 70/408). The being of the non-ground also affects is own transformative trajectory over and through the life of "spirit" in yearning and consciousness to, as it were, accomplish the "general unity" of the whole in a loving act "which is all in all" (70/408). We may then say, in the least, that to speak of the being of the non-ground is to exercise the deepest possible standpoint on the whole without compromising the essential course of differentiation, severability, and opposition so crucial to the capacitating sense of freedom.

If one desires a conceptual approximation to *Indifferenz* in Schelling's oeuvre thus far, the best candidate is a term never thematized in the treatise: *Ineinsbildung*.

The sense of 'mutual informing into unity' has colored every major elemental motion in the life of the 'whole' (as *hen kai pan*) Schelling has sought to disclose. Though it first appeared in the context of his conception of artistic creation (the art lectures), it then surfaced again in the *Further Presentations* as the "living artistry" of "the one-in-all and all-in-one" (FP 397/SW4 411), a phrasing similar to the "all in all" ascribed to the loving beneficence of *Indifferenz* (F 20/SW7 348). If we read Schelling by way of Boehme then a potential relationship between *Indifferenz* and *Ineinsbildung* is all the more plausible. Boehme opens his *Mysterium Pansophicum* by contending that the non-ground "is an eternal nothing but forms an eternal beginning as a craving [*Sucht*]."[39] Though in one sense this pertains to Schelling's aforementioned conception of yearning (*Sehnsucht*) in the dark ground, Boehme goes on to speak of the "being of all beings" as a "magical being" that not only births the will, but also "from whence all things, evil and good, originate, namely from the *imagination* into the great *mysterium*, since a miraculous essentialistic life gives birth to itself."[40] The formative, essential movement of the imagination—and not simply yearning—reveals the non-ground to be "an eternally lasting beginning"(for God and nature) in addition to "an eternal nothing."[41] The difference, to return to Schelling, is that *Ineinsbildung* stands rooted in absolute identity as divine artistry, and *Indifferenz* consists in the being of the un-ground before the divine itself is born. But there remains a similarity of outcome: both concepts point to the human being (as artist and as thinker) as the site in which the unity of the whole is imaged, reasoned, and spoken.

Among the first matters addressed on the heels of the un-ground discussion is the privileged role of man in the system, the very point left in the wings since "highest point of the entire investigation" (F 68/SW7 406) found man standing in the light of divine personality. Why align a brief yet provocative treatment of the being before and 'of' the whole with a singular appraisal of man's position in it? The reason, so it appears, is to situate the measuring word in view of the measureless origin. Attuned to *Indifferenz*, Schelling means to pass once more the very 'word' of the whole through the dark, irrational principle of the ground, the contingencies of the selfish imagination, and onward to the mediation of God and nature within the whole. "Only man," says Schelling, "is in God and capable of freedom exactly through this Being-in-God" (72/411). Man's capacity positively concretizes something of the sheer 'inner core' of what must remain in withdrawal. Man is a creature born in the birth of God *from* the being of indifference. Though vulnerable in his propensity toward self-assertion, he is the being of the word that will mediate nature and its "typology [*Vorbilder*]" and God. The absence of figuration in the *Ungrund* stands matched by the presence of articulation in the word. "The word that is fulfilled in human beings," says Schelling, "is in nature as a dark, prophetic (not yet fully pronounced) word" (73/411). We know this word to be the word of unity and love, the bonding measure of the whole. We also know that the movement from darkness to light occurs by way of an *Ein-bildung* amid divine self-revelation, and that the understanding's generative division allows this idea or awakening to be *hineingebildet* (impressed) into nature. What the depth of indifference enables and anticipates, it seems, is the eventual transfiguration of what is *Vorbilder* and what is *Ein-bildung* at the summit of man. The word in man is invested with the vocation of annunciating the ordering of nature and 'bringing-forth' the anticipated mediation with nature in God.

Not incidentally, Schelling passes through this point about the word to a more concrete point about the vocation of *reason* (F 74-7/SW7 412-16). One of the effects of *Indifferenz* as a matter was that it arrested all speculation, abstraction, and representation. In this sense, Schelling chastened reason in order to then retrieve it as a measure. But what kind of measure is reason? A system "of reason" is a system in which human reason recognizes itself in an accord with divine understanding (74-5/413-14). Reason not only is the business of inquiry, but is also an agency at work in the life of the system—the logos or word 'of' the whole. We have seen this agency in motion as "the understanding that develops what is hidden and contained in [the] ground" (75/413), a dialectical drive that is *in* the act of divine self-revelation and *in* the investigation disclosing it. And we have seen it delivered into the voice of human being. Human reason is by no means the apotheosis of divine understanding (for personality still reigns) but the agent spirit of personality is to be active in inspiring the science and dialectic of systematic reason. Human reason must be inspired, artistic. Inspiration (*Begeisterung*) "in the genuine sense is the active principle of every productive and formative art or science," what Schelling in 1807 called the "innermost energies" by which spirit "is diffused through the whole" (PA 355/SW3 426). In view of this there must be "a dialectical artistic drive" and a "dialectical philosophy" (F 75-6/SW7 414). The point is not to heap together philosophy and art, but to recover for the science of reason its own distinct inheritance—it is inspired by the same creative spirit that authors the procession of things from God. Specifically, this means reason is, like the word, "the measure *and*, so to speak, the general place of truth [*das Maß und gleichsam der allgeimeine Ort der Wahrheit*]" (F 76/SW7 411).[42] Just as the human being may well run afoul of the word, human reason may shirk the archetypal principle by which it measures. The mark of an inspired dialectics, on the other hand, consists in its ability to perform a task also invested in the word—to interpret the typology (*Vorbilder*) of nature and thereby surmount the oldest opposition on behalf of the whole. The answer to the question of the essence of human freedom lies in this capacitated measuring that marks the life of man at the summit. The task of the thinker is not only a task of freedom, but also a deed allotted for the sake of a necessary whole. Could it be that Schelling means for philosophy to exhibit the same "flower of life" he finds in Raphael, whose works show things "ordered in eternal necessity" and bear the seal of one who is "a philosopher, a poet at the same time"? (PA 351/SW3 420).

Conspicuously absent from Schelling's *Freedom Essay* is the ensemble of systemic possibilities and accomplishments hitherto orbiting around the identity philosophy's emphasis on *intuition*. If in Chapter 2 we based the primacy of the productive, creative, and artistic imaginations for Schelling on the project assigned to intuition, do the present investigations require us to speak of a different Schelling and a different imagination altogether? As I stated at the outset of this chapter, the *Freedom Essay* envisions a task distinct from those of ascertaining the unconditioned principle or attaining the standpoint of absolute reason. To broach the tension between necessity and freedom is to enter the matter of absolute identity through the cellar door—to set aside all deductive or logical renderings of the structure and test the very foundations of the 'whole' from the bedrock of possible harmony. Do the primacy of intuition and identity fall to the side? Yes. Is Schelling now averse to his prior hopes for a system of knowledge? No. As in Kant's *Critique of Pure Reason*, the decision for the *Freedom Essay* marks a decision to treat the work of thought at its elemental level. In Schelling's case this means coming up into the unity of the whole by means of matters invested in the integrity of its very *life*, not its slated coherence. We may call this a new stage in Schelling's philosophical work, a departure into the Ages of the World period, but while this is useful from the point of view of an external catalog it does little to report on the inner agitations of his thought. Even as we highlight the new—indeed, radical—considerations of ground, identity, and the irrational genesis of all things in this essential inquiry, Schelling's orientation to and from the imagination here binds the intensity of his thought, the character of his subject matter, and the style of his argumentation to those elements of imagination in his prior works. Schelling remains a thinker of standpoints consistently attuned to the real and ideal, primordial and performative, work of the imagination. The primacy of intuition and identity in his idealism is not so much overcome in the *Freedom Essay* as displaced by the rising force of imagination's ontological currents. Not only philosophy, but also the life of primordial principles becomes sensuous, aesthetic. The poetic imagination is, for Schelling, alive in the genesis of God and man, and afoot in the *poietic* resolve of reason itself. Figuration precedes logos in the drama of self-revelation, and measurement must repair understanding in the sojourn of thought. All things point to the creative life of the *word*, both in Schelling's history of ontological becoming and in his vision for inspired reason.

Heidegger on Schelling's Impulse
and Poetizing Impasse

In this chapter, we resume our study of Heidegger by tracking a pronounced tension crystallized in his encounter with Schelling—the tension between a *poietic*, asystic, and fugal impulse arising at the very limit of metaphysics, and a poetizing, representational essence of reason that holds this impulse at an impasse. Turning directly to Heidegger's 1936 lecture course, *Schelling's Treatise on the Essence of Human Freedom*,[1] we will discover that his dictum, "all great thinkers think the same [*dasselbe*]" (N1 35–36/ GA43 43) is especially true where the impulse to primordial jointure and the strife of ontological questioning is concerned, but also leaves room for pronounced *differences* in carrying out this impulse. I will argue that though Heidegger celebrates (and is inspired by) Schelling's impulse *beyond* willful subjectivity and will to system *toward* the open occurrence between ground and existence in the jointure of Being, he finds in Schelling's thought a point of necessary arrest best understood as a problem of production and therefore imagination. Drawing on material from his Nietzsche Lectures, I will situate this problem under the orbit of what he calls the *poetizing* essence of *reason* in order to show that the implication of the imagination is specific and severe, though by no means final. Manifesting the precise nature of Heidegger's strained relation to the imagination is, I will show, *the* condition for the possibility of understanding his contemporaneous transformation of poetizing reason as a representing, concealing force into the poetic imagination as a revealing, *poietic* force (a matter for Chapter 5). Along such lines, the chapter will conclude by entertaining a dialogue of sorts between Heidegger's Schelling critique, related elements found in his *Introduction to Metaphysics* (1935) and "On the Essence of Truth" (1930), and two later Schelling texts.

In a 1926 letter to Karl Jaspers, Heidegger remarks: "Schelling ventures forward philosophically much further than Hegel, even if he is more disorderly conceptually. I have only begun to read the treatise on freedom. It is for me too valuable than whatever I might pick up in a rough first reading."[2] His readings continued, resulting in the lecture course of 1936, a seminar of 1941, and informing the focus of seminars in 1943. What, precisely, did Heidegger find in Schelling's treatise that warranted such sustained attention? Two passages provide a hint. At the end of his 1936 course, Heidegger summarizes the experience Schelling provokes: "man is experienced in the insight into the abysses and heights of Being, in regard to the terrible element of the godhead, the lifedread of all creatures, the sadness of all created creators, the malice of evil and the will of love" (ST 164/GA42 284). In later notes, it is "the experience of how the history of Being penetrates us and thus bears us to unattained regions of dwelling in which a decision to ground the truth of Being must be made" (ST2 169/GA49 140). In short, Schelling's work opens up an experience of man, in which man is not the author and arbiter of all things. There is an agency beyond the subject and a history of Being in which man is instantiated. And the thought that brings forth this experience itself stands within an impulse of inquiry exceeding the faculties of understanding and reason, an impulse kindred to what Heidegger, in 1935, characterizes as an inceptual *leap* into *questioning*:

> [G]iving up the ordinary and going back into questioning interpretation is a leap. Only one who takes the right running start [*Anlauf*] can leap. Everything is decided by this run, for it means that we ourselves actually *ask* the questions again, and that we, in these questions, first create the perspectives. However, this does not happen in wavering arbitrariness, nor in relying on a system that has been set forth as the norm. Instead, it happens in and from historical necessity, from the urgency of historical Dasein. (IM 188/N 134)

To what extent is Heidegger's Schelling engaged in this 'running start'? To what extent does his 'system' stand in the way of the leap and its 'urgency'? And does the *imagination*, for Heidegger, furnish the footing for the leap or the wavering that hinders it? Heidegger's Kantbuch remains an instructive preface to this 1936 encounter. Where the former is a 'deduction' of the thinking of Being in fundamental ontology by way of the 'transcendental imagination' (*Einbildungskraft*), the latter is best understood as a 'deduction' of the thinking of the history and jointure of Being by way of 'appropriation' (*Ereignis*). In both cases Heidegger risks the 'violence' of a reading that seeks to make explicit the implicit, though decisive, aspects of the works in question. This entails a "creative transformation," an entry into the "new beginnings" and "impulses [*Antriebe*]" opened up by the work. In both cases, however, an impulse is initiated, then resisted. In Kant it was the failure to follow the logical unity of intuition and thinking "out beyond itself" to imagination taken as the structure of possibility in ontological knowledge; in Schelling, the failure will be to follow the freedom inquiry "beyond itself" to the "openness of Being," in which "creative [*schöpferisches*] Dasein" takes its stand (ST 11/ GA42 18, 98/169, 105/183). The task for the remainder of this chapter is to identify the main impulses Heidegger finds in Schelling, distinguish the shape of the experience he privileges, and demonstrate how the imagination becomes an implicit problem for Heidegger in this encounter.

Creative transformations

The initial allure of Schelling's treatise is, for Heidegger, that its inquiries are "driven beyond man" (ST 9/GA42 15). In light of the singular position of man and the measuring task of man's reason noted in our Schelling discussion, the comment appears strange. How does Heidegger understand and applaud this accomplishment? To go 'beyond' implies both a departure and a recovery. What is surpassed is the traditional regress to subjectivity. We have observed this in our discussion of the meaning of an 'essential' investigation in terms of the matter's 'whole.' As a question of essence, then, freedom becomes for Heidegger

> not the property of man, but the other way around: Man is at best the property of freedom. Freedom is the encompassing and penetrating nature, in which man becomes man only when he is anchored there. That means the nature of man is grounded in freedom. But freedom itself is a determination of true Being in general which transcends all human being. . . . the nature of true Being as the nature of the ground for beings as a whole. (ST 9/GA42 15)

There is a precedent in Heidegger's itinerary that supports his enthusiasm for this reversal. In *Basic Problems of Phenomenology* (1927), for example, he traced Kant's understanding of being "in the sense of being-produced [*Hergestelltsein*]" and of the subject in an "ontological mode of extantness [*Vorhandenheit*]" (BPP 147/GA24 209) back to the ancient and medieval conceptions of *eidos* and *ousia* so as to position the question: "What positive problems grow out of this problematic situation in which the subject is primarily determined by means of subjectivity, self-knowing, so that the question of its ontological constitution still remains fundamentally neglected?" The question of determining "the being of the being that we ourselves are" in light of an "original concept of being" (153–54/218–19) would thus have to overcome the notion that "being equals extantness" (176/251) by working through the "diversity of being as *a multiplicity of ways of being*" (154/219), the structure of Dasein's being-in-the-world, and the disarming mystery of the "indifference of being" subsisting beneath our everyday understanding of beings (175–76/251). Early in *Being and Time* he observed that the meaning of Being is "veiled in darkness" (BT 23/GA2 6), incommensurate with "dogmatic constructions," yet fundamentally attached to Dasein's pre-ontological understanding such that the whole analytic of Dasein consists in a questioning of what is 'beyond' (or rather, 'before') even though it is ontically closest. To investigate the meaning of Being, then, is first of all to allow an altogether implicit understanding to "show itself in itself and from itself" (36–37/21–22).[3] In the years following his 1936 Schelling course, Heidegger likewise explains: "That man . . . becomes the executor and trustee and even owner and bearer of subjectivity in no way proves that man is the essential ground of subjectivity" (N4 139/GA48 260)[4]

In like manner, what is of decisive importance in the 1936 course is that Schelling's inquiries are 'driven' (*getrieben*)—as though something about the matter itself propels the inquiries beyond man as their gravitational center. Just as Schelling's copula 'is' before man in the procession toward actual existence, matters pertaining to identity and essence are beyond man's interrogative position. The Cartesian *res cogitans* and the Kantian transcendental subject, for example, cannot perform an essential inquiry from their own necessary points of departure. Schelling's position affirms Heidegger's contention that "We philosophize only when the position of our human being becomes the real need [*Not*] of the question about Being as a whole" (ST 11/GA42 18). What is the meaning of this need? The answer, in part, is revealed through Hegel's misreading; Hegel, says Heidegger, fails to see that freedom "was not single for Schelling, but was thought and developed as the essential foundation of the whole, as a new foundation for a whole philosophy" (13/22). As soon as the question of human freedom becomes a question concerning the nature of true Being, the matter 'needs' to be understood (and is so driven) from within a horizon that exceeds man:

> Because it asks about the whole of Being, we cannot find anything outside of it from where we could, in addition, particularly explain why the inquiry deals with freedom. For the sufficient reason for the question of Being as a whole lies in Being itself and there alone. But man cannot withdraw from Being as a whole. For he is what he is, only be standing in the middle of beings as a whole and perduring this stand. (ST 10/GA42 16)

In the moment the question of ground and grounding enters Schelling's discourse, one could say, man and his inquiry are displaced into a horizon of the whole, which already anticipates a creative transformation in the inquiring agent, and which may in fact take Schelling's own project "beyond itself" by way of a "hidden, but disturbing force [*Kraft*]" (ST 11/GA42 18, 13/22).

The inquiries are also driven to the limit of *system* itself, a motion we have noted in Schelling's comments on dependency and becoming, living ground and divine personality. But Heidegger's position is critical in a broader historical sense. He understands "*the system*" to be "the decisive *task* of the philosophy of German idealism," and likewise appreciates the challenge Schelling faces in overcoming the supposed incompatibility of system with the concept of freedom ("Freedom excludes the recourse to grounding") (ST 19/GA42 42, 22/26–27). But in order to facilitate the larger creative transformation of understanding into the 'need' of Being, Heidegger must identify and isolate the cargo of idealism that the force of Schelling's project will, initially at least, jettison. In so doing, he continues a critique of German idealism that has been underway since his early work and is related to his noted concerns about subjective determinacy. When, in the 1936 course, he identifies "the self-certainty of pure thinking with regard to its correctness" (31/54) as a condition for system formation, he is extending his earlier observation that "in an extreme version of Kant's or Descartes' thought, German idealism (Fichte, Schelling, Hegel) saw the true actuality of the subject in self-consciousness" (BPP 152/GA24 216).[5] The confidence of a self-understanding "equated formally with a reflected ego-experience" (BPP 175/GA24 248) in a thinker such as Fichte, when added to the Kantian impetus to represent the world as totality[6] makes for a "flight to the objective" (ER 97/GA9 161–62) under the auspices of a self-certainty poised to decide "what 'is', as a principle and thus fundamentally" (ST 30/GA42 53). The developmental conspiracy of self-consciousness and self-certainty thus positions an "external manipulation" of beings, a "will to system" in which "thinking understands itself as the court of judgment over Being" (ST 26/GA42 45, 32/56–57). As a consequence, Heidegger later notes, metaphysical systems ultimately "merely attest to an accelerating *flight* in the face of the unknown ground" (N4 155/GA48 286).

Heidegger is no doubt critical of the will to system, but this is different from an indictment. In his Schelling course he means to nuance the difference between an external and a manipulating approach to system (the *Weltanschauung* contrived to satisfy the aspirations of the *Wissenschaft*, ST 16–18/GA42 26–29) and an internal disclosure of "the jointure [*der Fuge*] and coherence of Being itself" (28/50). To philosophize from a position of 'need' with respect to Being as whole is not utterly distinct from systematizing from within a position of reason's own creative demand. In 1928 and 1936 alike Heidegger appreciates the drive to system by way of reference to Kant's *First* critique. In 1928 he quotes directly: "But by system I understand the unity of the manifold items of knowledge under an idea. This idea is the concept, produced by reason, of the form of the whole" (CPR A832/B860 at ER 65–67/GA9 149–50). In 1936 he paraphrases:

> Reason is what makes all the actions of our understanding 'systemical' (A664, B692). Reason makes us 'look out' from the very beginning for the unity of a fundamental connection with everything we meet (A655, B683). Reason is the faculty of looking out into a view, the faculty of forming a horizon. Thus reason itself is nothing other than the faculty of system, and reason's interest is concerned with making evident the greatest possible manifold of knowledge in the highest possible unity. (ST 37/GA42 64)

In each case there is a sense of reason's necessary drive to system, and in each case the drive obtains by way of production and formation. The later statement is more pronounced, emphasizing the visual and constructive elements of the system demand. Indeed, he goes on to cite Kant's appeal to a "*focus imaginarius*" in which reason is the faculty "of anticipatory gathering," an 'art' of *logos*, *legein* in reason itself (ST 37/ GA42 65). The visual and architectural sense is crucial, for in it lies the incipient difference between exercising system as an "*absolute requirement*" (35/61) rooted in an intellectual intuition purporting to possess a "nonobjective knowledge of beings as a whole [which] knows itself as the true and absolute knowledge" (45/77),[7] and understanding system as "the jointure of Being itself" (39/68). These different accents on system reveal Heidegger's position regarding the tension between external and internal deployments of reason to be a result of the Kantian legacy of creative knowing. In the leading sense, the movement from without to within wagers on Kant's determination of reason as "a *creative faculty* [*schöpferisches Vermögen*]" (41/72), an "art" of gathering still poised to overtake the "idealistic shaping of system" and its totalizing assumptions (37/64, 42/74). Attuned to inner jointure, not external manipulation, creative reason may pursue "the nature of true Being . . . the nature of the ground for beings as a whole" (9/15). The immediate tension, however, is that the 'creative' shape of reason is also implicated in the way system has contrived its "framework of knowledge of beings," a production of reason performed according to the view that system alone "guarantees the inner unity of knowledge, its scientific character and truth" 39/68, 42/74).[8]

Heidegger thus reads Schelling's *Freedom Essay* from a horizon of great anticipation: the nature of Schelling's problem is poised to retask the will to system with an obligation to the whole of Being, an obligation that will displace the external construal of "unified fullness" (ST 39/GA42 68) in favor of a more primordial ontological attunement. The critical question is how to adjudicate the agent of prefiguration in creative reason—is it the eidetic figuring of the subjective knower or it is the primordial *legein* of thought in and of the whole of Being, the whole in which man "stands"

(45/77)? Heidegger's anticipation is thus tempered by the suspicion that the will to system, even in Schelling, will prove unable to forsake the manipulative use of reason's representational and determinative *legein*. Will the shape of the whole be drawn forth in terms of the ground and inner jointure of Being or will it be prefigured from a position of withdrawal and elective totality? These questions ask whether the pitfalls of the inquiring imagination in fact run deeper than Schelling realized, to the point where even the resoluteness of man and his reason are beset by an irresistible course of representation and production.

The poetry of thought

Eclipsing man and system with a position recovered within Being's own need is, as we have begun to see, an impulse that Heidegger finds specified in elements of philosophical *questioning* and ontological *jointure*. Heidegger observes that Schelling establishes the possibility that the system (of freedom) will be present in the "divine understanding," in which case the course of prefiguring the whole will be attributed to a ground of being, as *theos*, in God. This means the systematizing standpoint is passed through a "theological" turn such that the question of freedom "essentially moves within the realm of this primordial theo-logy of Being" (ST 50–51/GA42 87–88). Though this bearing is fundamental to the new impetus Schelling's elaboration of jointure will perform, we may rightly expect that the decision for theological comprehension shall remain a limiting factor. But the appeal of the turn toward divine understanding is that it establishes a *question* about "beings as such, about the essence of Being in general" (51/88).[9] There must be a primal ground of Being (for Schelling: in God), an ontological relation in which man stands and from which man's knowledge of manifest beings unfolds. The necessity thus situates human cognition in a ground that capacitates the knowledge of beings, says Heidegger, and the very "grounding of Da-*sein*" itself (53/93). The potential for being driven beyond man thus begins in the position of the grounding relation of the whole: "Schelling must deal namely with the question of *what* man *is* in relation to beings as a whole, what this relation is and what this relation of *one* of the beings (man) in the whole means for beings" (53/92). Heidegger believes Schelling realizes this initial necessity by transferring the force of intellectual intuition to the genitival and generative knowledge 'of' the divine understanding. We apprehend a likeness to which we belong, a primal being that exercises an understanding prior to cognition, yet in which the strife between necessity and freedom proves fundamental to disclosing "a *new path* and a *new horizon* to the relation of beings in general," a path of emergence in which philosophy itself arises "from a fundamental law of Being itself" (58/100).

The spirit of such a remark evidences Heidegger's intention to capture the primordial bearing of Schelling's standpoint without concerning himself (for the moment) with its theological milieu. The tension between necessity and freedom presents system with a reflection of philosophy's own constitutive position *as* "intrinsically a *strife between necessity and freedom*" (ST 58/GA42 100). Here the term 'strife' is captured from Schelling's oeuvre and set in the motion of primordial questioning. As this strife philosophical questioning attains the intention to draw "the truth of Being . . . out into the open [*ins Freie*]" (57/100), to the region in which strife's unifying course is enacted. On this new path of questioning from the law of Being, then, this interest in the 'open' translates into a path of return to the horizon of the "*world occurrence*" wherein "the world itself arises anew in its actual origins and rules as world" (58/100). Somewhat ambiguously, Heidegger likens such an enactment to "the poetry of the poet" in the essential sense of opening upon the primordial and not reworking the knowable realm (58/100). To think from the basis on which necessity and freedom arise in a primordial strife is then to think from the occurrence, from the "*unconditioned*" (60/105) ground of beings and not, for example, from a delimitation of freedom under the province of practical philosophy. Schelling's 'realm' recalls systematic knowing to the position that Heidegger has, since *Being and Time*, ascribed to the being of Dasein—that position for which the meaning of being is an issue.[10] Positioned thus, inquiry will no longer assume any distinction between Being and knowledge of being but will heed a more fundamental ontological difference. Heidegger characterizes what Schelling's standpoint has won as follows:

> The question of the principle of the formation of system is thus the question in what does the essence of Being consist, in what does Being have its truth? And that is the question in which realm something like Being can become manifest at all and how it preserves this openness for itself and preserves itself in the openness [*Offenbarkeit*]. . . . The real question of beings, the primordial ontological question, is that of the essence of Being and the truth of this essence. And now we recognize that to search for the principle of the formation of system means to ask how a jointure is grounded in Being and how a law of jointure [*Gesetz der Fügung*] belongs to it, and that means to think about the essence of Being. Searching for the principle of the formation of system means nothing other than asking the real ontological question, at least striving toward it. (ST 64–65/GA42 110–112)

Schelling's gesture toward the divine understanding shares with pantheism a theological formulation of the question of ground in which "The question of Being in general *is* meant" (ST 80/GA42 142). In the search for system's principle he allows a more dialectical and primordial impulse to flow in and over the idealist currents of intellectual intuition and external systematizing. In this way, Schelling's path, for Heidegger, exchanges the immediate egoistic occurrence of idealist intuition for the eventful world occurrence of Being's truth. His work returns the creative art of reason to interior strife of all productive gathering. But here an inevitable question arises: Why is Heidegger willing to embrace, for the moment, a primordial strife of questioning toward the question of Being under the auspices of a systemic standpoint? Why allow the *grounding* of Da-sein and the path of *occurrence* to enjoy the traction of an inquiry into the necessary origins of divine understanding?

The answer consists in the manner by which Schelling's question of Being is *meant*. This does not say the question is implicitly alluded to or stowed in the cargo of system formation. It says, rather, that Schelling's standpoint marks the domain of the question and that his thought advances as far into this domain as his standing in the inheritance of Kantian creative reason could allow. Specifically, the question is meant—is allowed to become meaningful—insofar as the attunement toward thinking this grounding occurrence arises through the *poiesis* of the *copula*, for Heidegger understands Schelling's treatment of the law of identity as an opening through with the question of the meaning of Being may be asked. The creative life of the copula accords with the 'open' into which the truth of Being is drawn. Identity, Heidegger observes, "is the belonging together [*Zusammengehörigkeit*] of what is different in one . . . the unity of a unity and an opposition," and this relational significance positions the question of Being's meaning in terms of a 'unity' that is "directly productive, 'creative' and progressing toward others. . . . in truth a progression and a bringing forth is contained there" (ST 77/GA42 133, 78–79/136–37). Heidegger goes so far as to say that "the true metaphysical accomplishment" of Schelling's treatise is "the grounding of a primordial concept of Being—in Schelling's language the more primordial grounding of absolute identity in a more primordial 'copula'" (85/147).[11] Primordially then, identity becomes "a band and a binding," and thus a conceptual opening toward "the possibility of a more primordial understanding of Being in general" (89/154). Schelling understands the nature of the band as spiritual—as divine will engaged with God as "creative life [*schöpferisches Leben*]"—and thus casts the band of Being as an emergence of "what is creative, and that always means what gives measure" (87/150, 90/150). And yet, it is at this precise moment in his reading that Heidegger sides explicitly *with* Schelling's impulse and *against* Schelling's idealist milieu: Schelling has transferred "the foundation of his philosophy to a deeper ground," a depth that requires idealism "to be shattered" (91/157).

The shattering

Namely, what is to be shattered is the idealist preoccupation with an eidetic, representative interpretation of Being: "Idealism is the interpretation of the essence of Being as 'Idea', as the being represented of beings in general" (ST 92/GA42 158).[12] As we have begun to note, this representational bearing, formalized as act of freedom in Kant, purports to capture beings on the basis of the ego and as "beings' appearing to themselves in absolute knowledge" (95/164). What is to be shattered, then, is the presumption that the will to representation assures the ontological acumen of absolute knowing. Until now the indications were that Schelling's treatise was already an accomplice in this shattering. In a certain sense this remains the case. At the same time, however, Heidegger observes that Schelling's system of freedom is itself founded in a questionable concept of Being—"primal being is will [*Ursein heißt Wollen*]"—and thus one wonders if Schelling's own adherence to will must, like the representational will, necessarily fail to pose the question of Being "in a sufficiently primordial way" (96/165–66).[13] Heidegger's interpretation is caught between the promise of one impulse and the derailing influence of a more historical, modern impulse. Schelling stands beyond the 'I represent' idealist drive of Descartes, but to some extent within the 'I am free' drive of German idealism. His system of identity combines idealism and realism, but does he escape the circle of will and representation?

> The system of Idealism is a 'system of freedom' because the principle of forming the system, the determining ground for the fundamental structure[14] of Being,

'the Idea,' is understood as freedom. It is not a matter of chance that the last section of Hegel's *Logic*, on general metaphysics in German Idealism, is entitled 'The Idea.' Idea has now long since ceased to mean the outward appearance of objective beings which we see. Rather, it means the being represented of beings [*die Vorgestelltheit des Seinden*]—represented, on the way through Descartes' 'I think.' That means that this representing of being represented represents itself. (ST 95/GA42 163–64)

The problem will and *Idea* pose to the impulse is the leading edge of a larger hesitation in Heidegger, and thus an interpretive difficulty for the reader. To be clear, Heidegger has applauded Schelling's intentional absorption of the striving his subject matter requires—the dissolution of the egoistic conception of Being's unity in the deeper currents of a primordial jointure. The advent of a higher realism upsets the reign of a representational absolute knowing, and portends the manifest "boundary" (ST 96/GA42 166) beyond which idealism cannot pass. And yet the extent to which Schelling consciously orchestrates the revision in deterministic thinking is unclear, almost beside the point. Schelling is something of a vehicle for a "new kind of questioning," a questioning through which the reality of evil will necessarily "split open" (98–99/170–71) the ambitions of system. Indeed, Heidegger borrows from Schelling the language of 'beginnings' then accredits the problem itself (and not the thinker)—evil—with determining a "new beginning in metaphysics . . . a transformation of the question of Being" (97/168, cf. 103/180). In Schelling the question of the ground of beings "as a whole" is "raised anew" (96/167), yet in Schelling one also finds a necessary point of arrest, a failure to sustain the question of Being. At the same time, it seems we are faced with a preponderance of elemental engagements between Heidegger and Schelling and yet none pertains explicitly to the *imagination*. Heidegger is alert to the *poietic* bearing of Schelling's copula and band, and the poetic path of thinking from the need of Being, but has yet to address the divine imagination or the measuring word in depth. Either our topic is at an impasse or is submerged within the shattering transformation of questioning.

The mood of the moment

Clues to resolving these predicaments begin to appear as Heidegger deepens his sense of the "essential impulse" (ST 98/GA42 169) by focusing more rigorously on the *attunement* of questioning and the *creative* occurrence of the jointure. *First*, the impulse presses for continued questioning, and it is through questioning that the "openness of Being" becomes manifest (98/169). Schelling's system of freedom "wants to answer the fundamental question of the essence of Being in a sense which comprehends all impulses to thought" (104/181). Rightly attuned, the motion of questioning evokes the "primordial fundamental mood [*Grundstimmung*]," which shall "ignite" the release of forces intrinsic to "creative *Dasein* [*schöpferisches Dasein*]" (105/183). The mood, that is, and not the resolution of the system, is the decisive matter.[15] Just as Schelling is interested in moving inquiry into the motion of divine self-revelation, Heidegger is interested in holding thought in the motion of an open inquiry. Heidegger confesses a "one-sidedness" in this approach to Schelling's text, but even the question of evil's inner possibility seems to require of Schelling the 'open' question: "What belongs to the determination of a self-contained being?" (106–07/185–86). "As with every actual interpretation of a work of thought," Heidegger explains, "it is true here that it is not the opinion which a thinker ends up with that is decisive . . . Decisive rather is the movement of questioning that alone lets what is true come into the open [*das Wahre ins Offene kommt*]" (106/185).

Second, the distinction between ground and existence marks an impulse toward primordial occurrence that must remain a matter for questioning. As Heidegger understands it, as Schelling's ground is a nonrational substratum, existence (as *Existenz*) is "*what emerges from itself* and in *emerging reveals itself*" (ST 107/GA42 187). Both principles serve the unity of the *Wesen* understood as self-contained Being as a whole, and abide as a distinction in the will. The motion of the jointure, then, is irreducible to objective presence, and the occurrence of this motion does not obtain in temporal succession. The being of the principles, rather, happens as a "Moment [*Augenblick*]" of simultaneity, a "*true temporality*" understood "poetically" as "the most primordial temporality" (113/197). Distinct from the 'immediacy' of something like intellectual intuition, this simultaneity measures the being of the jointure, the *Wesen* of the primordial whole. Heidegger also characterizes it as a moment of "clearing [*Lichtung*]" for the "possibility" of creation (114/199, 118/205–06) as the self-revelation of God. We have then a motion of questioning poised to capacitate *creative Dasein*, and a matter of such questioning that opens forth as a temporal depth and capacitating *creation* in the clearing of the jointure.

With these points the impulse in Schelling returns again to the threshold of will and, in so doing, specifies the questionable status of the imagination in Heidegger's reading. To think together in the primordial occurrence the force of creative Dasein and the creative moment of the clearing is to embrace two elements within the jointure's world occurrence. Being 'is' as a whole *and* as an issue for the poetic impulse here situated. But is the elemental creation here afoot going to remain an 'open' question of the open or will the will of system (and to system) confuse the course? Schelling's sense of artistry and creation in the motion of divine self-revelation is now at hand in a specific way, and Heidegger's interest in this aspect of the jointure's occurrence is uncertain. In one sense, he cautions against recourse to "the idea of production [*Herstellens*] which all too easily obtrudes itself" (ST 118–19/GA42 207).[16] But who is the target of this caution—Schelling, his interpreters, or both? Evidently, Heidegger means to advance a distinction between *production* and *poiesis*, between creation in the sense of willful manipulation and creation in the sense of gathering and saying. Their difference is not yet explicit. He allows that, on Schelling's view, understanding becomes as a "clearing [*Lichtung*]" (119/207, cf. 140–41/244, 128/223) in which imaging and utterance obtain. God's reflexive self-representation is a 'gathering' (*legein*) of image as word, a word of longing and love by which the "the jointure [*Fuge*] of Being is uttered [*augesprochen*]" (126/219, 128/223). Seen this way, creation in the jointure's moment "is not the manufacturing of something which is not there, but the bending of the eternal will of longing into the will of the word, of gathering

[*Sammlung*]" (130–31/226). The nuance allows Schelling some distance from the deterministic instruments of absolute idealism. But the will of the jointure and the will of its thinker remain an obtrusion, and any path of primordial questioning must also tread carefully. The being of Schelling's jointure is creative insofar as it concerns "what becomes in willing" (131/227), in which case we are again put on watch to wonder whether such a primordial band of necessary freedom is an adequate treatment of the clearing and its moment.

The moment of language and justification

As if to read Schelling's account of evil as evidence for this very worry, Heidegger finds in the impetus to *dis-jointure* (*Ungefüge*) a more primordial obtrusion of production, specifically in the saying measure of man. Evil is capacitated amid the clearing of light and dark principles as a counter-utterance and a presencing of man. Man "utters himself and becomes present in language," elevating himself over the universal will by uttering the 'light' of understanding (ST 141/GA42 245). Dis-jointure arises as a 'turn', a "reversal," an "upheaval against the primal being" (143/247–48). This possibility is 'prefigured' in the ground, but the free knowing that "wills in the will" (158/274) becomes adversarial in a collusion of language, light, and presencing. This is a fair reading of Schelling, but we must hear in Heidegger a focus on the willful and productive that stops short of characterizing man's 'rising-up' in terms of sin (145/248). The integrity of the jointure's creative work comes down to a specific situation of utterance and production—both in the primodial 'igniting' of Dasein, it would seem, and in the question that attends to this world-occuring clearing. Still, how and why Heidegger implicates Schelling in a misguided 'idea' of production needs clarification.

We have already noted Schelling's own concerns with the *Gedanken des Herstellens* in the emergence of man's self-assertion, the covetousness of yearning, and, from a different angle, in representational abstraction. Heidegger's concern on this point is with the way Schelling purports to resolve this issue by retreating from the problem of production and disjointure into an enterprise in *justification*. The retreat, as it were, marks a missed opportunity to hold in question the tension between the creative life of the jointure and the representing will impressed upon it. Such questioning would inevitably interrogate (and potentially refine) the productive character of the imagination, both in the moment of jointure and in the thought that strives to comprehend it. But Schelling, by Heidegger's reading, decides to justify the basis of necessary freedom and evil by appealing to a higher unity on the basis of divine production and will. Schelling's original "impetus" and "questioning," says Heidegger, diminish as the "more primordial interpretation of being" falls beneath the "polemical" (ST 159/GA42 276, 161/278) account of divine personality. A metaphysical gathering deflects questioning from the more essential gathering sought by the impulse. Schelling's "impasse" (*Scheitern*) thus arises in its most specific form when he attempts to limit 'system' to the being of *existence* in God, and thereby advance the larger being of God as a life, a life in which the bond of unity is assured (160–61/279). The drive toward unity, in short, distances the principles of jointure and occludes the opening in which questions of production, creation, and will could persist. Heidegger explains:

> At this stage of the treatise on freedom it is not yet clearly evident to Schelling that precisely the positing the jointure of Being [*Seynsfuge*] as the unity of ground and existence makes a jointure of Being as system impossible. Rather, Schelling believes that the question of system, that is, the unity of beings as a whole, would be saved if only the unity of what truly unifies [*die Einheit des eigentlich Einigenden*], that of the Absolute, were correctly formulated. (ST 161/GA42 279)

The impulse is lost beneath an ensuing apologetic, one that resorts to the same determinative instruments and will to system it has already placed in question. System requires unity, unity is best secured on the side of existence (the principle of light), and existence is itself assured in the life of divine personality. The internal impetus gives way to external assurance. The dark remainder of ground falls by the wayside, and with it the fundamental 'between' of the two principles—the precise opening within the jointure. Schelling's elusive discussion of *Indifferenz*, moreover, confirms the shape of this impasse as a misguided production of gathering. Thought, as strife, is lost in a comprehending act of divine love. Where the "knowing perdurance" of all beings (ST 162/GA42 281) wrought in the primordial opposition of ground and existence should have pointed to a *finite* essence of Being and of what stands in Being, Schelling elides the standing destiny of historical being in favor of a transcendent indifference positioned to author absolute unity. It is as though Schelling fell into a visible representation of the necessary, primordial strife of the jointure, then modeled an assurance for the word of unity in a still more primordial seat of systemic determination. The move to indifference is thus an effort toward comprehending and representing the incomprehensible essence of freedom that "transposes us into the occurrence of Being" (162/281). At the same time, Heidegger believes indifference and personality reflect a lingering appeal to the absolute on the basis of anthropomorphic analogies, which, ironically, occlude the underlying question of finitude.[17] All told, the investigation shrinks before the weight of destiny otherwise attached to historical, finite beings.

Imagination at a poetizing impasse?

Although Heidegger's interpretation, particularly on the matter of *Indifferenz*, is open to questioning[18] and merits more rigorous interpretation on the basis of his other works since *Being and Time*, our immediate concern is to ascertain whether Schelling's impasse marks an impasse for what we have called the poetic imagination. Clearly, we do a disservice to Heidegger and to Schelling if we reduce the impasse to a cul-de-sac of ontotheology, then leave the matter aside. According to Heidegger, Schelling fails to relinquish the will to system and remain within the primordial clearing, strife, finitude, and moment of the jointure. In broad terms, his error is not in reaching the impasse by way of misdirection, but in resisting the moment of the impasse as an "occurrence of Being [*Vollzug des Seyns*]" (ST 162/GA42 281) in which thought/questioning may take an essential stand. The impasse marks that site in which the necessity of a second beginning for thought is to arise through the transformation of the first. In more narrow terms, Schelling's path of primordial questioning becomes a vulnerable account of creation, representation, understanding, and measure. From Schelling's point of view the ontology of will is framed between the indifferent depths of the un-ground and the assuring heights of the divine personality, a frame that accomplishes a system of human freedom while enlivening the very meaning of system. From Heidegger's point of view, Schelling loses sight of the fundamental "disruption of Dasein" (164/292) disclosed in the capacitating ground for freedom and evil, and the deep moment of temporality there manifest. The ontological primacy of the eternal will, in effect, obfuscates the ek-static essence of time (an impulse from BT) as well as Dasein's sojourning *Inständigkeit* (instantiality) in relation to the be-ing of beings.[19]

The specific balance of these critiques is this: the obtrusion of production within Schelling's essential impulse stirs in Heidegger a resistance to the imagination in the very moment in which he envisions a more poetic bringing-forth for thought. Curiously, the promise of the imagination stands in a position of withdrawal beneath the gathering of systemic reason, yet the poetic gathering of questioning in and from the open jointure unveils the creative measure-giving of both Being and thought. While we are forced to admit that Heidegger's early devotion to the impulse of the productive imagination has waned, we must also recognize that the very touchstones of the impulse beyond man, system, eidetic configurations of being, and toward the open event of fugal jointure are constituent elements *of* the imagination, particularly the Schellingian imagination: creation and *poiesis*, measure and utterance. In short, the status of the imagination at the 'end' of metaphysics and on the brink of a 'leap' into inceptual thinking is not easy to ascertain. One is tempted to minimize the issue for Heidegger, consign it to a closing stretch of transcendental reflection and absolute identity, and characterize the turn through fundamental ontology to inceptual thinking as the turn from imagination in the meaning and thinking of Being to poetry in the open disclosure of Being and truth.[20] I believe our discussion thus far shows such a temptation to be simplistic and misleading. The poetic impulse in Heidegger (only briefly noted in this text, though contemporaneous with it) is indeed vital and will concern us in the following chapter, but in order to grasp this impulse in full and regard it as a possible reorientation of the imagination we must further specify the source of Heidegger's hesitation over *Einbildungskraft*, *Ineinsbildung*, and the fleet of representational maneuvers through which Schelling's 'essential' inquiry discloses its matter.

The critical lacuna

Based on the 1936 course, it appears as though Heidegger did not deign to treat or explicitly embrace Schelling's formulations of the imagination because the sense of becoming, creation, measuring, and inspired reason stood contaminated by the obstinate instruments of *willful production* and its externally bound 'ideas'. In this sense, Schelling's treatment of, and vision for, the imagination confirm Heidegger's long-standing worries about the Kantian tendency to understand *being* as producedness

(BPP 150/GA24 213–14) and *reason* as a productive *legein* (ST 37/GA42 64). The fault is not exactly Kant's, but belongs to an ontological orientation in Kant that the age of idealism rectifies in its will to system. To be clear, production (and its 'obtrusion') names a problem with two tiers: the assumption that the meaning or essence of primordial being is will, and the exercise of willful production in the thinking that treats the primordial. Heidegger's texts of the 1930s offer many avenues for parsing this concern. But the best treatment for our purposes—the most troubling diagnosis of the imagination on the face of it—is found in his course lectures on Nietzsche (1936–40). If in prior years (works of 1927–29 noted earlier) Heidegger identified the Kantian deployment of the creative character of reason, so too in his *The Will to Power as Knowledge and as Metaphysics* (1939) and *Nihilism* (1940) he surveys the movement through Plato, German Idealism, and Nietzsche of this reciprocity between Being as "at bottom experienced as will" and subjective reflection's assumption of willfulness in ontological, theoretical, and practical domains. Through this itinerary, says Heidegger, "man first of all comes to know himself as a willing subject in an essential sense on the basis of a still unelucidated experience of beings as such in the sense of a willing that has yet to be thought" (N4 205). In the directional vector of these emphases through absolute identity, the *beingness* of beings was regarded in terms of effectiveness (actuality) and objectivity (N4 181/314–15)—ultimately consummating the subjectivization of beingness. To 'think' this larger experience, Heidegger adopts the phrase, the "poetizing character of reason [*Das dichtende Wesen der Vernunft*]" (in his *The Will to Power as Knowledge and as Metaphysics*, §15) (N3 97/GA47 177) as a title for the fate of the transcendental imagination in Kant, a doctrine he still regards as an "incomparable" step (96/180). How might the tensions within such 'poetizing' serve to situate the concerns about production in the Schelling course and clarify Heidegger's silence on the Schellingian imagination?

In the section thus entitled "The Poetizing Essence of Reason" the interpretive point of departure is an isolated remark in Nietzsche's "On the Advantages and Disadvantages of History for Life" (1873). Nietzsche notes: "The development of reason is adjustment, invention, in order to make similar, identical—the same process that every sense impression goes through!" (at N3 94/GA47 177). Poetizing denotes a necessary inventiveness in the exercise of reason that "must always occur before there can be thinking in the usual sense" (95/178). This has little to do with a 'poetic' essence; it does, however, suggest how the fictional bearing of poetry (which Plato resisted in *Republic* Bk. X) is always already operative in the prefigurative and categorical constitution of entities by reason in encountering them. But in what sense is poetizing a term of necessity and not, per se, a term of prognosis?[21] In simple terms, reason finds itself thrown into a situation in which it has a task to perform, and if the situation is first manifest as a surrounding sensuous field, then it will take the cues for this task from its default comportment to this field. Nietzsche's insight is that reason is underway as a commanding force invested in efficacy by way of securing order and constancy in the entities it determines. This accounts for the appeal of constitutive 'Ideas' in the Greek sense, a "higher origin" to which objects may be referred, figured, and drawn into the sphere of the "utility" of a reason "intent on something constant" (95–96/181, 97/181 99/183). Descriptively speaking, poetizing is a choice for order over chaos, and reason requires order if it is to attribute purpose or finality to the purportedly "actual" (100/185) field of experience. Heidegger repeats a consistent point of reference:

> Kant first explicitly perceived and thought through the creative character of reason [*dichtenden Charakter der Vernunft*] in his doctrine of the transcendental imagination. The conception of the essence of absolute reason in the metaphysics of German Idealism (in Fichte, Schelling, and Hegel) is thoroughly based on the Kantian insight into the essence of reason as a 'formative', creative 'force' ['*bildenden*,' *dichtenden* '*Kraft*']. (N3 95–96/GA47 179)

Kant is by no means the author of this character, but formalizes a necessity that expresses "what had to be said about the essence of reason on the basis of modern metaphysics" (N3 96/GA47 180). By 'basis' Heidegger means the correlation between subjectivity and reason previously noted in terms of the reflection of the ontological will in the commanding willfulness of subjective knowing, and here identified as "the self-certain representing of beings in their beingness, that is, *objectivity*" (96/180). But did not the Schelling interpretation already treat this tendency as a problem manifest in production? How can this sense of poetizing be necessary and problematic at the same time?

Calculative representation

Before answering this question we must consider how Heidegger finds in poetizing a scope of necessity that attaches to reason's *representational* drive. Representing, understood as the offspring of subjectivity's self-understanding in modern metaphysics, is wrought in terms of willing. The target of representing of course becomes objects (beings), but the character of reason that enacts this representing is, one could say, derived from (and derivative of) the appearance of Being as will. Representing is reason's way of attaining the traction required for its certain determinations of beings and Being. Accordingly, the willful and creative character of reasoning further capacitates itself as a faculty—as the transcendental or intuitive receptacle in which appearances of beings are, so to speak, schematized into objectivity. Heidegger's statement to this effect merits quoting in full:

> Representing [*Vorstellen*] must be self-certain because it now becomes the *re-presenting* of objects that is established purely on itself, that is, as bound up with a subject. In self-certainty, reason makes certain that with its determination of objectivity it secures what is encountered. It thus places itself in the scope of a ubiquitously calculable certainty. Thus, reason becomes more explicitly than ever before the faculty that forms and images to itself everything that beings are. Hence it becomes the imagination [*Einbildungskraft*], without qualification, understood in this way. If we emphasize that Kant 'only' more clearly foresaw and expressed this essence of reason for the first time as a whole and in terms of the actual dimensions of its capacities as a faculty, this 'only' should in no way diminish the Kantian doctrine of transcendental imagination. The only

thing we wish to do and can do here is to concentrate on rescuing this step of Kantian thinking by noting that it is incomparable [*Unvergleichliche*]. (N3 96/ GA47 180)

The passage is perplexing. If one comes to it by way of the *Kantbuch* the destiny of reason as imagination, and the need to 'rescue' this step, is plausible. If, however, one comes to it by way of "The Essence of Truth" and *Introduction to Metaphysics* (texts we will soon discuss in Chapter 5), the conspiracy of imagination and 'calculable certainty' appears starkly opposed to the conception of truth as *aletheia*. Read by way of Heidegger's 1936 course, one cannot help but hear in representation and calculation the external, manipulating, and mathematical approach to system and thus Being as a whole that Heidegger's Schelling, to his credit, opposed. In what sense is Kant's step 'incomparable'? And in what sense is the representational, poetizing force indeed 'essential' in reason? If this is the *Wesen* of reason then the creative character of thought would seem in the very least incongruent with the celebrated structuring of freedom's essence in and from the open jointure of Being. The schematizing subject of such imagination seems more an acolyte of *Wissenschaft* and *Weltanschauung* than the ek-sistent Da-sein instantiated in the ecstatic expanse of the jointure's moment.[22] Perhaps what Heidegger means to rescue is Kant's foresight—that reason's stake in representation would accelerate down a path of self-fulfilling determination, and, in so doing, amass in itself a quantifiable, schematizing decisiveness. The more reason, as a faculty, wagers its authority on the ability to represent standing objects in their beingness, and Being as Idea or "representedness," the more it must strive to equate its grasping and seeing of beings (its *thea* and *horan*) with a "beingness of beings" (as *ousia*) presumed to be "the *a priori*, the *prius*, the prior" (N4 157–58/GA48 288–89).[23] Creative reason finds itself in the aftermath of a deal brokered with representation and representedness, in which case the so-called faculty of reason must avail itself of its productive, poetizing resources.

It is by virtue of being alert to this sense of necessity in poetizing (though without affirming it as the *only* possible sense of poetizing or, for that matter, thinking) that Heidegger further elaborates the pressure toward identity and constancy in the performance of representational determination. Combining the sense of Kantian transcendental function with Nietzsche's use of categories of reason, Heidegger announces that "Nietzsche too must retain the poetizing character of reason, the 'pre-existent', that is, preformed and prestabilized character of the determinations of Being, the schemata" (N3 97/GA47 181). Sense impressions require of the rational subject a poetizing stamp of "identity and sameness" if the sensuous is to be gathered and secured as permanent: poetizing "first clears for what is encountered that free place from which and upon which it can appear as something constant, as an object [Gegen*stand*]" (98/183). But the "pressing 'tumult'" of sensations, says Heidegger, are already a "fictionalized manifold," what Nietzsche understood to be an advance representation of something "*as* something *re*-presented" (98–99/183–84). In short, reason, intent on constancy, 'produces' beings and categories for determining them— 'effecting' them and, in turn, further substantiating the ongoing course of "poetized schema[s]" (99/184) such as 'finality' for Nietzsche. Nietzsche's own preoccupation with the 'developmental' and 'biological' essence of reason, as well as the "fixation" of knowledge in art, further reveals the "subjective compulsion" (102/194) to grasp the world through reason and thus secure a certain permanence in life.[24] The inventiveness of poetizing, observes Krell, is but one way by which Nietzsche may capture the tense situation in which truth, masquerading as "correctness of assertions about beings," is in fact an illusion, "an illusion that is essential yet also inimical to life." Of course, the judgment that terms something an illusion assumes some alternative measure of correctness.[25]

In view of these insights, the sense of poetizing as necessary in terms of both reason's character, *and* problematic as ultimately a "projection of the beingness of beings as permanence and presencing"[26] comes down to the phenomenological experience of reason when it discovers itself thrown amid a sensuous field of entities. Reason must take its cue from something, and since the tradition of ontology has disposed it to keep knowing and Being separate, to understand both in a representational way, it takes its cue from what appears to be most immediate—the sensuous field. This necessary state of affairs is comparable to the average everyday understanding of Being charted in *Being and Time*. But as in the analytic of Dasein, we may expect to learn that what appears most immediate is neither most authentic nor indeed what is 'closest' to the inquiring entity. Poetizing's figurative, representational track proves to constitute an illusory *legein*, but it would accomplish something far different, and far more creative in the *poietic* sense, if it oriented its questioning to and from the 'open occurrence' of the primordial jointure.

How then does it stand with the imagination? In this chapter and the last we have asked this question in the context of (i) Schelling's pursuit of human freedom's essence in the fugal ground of what he advances as a living system, (ii) Heidegger's engagement with this essential impulse and his strained relation to the course of representation and production in the systematization of this creative jointure. If, in Kant's first *Critique*, Heidegger found "an advocate" for fundamental ontology's question of Being,[27] in Schelling, Heidegger finds an advocate for recalling philosophical questioning to the primordial strife of the ground. The criterion for advocacy is (in the very least) a resolve to think what is 'inner' on the bases it determines, bases before and beyond the external determinations of logic, abstraction, and externalizing ideas. Where Heidegger's Kant revealed the power of imagination "as the ground for the inner possibility of ontological synthesis" (KPM 94/GA3 131) in a transcendental sense, but ultimately placed his signature beneath the mastery of the understanding as opposed to the "primordial productivity [*ursprüngliche Produktivität*] of the 'subject'" (MFL 211/GA26 272), Schelling vested in the divine imagination and the measuring word a far more original and originating capacity for creation of and order for the 'whole.' But Heidegger's Schelling is not quite the fulfillment of what was found wanting in Kant, and this state of interpretive affairs is not reducible to a difference of interest or project in Heidegger's *Wiederholung*. Schelling's impasse is more subtle than Kant's, for the 'mastery' is given not to a faculty of understanding but to imagination in the role of production—to creative reason as a poetizing force of willful questioning presumed to accord with a willful primordial Being. The imagination that slipped through Kant's fingers is grasped all too tightly in Schelling's systemic gathering.

Our consideration of poetizing not only has elucidated this quandary, but it has also allowed us to consider an important possibility: the reason Schelling "had to get stranded" (ST 97–98/GA42 168) in his service to the 'impulse' is because he in fact typifies, for Heidegger, a betrayal of the imagination, or what the imagination might have become. Heidegger's specific affinity for the capacitating creativity of the jointure, for the strife of questioning, and for the originary sense of measurement and saying stand as indicative remainders of an imagination that must be rescued from the concealing productions of poetizing. If in Schelling they comprised the footing for a 'running start' for the leap into questioning that nevertheless staggered, it remains to examine the traction they provide for a leap by way of a different question of essence and a different path of poetizing—that of poetry and art. These concerns will occupy us on the side of Heidegger in the next chapter. But before turning our attention to those advances in his discourse, it will serve to make one further push back through Heidegger and allow Schelling to speak, on his own terms, to the shape of the impasse in which Heidegger has left him.

Asystic form and the truth of the mirror

In his 1935 *Introduction to Metaphysics* Heidegger clarifies the "higher order" of philosophy, as compared to the sciences, by likening it to poetry: "Only poetry is of the same order as philosophical thinking, although thinking and poetry are not identical" (IM 28/N 20). Their likeness has to do with their ability to "talk about Nothing"— as opposed to fixing beings in their beingness as something—and this is a mark of superiority, for "the poet always speaks as if beings were experienced and addressed for the first time" (28/20). To speak of the Nothing is to enact expression on the brink of a *beginning* within the relational whole of being. This is the kinship Heidegger had in mind when, in his Schelling interpretation, he likened the impulse beyond man and system into the origins of a world occurrence to "the poetry of the poet" (ST 58/GA42 100)—a venture into the open terrain of the primordial as opposed to the manipulation of the knowable. The higher order of poetry and philosophy cannot be understood apart from this more prevailing tendency toward willful representation and subjective production. The distinctly *expressive* abilities of philosophy and poetry cannot be appreciated unless held in tension with the objectivizing expressiveness that intends constancy and fixation in the will to truth. But Schelling, as well, likened what is highest in thought to the poetry of the poet.[28] Might this interest signal a portion of the 'essential impulse' that is shared by the two thinkers? Is there an orientation in Schelling that in fact did not 'get stranded' and may support Heidegger's efforts to rescue the *poietic* bearing of the imagination from the concealments of production and system?

The indefinable and originary

On the face of it, Schelling's 1821 lecture, *On the Nature of Philosophy as Science*, sounds decidedly unhelpful to Heidegger's distinction between philosophy and the sciences. Upon closer examination it reveals a moment in which Schelling strains to step through the impasse toward the strife of philosophical questioning, thereby affirming Heidegger's interpretive concerns and gesturing, in its own way, toward the 'right running start' he envisions. Recalling the necessary place of the dark ground beneath the being of all existence and actuality, Schelling opens his lecture by pointing to a necessary *asystation* (in the Greek sense of a matter in internal conflict) prior to any system. The difficulty inherent in any attempt to locate human knowledge within a system evidences the fact that knowledge "originally and of itself" is not in a system (NPS 210/SW9 209), but is in a state of disharmony longing for harmony. The aspiration to 'one' system of knowledge thus assumes one original discord beneath all systems. Schelling explains: "Hence the idea of the system as such presupposes the necessary and irresolvable conflict of the systems: without the latter the former would not arise" (212/211). How then does the "*principle*" of a system's possibility arise? Though the grounding principle would seem to require a "subject" of movement that must "proceed through everything and cannot remain in anything" (215/214–15), this subject is difficult to ascertain. Descartes' *cogito ergo sum* and Fichte's *I am I*, for example, are failed principles because they substantiate systems of mere laws, as opposed to a "living system" (216/216). Moreover, the search for the subject of the principle is itself misguided as a question of *quid*—'what' the principle 'is.' A question of definition cannot treat "the indefinable itself" (216/216).[29] The point recalls the difficulty inherent in treating *Indifferenz* noted in the *Freedom Essay*. 'Whatness' assumes delimitation and form, but the basis for a system of knowledge must resist all limitations and forms—must be "truly infinite" (217/217). The principle that moves in the disharmony of asystation cannot be finite, cannot be an entity, and indeed cannot even be God. What appears to be a basic exercise in presenting the necessary conditions for the possibility of system thus amounts, quite remarkably, to a bracketing of the 'absolute' subject and the divine personality.

The asystic principle must maintain mobility and infinity. It must, potentially at least, 'be' everything. Though Schelling does not here thematize the 'Nothing,' he does allow that the principle must have a capacity to be both God and not God; and "in this respect it is above God" (NPS 217/SW9 217) and before all determinative footholds. But is not the question of a principle for system itself a question of logical deduction asked from a horizon of systemic, determinative reason? Possibly so, but to his credit Schelling is speaking from the edge of all systems, from the preparatory limit of Idealism, from the line between system and *asystasy*, coherence and conflict, 'God' and the 'superdivinity' (217/217). He avers that if the necessary possibility of a system of knowledge requires as its principle something unlimited, and if thought is to apprehend this principle, then this means the philosopher of such a system must enter a realm of 'being' beneath the ground of any system. Philosophical questioning, one could say, must take a stand in the space between ground and existence, darkness and light:

> Those, then, who want to find themselves at the starting point of a truly free philosophy, have to depart even from God. Here the motto is: whoever wants to preserve it will lose it, and whoever abandons it will find it. Only those have reached the ground in themselves and have become aware of the depths of life,

who have at one time abandoned everything and have themselves been abandoned by everything, for whom everything has been lost, and who have found themselves alone, face-to-face with the infinite: a decisive step which Plato compared with death. . . . It is a grim step to take, it is grim to have to depart from the final shore. This, we can infer from the fact that so few have ever been capable of it. (NPS 217–18/SW9 217–18)

The passage is notable in the way Schelling's structure of abandonment and departure anticipates what Heidegger believes to be essential to poetry and art. But the assumption that the ground is to be found 'in' the 'self' and in an encounter with the 'infinite' (as opposed to the *abgrund* or Nothing) keeps us mindful of a telling difference from Heidegger's step of departure.[30] But it is with this sense of necessary departure, Schelling explains, that the turn from 'negative' to 'positive' philosophy is positioned. Instantiated in the space of the infinite, philosophy faces the possibility for system in the *freedom* to, or not to, take up *form*. The principle for system is an activity, a will: freedom. Schelling is quick to insist that this "pure absolute freedom itself" is not a freedom 'from' determination but at once a freedom 'for' form (existence)—it is "eternal, pure ability," "pure will itself," and indeed "complete indifference" (NPS 220/SW9 220). The point is consistent with his discussion of indifference in the *Freedom Essay*, and confirms my sense of the unground as an emergent force conceived in terms similar to those of imagination. Heidegger, had he commented on this text, would likely mark this asystic quality of freedom and formation as further evidence of Schelling's 'productive' impasse. And though Schelling here affirms a freedom "antecedent" to human subjectivity, and speaks of the "open space" where "wisdom can still search for and mind itself" (242/245, 224/224–25)—even to the point of distinguishing 'thought' (as free) from 'knowledge'—the way in which the science of philosophy becomes "*aware of this eternal freedom*" (242/245, 221/221) involves the same constituent elements of imagination that provoked Heidegger's 'poetizing' hesitation: likeness, recognition, production, creation, light, mirroring, and artistry.

Though the features of Schelling's 'impasse' remain evident in the stated turn toward positive philosophy, the sharpening of the asystic path of philosophical questioning underscores those elements of the *Freedom Essay* that Heidegger applauded. Schelling is intent, once more, on the mystery of original discord and darkness, on the open horizon beneath determinative reason, and on unsettling the pretensions of logical or categorical inquiry. Whether or not he is as alert to the risks of poetizing as Heidegger would like depends on how he would understand this primordial collaboration between freedom and form. There is, however, a later confirmation of his intensified interest in pressing philosophy toward the matter of originary meaning and a poetic sense of 'ground.' In the *Historical-critical Introduction to the Philosophy of Mythology* (1842), the Greek sense of *asystation* is found embodied in Greek mythology's performance of "a certain meaning as originary [*Bedeutung als ursprünglich*]" that mirrors the "immemorial . . . question of meaning" in philosophy (PM 10/SW11 10). The association presses the far boundaries of philosophy as a 'science.' The way Schelling proposes to treat this element of mythology is much like the way he approached the *essence* of human freedom in the *Freedom Essay*, and of equal kinship with Heidegger's basic phenomenological devotion to letting-be his own matters: Schelling's intends "an immanent development, a development *of the matter itself*" (20/22). Specifically, the intent is to allow mythology's "free art of poetry [*Dicktkunst*]" to exhibit the "ground from which it springs forth" (19/21, 13/14). The method and the matter, then, appear at considerable remove from the ontology of will and obtrusive production. Schelling does not speak of representation in this context, but of how mythology "mirrors a meaning for us . . . or points to it in the distance, but a meaning that itself perpetually withdraws from us, after which we would be compelled to hasten without ever being able to reach it" (13/15). Mythology thus enacts the position of departure from the 'final shore.' There is a sense of showing or shining within the work to which a poetic look attunes itself: "The poetic view is able to allow for the idea that natural phenomena shine forth [*hindurchschimmern*] through the figures of the gods. It can believe to perceive in itself the first experiences concerning powers operating invisibly in human things—why not even religious shudders?" (14/15). As a scene of mirroring and withdrawal, then, a poetic attunement hosts an illumination of the creative possibilities in man. The work of mythology—like a 'convulsion' of the imagination noted in his Plastic Arts address—is thus a springing forth of meaning and a shining forth of possibilities. And not only poets, Schelling elsewhere writes, "but also philosophers, have their ecstasies."[31]

A resoluteness before willing

To qualify as a recovery of his own essential impulse, Schelling's departure from the shore of system and divine assurance would, for Heidegger, require a new species of resoluteness and a new horizon of questioning in the neighborhood of what is 'nearest.'[32] A willful resolve must become an "open resoluteness [*Ent-schlossenheit*]," the essence of which "lies in the de-concealment [*Ent-borgenheit*] of human Dasein for the clearing of Being and by no means in an accumulation of energy for 'activity.' . . . But the relation to Being is letting. That all willing should be grounded in letting [*im Lassen*] strikes the understanding as strange" (IM 22–23/N 16).[33] Schelling's sense of departure and abandonment is apt, but it would require specification as a "questioning that pushes us into the open [*Offene*], provided that it itself, as a questioning, transforms itself (as does every genuine questioning), and casts a new space [*neuen Raum*] over and through everything" (32/23). What arises as 'strange' yet vital is the nature of this open space as a site in which one experiences "things as they are in whatever may be nearest" and one stands in the *truth* as "the openness of beings" (32/23, 23/17).

To continue our comparison, an attunement to the asystic would hasten a question of the truth of Being without ready recourse to 'being' or beings in the available sense of the Greek *to on* or 'beingness' as *to einai* (*esse*) (IM 33/N 24). The open space thus reopens the question "where in all this is the Being of beings, and what does it consist in?" (34/24). For Heidegger, this question of Being's originary meaning is also, at the same time and in the same space, a question of the essence of *truth*, of "the one thing that in general distinguishes every 'truth' as truth" (OET 136/GA9 73). Both inflections of the question ought to arise in the departure from determinative poetizing and the withdrawal from all that creative reason takes to be 'obvious,' but the strife incumbent upon such movements is not so easy to sustain. Heidegger notes that though German idealism is, on the ordinary view, lauded for its "originary questioning about grounds and the bonding [*Bindung*] to such grounds," it is still of an irresolute age in which "[a]ll things sank to the same level, to a surface resembling a blind mirror that no longer mirrors, that casts nothing back" (IM 48/N 34–35).[34] Heidegger, like the later Schelling, returns through Greek thought to Greek tragedy, Heraclitus and Parmenides in order to capture the roots of this reflex toward poetizing measure as well as the alternative possibility that the originary is that which springs forth (*Ursprung als Entspringen*) in a way that "'belonging-together reciprocally are apprehension and Being'" (*to gar auto noein estin te kai einai*) (154–55/111).[35] Schelling's *Freedom Essay* was already an exercise toward thinking this reciprocal belonging-together, and his later emphases on the experience of asystasy in the face of the infinite imply a continued resolve, but what Heidegger wants to spring forth and shine forth from his 'mirror' in the scene of open withdrawal is the manifest essence of Being and truth (a scene which the *Beiträge* will distinguish in the verbal sense of *die Wesung des Seyns*). This means we may supplement our understanding of the production/poetizing concern from the last chapter with the insight that one of the reasons Schelling 'had to get stranded'—had to resign his impulse to the poetizing essence of reason—is that he failed to let the immanent development of his 'matter' turn his questioning back toward a deeper consideration of the essence of truth. Where the divine imagination, in one sense, and the inquiring imagination, in another, are bent on representing beings in their 'beingness,' the measure of *letting-be* gives way to a measuring *will*, and the opportunity to "engage oneself with the open region [*das Offene*] and its openness into which every being comes to stand [*hereinsteht*]" and "reveal themselves with respect to what and how they are" (OET 144/GA9 84) as an event of truth in the Greek sense of *aletheia* is passed over, and forgotten.[36] An 'open resolutenes' is required in the scene of departure and withdrawal because it honors the 'freedom' of the scene to emerge from the side of the matters as a disclosure of the eventful meaning 'of' Being and the standard for the truth 'of' beings. Questioning arises in the interest of disclosedness, in the opening of the open region as being upsurges into presence and as "every measure [*jegliches Maß*]" (145/85) for being and truth.

To depart for the strange nearness of beings is to attune oneself to the essential needfulness of Being and truth. Schelling approximated this sense of need in his account of divine self-revelation and in man's service to the unifying 'word' of order over the whole. In so doing, he assumed a life of truth moving in and from the jointure but failed to pair man's original becoming and instantiation in the 'summit' with the question of truth's essence, a question the immanent development of the open between ground and existence ought to disclose. If his "On the Essence of Truth" is any indication, Heidegger expected the account of Dasein's essential capacitation and creative force to allow for a retrieval of truth's bearing on human being and freedom. He explains:

'Truth' is not a feature of correct propositions that are asserted of an 'object' by a human 'subject' and then 'are valid' somewhere, in what sphere we know not; rather, truth is disclosure of beings through which an openness essentially unfolds [*west*]. All human comportment and bearing are exposed in its open region. Therefore the human being *is* in the manner of ek-sistence. (OET 146/ GA9 86)

The jointure's 'open' does not simply belong to a movement of will through divine becoming and into inspired reason, but must also be understood as *aletheia*'s clearing, the *Lichtung* in which "Beyng appears originally in the light of concealing withdrawal [*verbergenden Entzugs*]" (OET 154/GA9 97). If Schelling fails to let-be the question of the truth 'of' being in the being of jointure and neglects his own 'remainder' of the dark, discordant ground in favor of justifying the unity of system under divine personality, Heidegger finds in the illumination of *Lichtung* both an open disclosure of measure for the ek-sistent Dasein and "this innermost need [*innerste Not*] that thinking has" (152/95), as well as a doubling back into the region of concealment and withdrawal. Truth names the "sheltering that clears as the fundamental trait of Being," through which any measure of accordance between knowledge and beings is to unfold (153– 54/96–97). Before the logos of unity may be 'said,' proclaimed, or presented, freedom must be understood through a comportment toward accord before all assertions of correctness—a freedom "for what is opened up in an open region [and] lets beings be the beings they are. Freedom now reveals itself as letting beings-be" (144/83). In this way the matter of the essence of human freedom and the 'connected matters' of primordial ground/existence alike point toward an *erscheinen* of *ursprünglich* truth that would have preempted the poetizing tendencies toward production and efficacy.

In view of these considerations, it is evident that the question of the essence of truth must participate in and shape the question of the meaning of Being, and indeed the question of the essence of freedom. Any 'immanent development' of a matter of essence—any questioning willing to risk the *unheimlich* experience evoked through letting beings be—turns on an open "attunement" to aletheia's disclosedness and thus an "ek-sistent exposedness to beings as a whole" (OET 147/GA9 87). What we have thus far said regarding the *Gedanken des Herstellens* in reason's poetizing command may now be paired with the "knowing pro-ducing [*Hervor-bringen*]" (IM 18/N 13) of the will-to-knowledge in assuming that the truth of beings is thought on the basis of a correct conformity of object representations to their beings. If creative reason tends toward poetizing, determinative truth tends toward *technē*—in one aspect, a privileging of beingness as the expense of beings. Neither poetizing nor *technē* are *essentially* crippling or misguided, but when detached from a mindfulness of their grounds they adapt to a damaging course of *hervorbringen*. Truth becomes the "certainty of presentation" anchored in a view of being "defined as the objectness [*Gegenständlichkeit*] of presentation" (AWP 216/GA5 87), and the understanding of beings as a whole "shifts" to accommodate the human as "*subjectum*. . . . the referential center of beings as such" (AWP 217/GA5 88). But just as Being necessarily withdraws from the gathering grasp of poetizing, it also retreats from the arresting grasp of *technē* (OET 149/GA9 90–91). What Heidegger says of this predicament on the side of truth holds as well for the side of production:

Yet the seeming glimmer of *aletheia* that remains, no longer has the sustaining strength and tension to be the determining ground for the essence of truth.

And it never became such a ground again. To the contrary. Ever since idea and category have assumed their dominance, philosophy fruitlessly toils to explain the relation between assertion (thinking) and Being by all possible and impossible means—fruitlessly, because the question of Being has not been brought back to its adequate ground and basis, in order to be unfolded [*entfaltet*] from there. (IM 203–04/N 145)

He goes so far as to speak of the "collapse of unconcealment," a "happening" effected by a failed resolve, which in turn calls for "a thoughtful re-trieval" (IM 204/N 145). The collapse itself must be retrieved and "displayed," and, done 'thoughtfully,' the glimmer of unconcealment too may well "happen" in a specific kind of *work*—"the work of the word as poetry, the work of the stone in the temple and statue, the work of the word as thinking" (204/146). Where the dominance of *doxa* as "a type of logos" has deprived beings "of the possibility of turning themselves *toward* apprehension, appearing on their own right,"[37] an artistic work (as an *ergon* "pro-duced into unconcealment [*Unverborgenheit her-gestellte*],") is a "striving for the unconcealment of beings" (204–05/146).[38] Where the *pseudos* of *doxa* "distorts beings and twists them," the "struggle for truth . . . becomes the struggle for the *a-pseudos*, the undistorted, the untwisted" (205/146–47). In broader terms, when we speak of Heidegger's concern to 'twist free' of the concealments wrought by poetizing and *technē* this means, in effect, to straighten the path and focus the view toward the unconcealment of beings. In a very significant sense, it is to pair the striving of thought with the striving of a 'work.' But we must first understand such a pairing as a dilemma for Heidegger, rather than a clear decision for instantiation in the aletheiac opening. The dilemma arises in the desire to recover or adapt the direction of *pro-duction* as a measure of truth and being without falling into procedural *Erklärung* (see AWP 211/GA5 80), to honor the 'happening' of unconcealment without sliding into that *pre-senting* (*Vor-stellen*) of beings that forgets the simultaneous concealment of beings as a whole (AWP 216/GA5 87). How can the strife of questioning and the strife of a work bind itself to the open region without prefiguring the event of disclosure by way of a measuring outline (*Grundiss*) or presentiment for the objective (*Gegenständigen*) (cf. 209/77, 219/90–91)? It seems we do not depart from the final shore so much as we are delivered from it, and this too requires a crafted vessel, a work.

Heidegger's Hölderlin and the Aletheiac Imagination

In the last chapter, we sought both the central work and the implicit threat of the imagination in an investigation of essence and in a retrieval of an essential impulse. If in Chapter 2 we followed the opening of the imagination in the question, "what reality inheres in our representations?" these recent investigations have followed this opening to the more ontological question, "how is the being of the divine, of man, and of thought constituted as *reell* in a living ground and as a living system?" In Schelling's *Freedom Essay*, the generative work of the divine imagination and the inspired vocation of human reason constituted two creative elements intrinsic to the essence of human freedom at its primordial origin and in the life of the 'whole.' Heidegger's course on this text affirmed the fundamentally *poietic* bearing of this fugal occurrence, but hesitated over the productive character assigned to Being and afoot in the creative reason that gathered this occurrence under the unity of divine personality and for the unifying command of poetizing. Schelling's 'impasse,' I argued, was as an impasse for the imagination on account of the entrenched habits of representational determination and the figurative efficacy of a systematizing *legein*. The imagination was manifest in the being of the copula and between the being of ground and existence, yet proved too much of an accomplice in concealing the emergence of Being in a primordial clearing, the capacitating ground for creative Dasein, and the strife of philosophical questioning.

Our present task is to consider the possibility that the imagination, though still very much *in question*, remains a constitutive part of Heidegger's own service to the 'essential impulse' and in his endeavors to twist free of the poetizing essence of reason. This means we must be prepared to treat the imagination as 'underway' in conjunction with the momentum of the 'right running start' foreseen for the leap into inceptual thinking. As in our previous discussion, here we shall work from within operations of imagination that are intrinsic to questions of *essence*: the essence of truth, the essence of poetry, and the origin of the 'work' of art. The primary texts will be Heidegger's "Hölderlin and the Essence of Poetry" (1936) and "The Origin of the Work of Art" (1935/36),[1] followed by a brief study of the expansive scope of imagination as it appears in *Contributions to Philosophy (Of the Event)* (1936–38) and "Poetically Man Dwells" (1951). I will argue that the focal texts, as one sustained project, disclose the elements through which Heidegger intends a reorientation and re-tasking of the *poietic* bearing of the imagination, even at a moment in which he leaves the term (and its cognates) at Schelling's impasse. Among these elements stand the need to resolve the dilemma of production by way of the creative bestowal of projection, to specify the fugal event as an event of the poetic and artistic work, to oppose the measure of poetic naming and workly strife to figurative representation and aesthetic reductionism, and to retrieve in the endurance of poetic work a basis for the resoluteness of Dasein's dwelling and thought's questioning. By tracing the motion of these elements in Heidegger's discourse, and accentuating the affective shape of his phenomenological entry into the essential work of poetry, I will account for a poetizing impulse that allows the imagination to be at once *questionable* with respect to ascertaining the essence of projection in a poetic work's disclosure, and *question-worthy* with respect to fixing and figuring the clearing of truth as the openness of beings and the founding of Beyng in a work. To appreciate the instantiating, preserving capacity of language as intrinsic to the need of truth and the need for *poietic* work, we must follow Schelling's fugal impulse into Hölderlin's poetic impetus, and thereby recover *Dichtung* as the event of *aletheia* and the instigation of *Denken*'s measure.

The measure of poetry's quivering half-light

If reason is a work of language, as Schelling's *legein* of the whole is a work of word and measure, and if philosophy occupies a 'poetic' position above the sciences, then do creative reason and proclaiming saying stand in the inheritance of a poetizing imagination that pro-duces unconcealment without allowing the *ideas* of production to obtrude themselves? Can we speak of a poetizing impulse in a language which intends an 'open' event or happening, yet resists the schematizing immediacy of determination? Being, Heidegger reminds us, is never a being but "because Being and the essence of things can never be calculated and derived from what is present at hand, things must be freely created, posited, and bestowed" (HEP 124/GA4 41). This necessity amounts to a dilemma, which only a certain form of imagination and a certain event in language may resolve: to adapt the sense of creation to accord with bestowal.

In the portion of *Being and Time*'s first division that explores the shape of *being-in* as applied to everyday discourse, Heidegger's treatment of the existential–ontological foundation of language contains an oblique reference to the poetic possibilities in spoken expression. He notes: "In 'poetical' [*dichtenden*] discourse, the communication of the existential possibilities of one's state-of-mind can become an aim in itself, and this amounts to a disclosing of existence [*das Erschließen von Existenz*]" (BT 205/GA2 216). In the comparative section of his course, *History of the Concept of Time* (1925) he similarly observes: "The discoveredness of Dasein, in particular in the disposition of Dasein, can be made manifest by means of words in such a way that certain new possibilities of Dasein's being are set free. Thus discourse, especially *poetry* [*Dichtung*], can even bring about the release of new possibilities of the being of Dasein" (HCT 272/GA20 375). Language—as having to do with Dasein's expressive character—assumes a range of discursive possibilities, but poetic speech or poetry is especially capacitated with the means of disclosing something beyond mere declarative propositions and indications of one's mood. To poetic disclosure belongs a capacity for disclosing existence itself in a liberating way. At the end of Chapter 1 we noted Heidegger's more pronounced assertion in *Basic Problems of Philosophy* that "Poetry, creative literature, is nothing but the elementary emergence into words, the becoming-uncovered [*entdecktwerden*], of existence as being-in-the-world. . . . the world first becomes visible by what is thus spoken" (BPP 171–72/ GA24 244).[2] Together, these comments convey something of the capacity of poetic creation to disclose both the existential being of Dasein and the shape of Dasein's world. Poetical discourse is already 'beyond man' regarded as willing subject. The question is to what extent the *essence* of poetry is already beyond or before the will to prefigure and poetize beings and world into the utility and permanence of the objective. "True art stands in rank with the first reality," writes Russian avant-garde poet Daniil Kharms, "it creates the world and is its first reflection. It is necessarily real. . . . It seems to me that these verses have become a thing, and one can take them off the page and throw them at the window, and the window would break" (1933).[3] Things or not, the words of the poet stand poised to break *open* a world that is otherwise enclosed.

Impetus toward openness

In Heidegger's 1936 address, "Hölderlin and the Essence of Poetry," there is a singular orientation not just to the disclosive capacity of poetry, but also to a poet who "because of an excess of impetus, poetically thinks through to the ground and center of being" (HEP 128/GA4 47). Hölderlin's 'impetus' is of the same fashion as Schelling's 'impulse.' This is not simply a result of the contemporaneous standing of the Hölderlin text and the Schelling course, but is indicative of the fact that Heidegger is very much in dialogue with Schelling while reading Hölderlin. The sense of 'excess,' however, implies that the poet, more than the thinker, is so overwhelmed and provoked down the path of the essential that impasse is not an option. Hölderlin is a poet whose imagination risks the hour of "the quivering half-light" and stands in the night of "the fantastical"[4]— dwelling in the space of the 'enthusiastic' (*Schwärmerei*) imagination that Kant warned against and Schelling reclaimed. Is this the space in which creation is also a bestowal? If the stated purpose of the inquiry is to uncover that which is essential in poetry by considering what Hölderlin's poems evoke within and about language, the deeper aim is to escape the above 'dilemma' by allowing our "standing within poetry's sphere of influence" to become a "standing in the midst of the openness of beings" (118/34, 121/38). But what does the 'fantastical' have to do with the 'openness of beings'? The language of instantiality recalls the promising (if unsustained) movement of Schelling's questioning into the clearing and moment of Being's occurrence in the jointure, and evokes a sense in which poetry's essence will bring forth an opening for Da-sein to stand in language. Heidegger thus positions himself astride two parallel pathways of instantiation—one owing to the decisions of the thinker, and the other to what stirs in the poet. These are not as much rival paths as they are different accents on the same resoluteness.

Where Schelling's *Freedom Essay* arose within a time of estrangement between reason and revelation in the specter of immanence, between *reell* being and abstraction in the Hegelian apotheosis of system, and with a view toward the divine 'need' in self-revelation, Heidegger's turn to Hölderlin's poetry arises in a historical "*time of need*" (HEP 128/GA4 47)—an age of poetizing blindly detached from the deep 'Moment' of temporality disclosed in Schelling's jointure. Being, defined as *ousia* (in the sense of constant presence) and, in turn, *substantia* has become "intangible as a vapor" (IM 207–08/N 148, 41–2/30), *logos* as *katēgoria* "has become the court of justice over Being," *questioning* prefers counting and calculating to "the right moment and the right endurance" (IM 216/N 154, 221/157), and under the "purview of aesthetics" the work of art "becomes an object of experience and is consequently considered an expression of human life" (AWP 208/GA5 75). The 'need,' in short, surmounts the boundaries of culture and *Wissenschaft*: to maintain the impulse of questioning appropriate to the aletheaic essence of truth and the instantiation of Da-sein within the jointure, thought must navigate the impasse of metaphysical willfulness in general and poetizing in particular. Select phrases from Hölderlin's corpus will comprise an "emergency route [*Notwege*]" that accords with the 'right running start' for the leap through Schelling's impasse; along this route thought will pass before the innocence, danger, and expression that together deliver language into "the midst of the openness of beings" (HEP 118/GA4 34, 121/38). The time of need, in short, needs a truer *measure*. This in turn means an untwisted production; a 'straighter' poetizing that is like the fugal 'saying' of Schelling's jointure but distinct from Schelling's justifying production of God.

The promise and risks of poetic poetizing turn on the nature of human dwelling in language and the course of imagination there proffered. For Hölderlin, poetizing is the "most innocent of all occupations." Poetry is a playful making, a production that, says Heidegger, "freely invents its world of images and remains lost in thought in the realm of the imagined" (HEP 119/GA4 35).[5] It is "harmless" and "without effect," and "has nothing in common with the deed, which immediately intervenes in what is real and changes it" (119/35). These qualities stand Hölderlin's poetizing in marked anticipatory contrast to the poetizing character of reason highlighted in Heidegger's commentary on Nietzsche. The latter poetizing is also inventive, but deploys representation in the service of determinant effect, thereby exchanging the 'tumult' of impressions for the stability of beingness and the compass of categorical knowing. Poetry is a saying in the domain of imagination, and not a prefigurative imaging of the apparent world as actual (*wirklich*). But poetry also works from within the realm of language, and in this function it delivers a *dangerous* good. The free inventiveness belongs to a poetic imagination that, following Hölderlin, "dwells in huts" (at 119/35), an imagination set apart by virtue of being exercised in a *human* being. Dwelling thus overlays the form of play with a testimonial vocation—the human is the creature who "must bear witness to what he is" and must "stand" for this attestation (120/36). In the assumptions constitutive of poetizing reason, the human creature thought himself the representative of Being as will, in which case the 'whatness' of human being was answered by the commanding nature of subjectivity. Put in mind of his dwelling, however, human testimony must concern not "an additional expression of human being" but rather "belongingness to the earth" (120/36). Language, for Hölderlin, arises as a divine gift, a gift that equips the human to command through "the freedom of decision," yet tasks the human with testifying to the "belongingness to beings as a whole" (120/36).[6] Language, the very mode of attestation, is dangerous because its expressive capacity can as much preserve this belongingness as attenuate it. Language poses a threat to both Being and itself insofar as it is the creative site in which the intimacy between Being and beings either appears essentially or withdraws under the deceptive ambitions of understanding. Ensconced in danger, language, says Heidegger, "is tasked with making beings as such manifest in works and preserving them" (120/37).

We are already alert to the dangers of this vocation because we have noted how the poetizing drive to representing beings in beingness amounts to a coercive neglect of Being's own primordial and determinative agency. The word, says Heidegger, "never offers an immediate guarantee as to whether it is an essential word [*wesentliches Wort*] or a deception" (HEP 120/GA4 37), even though the word of reason, and the appearance it creates, trusts itself as the intelligible guarantor of the sensible. How then is the word an agent of creation and bestowal? As with the case of everyday discourse in *Being and Time*, Heidegger accredits language as a 'good' for communicating "moods" and facilitating "understanding" in which case it maintains an instrumental value. But language is also a good "in a more primordial sense" insofar as it grants the "possibility" not just of Dasein's being-in the world, but also of "standing" at the very site of the world's origin for Dasein in history (121/37–8). Adapting the sense of 'word' used by Schelling to convey the immediacy of will and becoming in the jointure of ground and existence, Heidegger calls language "that event [*Ereignis*] that has the highest possibility of human being at its disposal" (121/38, cf. 123/40). The appearance of this term, *Ereignis*, in conjunction with a sense of 'possibility,' marks a crucial moment in our investigation of the imagination since Chapter 1. It allows us to formalize a theme that has been implicit across a range of considerations: the immediacy of the mediating work of the productive imagination and the schematism in Kant's first *Critique*, the 'convulsions' of the imagination in Schelling's appraisal of Greek artistry, the reflexive and creative representations of the divine imagination, the proclamation of the measuring word, the reflection of originary meaning in the mirror of mythology, the capacitating 'moment' Heidegger finds in Schelling's jointure, the ecstatic, and the unconcealing event of truth.

What qualifies an event 'of' language as *Ereignis* is not yet clear, but as we have sought the imagination in transcendental, artistic, and ontological contexts we have encountered steadily a sense of 'happening' or 'occurrence' that overwhelms temporal order and supersedes rational determinations with a disclosure of possibilities. These eventful possibilities lack the fullness that Heidegger will ascribe to *Ereignis* but concern the human being and often arise through the human being, but are always already underway 'before' the human subject. Similarly, a statement from *Introduction to Metaphysics* sets the bar for what we want to understand of language as event: "Being is the fundamental happening [*das Grundgeschehnis*], the only ground which historical Dasein is granted in the midst of beings that are opened up as a whole" (IM 215–26/N 154). We thus meet the appearance of *Ereignis* as a term for what is essential in language with the anticipation that Heidegger will recover in poetizing a resolute letting-be that stands attuned to an event of opening and bestowal.

The poetic event

There are two essential ways in which poetry allows for the *event* of language. Both are crucial to resolving the apparent tensions between the fantastical imagination and the openness of beings, and the creative and bestowing. The *first* event is constitutive and is evident in Heidegger's statement, "language is only essential as conversation" (HEP 122/GA4 38). In the everyday sense, language, like reason, is an exercise in combination. But in the act of conversation we observe how language is in fact what "mediates the coming-together" (122/39) of interlocutors and the matter of which they speak. A conversation is a unity wrought through words, and if, following Hölderlin, we humans 'are' a conversation, then our mutual constancy and endurance require that "the essential word [*wesentlich Wort*] must remain related to what is one and the same" (122/39). There is an appeal to Schelling's understanding of identity behind these remarks, as well as an application of what must be the 'same' in the enduring 'unity' of conversation to the ecstatic nature of time—the historical opening of time toward the "present, past, and future" across which we move in conversation (122/39). Whatever is brought forth through conversation across the opening of "torrential time" (at 122/40) already assumes a belonging-together of humans and gods in conversation.

The *second* event essential to poetry maintains the sense of *poiesis* in language, but replaces the Schellingian paradigm of 'becoming' with that of 'enduring' (*das Bleiben*).[7] This event is the simultaneous appearance of gods, world, and language *in* the moment of divine address and poetic *naming*. Again following Hölderlin, Heidegger pairs the earlier testimonial stand of human belongingness to earth with the divine instantiation of the ground of human existence in the decisions of conversation. Humans arise (stand as Da-sein) in a response-ability to the divine address and measure out the time of belonging through "naming the gods" and promising or denying ourselves to them (HEP 123/GA4 40). The emphasis on decision echoes Schelling's sense of man as a summit in the motion of all becoming, here transposed into a decision to bring the divine into word, into the open of conversation. The response-ability of the word is not a question of man's moral destiny, but of the ontological decision to name "the gods . . . and all things with respect to what they are" (123/41). Poetic naming, like poetizing reason, concerns the deliverance of beings, gods, and indeed Being *into* the appearance or standing by which they will be known, but the sense of need and event informing this motion adapts the movement of 'becoming' into the spirit of 'enduring.' What *remains*, says Hölderlin, is *founded* [*stiften*] by the poets. This accredits the word with a privilege over presence, for what appears to knowledge as present is, in fact, "fleeting," and even what "is simple can never be directly seized from the chaotic" (123/41, 124/41).[8] Hölderlin thus appeals to the striving freedom of poetic work, to Schelling's *Dicktkunst* as the reflection of "a certain meaning as originary" (PM 10/SW11 8). Poetic naming, like reason's schematizing, is a creative event performed in the interests of security, constancy, and measure.[9] But naming is an opening in Being "so that beings might appear," in which case "the poet's naming first nominates beings to that which they are," not as objectified but as "the essence of things coming to expression so that they first shine forth [*aufglänzen*]" (HEP 123–24/GA4 41).

The naming saying of the poets, then, is a founding [*Stiftung*] understood as a "free bestowal [*freie Schenjung*]" (HEP 124/GA4 41) and not an expression of beingness, as though a universal concept of Being were already grasped then parceled out amid the appearing entities of experience. Founding, in simple terms, is a mode of creation but not an act of gathering in the sense of *legein* we have noted. Moreover, as a free bestowal, this founding event is not an act of the subject upon an object made present, but is an opening in Being whereby Dasein itself "is brought into a firm relation and placed on a ground." In this way, to say that the essence of poetry "is the founding of Being in words" (124/41–2) is to suggest that poetic utterance anticipates the relational whole within which the human dwells, and this is something altogether distinct from anticipating the figurative representation of Being or beings that the will to knowledge, truth, and system gathers in a calculative way. The poetic word, like Schelling's word of unity and proclamation, is a word 'of' emergence and *poiesis*, but Heidegger lays his emphasis more on the poet's care for the shining forth of beings from this ground than on the loving measure of divine understanding or the categorical gathering into idealist 'Ideas.' We may simplify the importance of these distinctions by returning to Schelling's own analogy; essential poetic saying is what happens in the departure from the final shore. Set adrift from instrumental representations and productive assumptions, thought endures the strife of the abyss and abandonment by crying out in language—a cry of alarm that is, in the poet, a call of rescue; not a return to the shore but a rescue of buoyancy, so to speak, amid the open ground. Hyperion's insistence that "*one* melody still sounds for me" here resounds.[10] The departure, more specifically, here becomes a departure *from* the blinding shore-bound light *for* the dark ground such that what shines will shine freely and alight on what the naming word shall preserve. In its domain of language, and as "the founding naming of the gods and of the essence of things," poetry thus evokes the sense of existence as being 'poetic' in its ground. The creative, *poietic* response-ability of the poet notwithstanding, such existence is a "gift." The gift obtains, as it were, in the dwelling—in the position of standing "in the presence of the gods" and being "struck by the essential nearness of things" (124/42).[11] Nearness is assured because, through poetry, "everything first steps out into the open" (125/43); and noble tones, writes Hölderlin, "must yet sound again in the symphony of the world's course."[12]

Heidegger's arrangement of these elements is curious. In one sense, he has retraced Schelling's steps into the emergence of will and word within the play of ground and existence in divine becoming. Naming and founding, on this view, correspond to the yearning of the dark principle to attain an image of standing unity, and that expressiveness by which things 'shine forth' corresponds to the reflexive self-representation of the divine imagination that delivers God and man into real existence. In still another sense, and insofar as Hölderlin's deities are outside the scope of the metaphysical God, Heidegger's emphasis on founding is removed from the horizon of becoming or divine self-revelation, and the concern is to establish poetry as "the primordial language" that capacitates Being and everyday language (rather than freedom and evil). Common to both views is the sense in which Heidegger, like Schelling, has pledged his inquiry to a question of essence (of poetry in his case, of human freedom in Schelling's), and the impulse of the matter itself in turn brings thought to a standing position *in* the gathering of the jointure. What was, nevertheless, lacking in Schelling is, to a certain degree, available in Hölderlin.

It is not by accident that Heidegger says of a letter by Hölderlin: "The excessive brightness drove the poet into darkness" (HEP 126/GA4 44). As a man, Hölderlin may arise at the 'summit' of God's creative production, but as a poet he dwells amid both the gift and the danger of the dark ground—he is "gathered into" existence, has "caught sight of the completed whole," and yet the brightness 'shining forth' from the Being his poetic word has founded is a 'quickening' and 'exhausting' force (126–27/45–6). Poetic freedom is, like human freedom, essentially a "supreme necessity," and just as Schelling's God brings man to a point of decision Hölderlin's gods "bring us to speak" (127/45). Schelling's man is tasked with a word that measures the unity and love wrought by divine necessity, but Heidegger's poet, though "mindful" of the belongingness of beings to a whole, stands "cast out . . . into that *between*, between gods and humans" (128/47). Since Heidegger takes no recourse to Schelling's divine personality or indifference, he is again disposed to link this standing, this dwelling, to a more historical "*time of need*," a time marked by "a double lack and a double nothing: in the no-longer of the gods who have fled and in the not-yet of what is to come" (128/47). To say that the essence of poetry "anticipates an historical time" is to withhold the assurance of a salvific eternal beginning, and instead reckon with the 'need' of a time measured in the thick 'moment' of "the nothingness of this night" (129/47–8).[13] Hölderlin's poets are "like those holy priests of the wine-god/Who traveled from land to land in holy night"—they are expectant of what is to come and bear the signature of a divine birth, but they remain between the dark and light principles, needful of "divine fullness" (at 129/48) but unable to bear it or trust understanding to measure it in full.

So what has Heidegger's engagement with Hölderlin's performative reflection on the "essential essence of poetry" won for the dilemma of pro-duction in the retrieval and preservation of the aletheiac opening? Notice that in asking this question, we do not ask what is *the* valid concept of poetry now (see HEP 118/GA4 34, 128/47). Heidegger has not sought a course of conceptual correction. Neither has he sought in poetry a mere device for substantiating the recovery of truth as aletheia. The question of the essence of truth led necessarily to the encounter with the essence of poetry, to the 'work' (*ergon*) of a poet who, by untwisting the distortions of poetizing and *technē*, stands attuned to the need of truth and thus spoke to a time of need.[14] We have learned that the direction of the *asystic* impulse, if pressed beyond the recourse to poetizing reason, comes to a path of the *a-pseudos* in poetic saying, naming, founding. Poets such as Hölderlin, one could say, lack the 'will' to neglect the perdurance of the dark remainder. Their path is an emergency route because they risk the refusal of *Grundiss* and *Gegenständigen*, turn toward *Ereignis* in lieu of complete *Erklärung*, and enact the creative as the bestowing. This does not mean the poetic imagination is a passive accomplice in the happening of Being and the truth of this occurrence. What shines forth in the 'between' springs forth in words, thereby eliding the short but consequential step toward presence and re-presentation. Hölderlin's words do a measuring work. His poems are a production of and for an event, a work of imagination irreducible to authorship or utility, mimetic cooperation or wistful wanderings of fancy.

Though the standing of the poet clearly outstrips the *a priori* position of the faculties, Kant's *Einbildungskraft* remains an instructive element for understanding this sense of poetic poetizing. More than a minor support in an outmoded transcendental structure, it is that indispensable event of receptivity and mediation that creates and bestows—an opening 'beneath' cognition and (arguably) before all sensible/intelligible dualisms that mirrors the poet's standing in the open region 'beyond man' and before the willful measures of understanding. In essence, poetry, for Heidegger, shelters this elemental event even as it extrapolates its schematic character into the mindfulness of the poet's measure. The difference between the Kantian and Hölderlinian imaginations, however, is of course meted out as a difference between creative horizons and instrumental functions. To think the essence of poetry is to allow for magnetism between the strife of philosophical questioning and the strife of a poetizing imagination that withholds itself from the poetizing essence of reason. The work of reason lets-be a work of *ergon*, an unconcealing production in poetry, which in turn reflects upon *thought,* a course of aletheiac retrieval. To think the full measure of the poetizing imagination in *art*—"as setting-into-work of truth" (OWA1 144/HS 17; cf. IM 204/N 146)—is, likewise, to think by way of a "leap [*Sprung*]" and raising a question of *origin* as a way of "making the right jumping-off [*Ab-sprung*] for this leap" (133/8). In Kant, the artistry of productive imagination in the soul later bloomed into the play of imagination in artistic taste. In Heidegger the *herstellend* word of the poet is the well from which the *Hervorbringung* of the work of art draws its truth. But how is the essence of poetry also the essence of art more generally? And on what grounds, if any, may we still speak of the imagination when we speak of art as an origin [*Ursprung*] that "can only begin as a leap" (OWA1 148/HS21)?[15]

Truth in the poetizing work of art

To draw philosophical questioning into the matter of the essence of poetry is to straighten what is twisted by the poetizing essence of reason and retrieve a more fundamental poetizing that comports with the aletheiac essence of truth. If we want to speak of what is at issue, for Heidegger, at the limit of metaphysics, then we must understand this straightening retrieval as a project of attuning all poetizing to the play of truth in the deeper sense of ποιεῖν—to 'bringing-forth' as *hervor-bringen* and to 'pro-ducing' in the sense of *her-stellen*. But is the imagination an accomplice or a hindrance in this sense of preserving the relationship between ποίησις and *aletheia*? When Heidegger comes to the question of the origin of the work of art this same project persists in the form of two directive necessities. First,

> the determination of the essence of poetry as projecting *does not exhaust* its essence. Without a glimpse into the *full* essence of poetry—i.e., of art—we also do not grasp the becoming of truth. We particularly do not grasp how something like the work is necessary for the becoming of truth. (The ground of the necessity of each work is its origin.). The full essence of poetry comes to light in the statement: Poetry—the essence of art—is *founding of Beyng* [Stiftung des Seyns].
>
> (OWA1 146/HS18–19)

To be clear, the statement does not say that art is the 'only' way in which truth occurs. Heidegger's emphasis, rather, is on the emergence of truth in the work's essential ground. This focus holds in our second passage, simply put: "The most concealed ground for the necessity of the artwork, its most authentic origin, is the essence of truth itself" (OWA1 148/HS21). That is not to say that truth somehow 'depends' on works of art in something like a causal relationship, but that the question of art's origin *is* the question of poetry's essence, and that the work of a work of art is a founding of Beyng and an occurrence of truth. Thus, we begin to see that "On the Essence of Truth," "Hölderlin and the Essence of Poetry," and "The Origin of the Work of Art" are texts joined by one project. The project concerns the gathering significance of a poetizing projection (*dichtender Entwurf*) for a time of need and for truth's own need. Schelling's fugal and *asystic* impulses are alert to these needs, and are indeed framed by an 'essential' interest in the plastic arts, tragedy, and mythology. But to discover in art "the poetizing founding of Beyng" requires that the ground from which ideas of production obtrude be reclaimed by a production of "the openness of the there into which all beings and nonbeings stand" (OWA1 146/HS 19). In one sense, this *Da* is the poet's word. In the same sense, more 'fully' explored, it is the 'work' *of* art—the *ergon* through which art lets the origin of truth originate. Stylistically, Schelling has taught us that matters of inquiry attain clarity by way of permitting them a course of strife and opposition. Heidegger's language of impulse and impasse, impetus and exhaustion, has put this lesson to use and accentuated it as a course of necessity within the needful history of Being. His study of art's 'work' will do the same, allowing its inceptual, poetizing significance to emerge in sharp relief against the background of concealing conceptions—namely those of creation, representation, expression, and object-being. If and how 'imagination' should be included in this list is a question that must remain open.

Alert to these points of departure, what we want to ascertain in Heidegger's *a-pseudos* of art, truth and Beyng can be represented by aligning a passage appearing early in the first (Freiburg) version of "The Origin of the Work of Art" with a caution appearing near the end of the full version.

> Truth is never read off from that which is already at hand. Rather, the openness of beings occurs by being projected, by being *poetized* [gedichtet]. All art is in essence poetry, i.e., the breaking-open of that open in which everything is otherwise than usual. By virtue of the poetic projecting [*des dichtenden Entwurfs*], what prevailed until now and was usual becomes non-existent. Poetry is no wandering contrivance of something random, no drifting-off into the unreal. The open that poetry, as a project, opens up (projects ahead) and holds open, first allows beings as such to enter and brings them to shine [*Leuchten*]. Truth, as the openness, occurs in projecting—in poetry [*Dichtung*]. (OWA1 144/HS 17)
>
> If we fix our vision on the essence of the work and its connection [*Bezug*] with the happening of the truth of beings, it becomes questionable [*wird fraglich*] whether the essence of poetry, and this means, at the same time, the essence of projection [*Entwurfes*], can be adequately thought in terms of the power of imagination [*vonder Imagination und Eindbildungskraft*]. (OWA 197/GA5 60)

Why and how does the poetic essence of art amount to a projection that casts the imagination in a questionable light? To answer this question, three avenues pertaining to the question of art's origin must be explored: (1) the manner in which a distinction between object-being and work-being confronts aesthetics with a reorientation toward the emergent *actuality* of art's work; (2) an entry *into* the experience of two works of art that reveals the pitfalls of a poetizing determination and, by contrast, discloses the essential event of truth and the openness of beings in the clearing of a work; (3) the relationship between the originary *strife* of the open region and the play of disclosedness and seclusion through which truth *exposes* all measure-taking in its name.

Object-being and work-being

The *first constitutive matter* signaled by the preceding passages is the tension between grasping the truth from the *at-hand* and glimpsing or fixing the essence of poetry as the essence of artistic *work*. We have tracked this tension already with respect to the being of truth and the originary standing of the poet and have highlighted it as a tension between poetizing in the sense of determination and poetizing in the sense of possibility. How does the tension stand with respect to works of art more generally? The everyday at-hand disposition to grasping artworks conceals a more essential relationship by masking the elemental with elementary assumptions. Foremost among these is the assumption that artworks are objects having a "thingly character" (OWA 145/GA5 3) and originating from the artist's creative determination. We speak of a 'piece' of art, a thing having an "object-being [*Gegenstandsein*]" (OWA1 131–32/HS 6–7), and handle such works according to the equations of the art industry, all the while praising them (if such is the case) on the basis of an aesthetic experience oriented to the thing's "createdness [*Erzeugstein*]" (OWA 145/GA5 3, OWA1 132/HS 7). This state of affairs specifies the reduction of beings to 'beingness' or 'representedness' under the domain of poetizing reason. Heidegger is not as much concerned in indicting this disposition as he is in manifesting its astonishing distance from "the work-being [*Werksein*] of the work" (OWA1 131/HS 6). Obviously, concrete works of art are created and are brought forth through an artist's presentation (*Hervorbringung*) (OWA1 131–32/HS 6–7), but structuring an aesthetic or enterprising view of a product on this basis will attain nothing of "the immediate and full actuality of the work" (OWA 146/GA5 4).[16]

The critique is similar to Schelling's concerns about an overreliance on *form* in his *Plastic Arts* address. Art theory and aesthetics, says Heidegger, attempt to grasp the thingly element by treating the work in terms of "matter (*hyle*), [and] form (*morphē*)" in a sensuous synthesis focused on appearance (*eidos*) (OWA 152–53/GA5 11–12). This representational framework, in effect, prevents what is 'actual' in the work from arising "undistorted" in a "free field" (151/10) (an early allusion to what will become, more significantly, the 'open region'). Aspiring to attain 'the actual' (*Das Wirkliche*, as opposed to *Abgeschlossenheit*) is, as well, a risk of inquiry reminiscent of Schelling's own endeavor toward the being of the ground (see F 27/SW7 357, 42/375). When Heidegger speaks of the "undistorted presencing" (OWA 151/GA5 10) of a work's character, it implies an exercise on the manner in which "the traditional interpretation of beings" (148/6–7) shapes a *subjectum*-based approach to works, much the same as Schelling's intended disclosure of the essence of freedom rooted in the being of ground and existence implied an exercise on mechanistic and representational abstraction. But Heidegger's parameters for 'actuality' are more severe—either we naively allow the work to vanish as a thing, or we seek it in its mode of steadfast "self-containment" (152/11). Just as poetizing reason cannot resist the reduction of beings to beingness, thus serving the interests of utility and calculation, an equipmental notion of beings falls prey to dictates of sensation and utility in apprehending the *ens creatum* as the "thingness" of the thing (156/17). Conceptual instruments masquerading as the self-evident presentation of thingness in "the unity of a manifold of sensations, as formed matter" must be bracketed if we are to allow the thing, or the work, to "rest in its own self." But *letting* a thing *be* turns out "to be the most difficult of tasks"; the "unpretentious thing," says Heidegger, "evades thought most stubbornly" (156–57/15–16). Though Heidegger would care little for the comparison (on this score), thought is here challenged in the same way as Schelling evoked the challenge of thinking the *Ungrund*: to think toward the indeterminate condition of possibility for the being of the ground and the being of existence is a structural foreshadowing of the challenge to think art as the "third thing" that somehow constitutes the being of the artist and the being of the work. If, then, the question of the origin of the work of art "asks about its essential source," and if this asking intends a passage into "the workly character of the work [*Werkhaften des Werkes*]" (143/1, 157/16), then a project that would have seemed manageable under the auspices of a poetizing 'aesthetics' becomes utterly frustrated. What and how, Heidegger asks "is a work *of* art?" (144/2, my emphasis). How does a work come *from* art? The question of origin, as a question of actuality, effectively jettisons both subjective command and artistic creation (in the causal sense). For the inquiry to proceed at all, a strenuous phenomenology is required, a freeing of the work and then a 'procession' from the work (cf. OWA1 131/HS 6).

Openings

A *second constitutive matter* following from our focal passages is the connection between a poetizing projection of the *openness* of beings and the *happening* of the truth of beings. We have already come across this connection in terms of the essence of poetry, where the *Ereignis* of Hölderlin's production consisted in a creative bestowal that enabled the appearance of beings to shine forth through a naming, founding word, and also instantiated Dasein itself 'in' the open region of nearness, need, and dwelling. But the connection is by no means exhausted, and we now want to ascertain its 'fullness' by turning to works of art that allow an experience of "truth setting itself to work" (OWA 162/GA5 22). By doing so, we will also learn how and why the work-being of an artwork transcends the possible, though limited, determination that art originates in a transfer from artistic "imagination" into artistic "product" (OWA1 131/HS 6). In his first version of the text, Heidegger treats this connection between openness and happening rather directly, speaking of the "worlding [*weltenden*]" (135/9) instantiation won by the setting-forth (*Herstellen*) and setting-up (*aufstellend*, in the sense of *Errichtung* and *Erstellung*) of the work's work-being before treating any concrete examples (136/10). In his later version, he first evokes the connection through a phenomenological description of two works—a Van Gogh painting and a Greek temple—then formalizes the 'how' (as opposed to the 'what') of truth's 'work' by gathering together a more emergent collection of 'matters connected' to our experience of the poetizing projection. One reason for prolonging the discussion in this way is that he means to place us in the passage through the equipmental bearing and into the workly character of these works. This approach affords a more immediate experience of how the ordinary pursuit of a work's 'actuality' reaches an impasse that, as it were, *opens* our inquiring vision in a way appropriate to the essential opening of truth in the work. As with any case of phenomenological description, one goal of bringing thought into the experience of these artworks is to reveal the stumbling block of unquestioned prejudices, the *pseudos* of *doxa* noted earlier. In this case, the interpretive matrix of 'use' and 'representation' must become questionable through the return to the work's projected *openness*, and this experience will begin to attune us to the motion by which truth takes a *stand* in the work.

Heidegger's entry into Van Gogh's *painting* of the 'peasant shoes'[17] occurs in the context of magnifying the distinctive meaning of 'letting-be' beneath the thingly-oriented sense of 'use.' We may understand this context as a specific study in two trajectories of poetizing—poetic projection on the one hand, objective command on the other. Peculiar to the painting is the fact that the shoes (the matter) *stand out* without any clear indication of where they stand. Heidegger's entry into the painting has nothing to do with form and matter, beauty, or symbolism, but focuses on "the dark opening [*dunklen Öffnung*]" within the shoes (OWA 159/GA5 19); this phrase marks a development of the "free field" (151/10) solicited for the display of a work's character (the development will continue toward the "open region"). The shoes are a piece of equipment, and justifiably so, but through our nearness to this opening we are led to hear "the silent call [*Zuruf*] of the earth," and thus a sense of 'belonging' to the earth encompassed by the *world* of their wearer. Heidegger deliberately avoids any mention of 'representation' instead drawing us into "the abundance of an essential Being of the equipment" (159–60/19–20) as a step toward ascertaining the 'actuality' of the work. Our viewing intentions join with the wearer's own standing amid earth and world, their mode of assuming the security and reliability of the shoes in the context of their lived engagement with both. We thus pass through the equipmental bearing into the "workly character of the work," a passage by which the artwork "lets us know what shoes are in truth" (161/21). Such a passage rivals the representational side of poetizing production because neither we the viewer nor Van Gogh the painter have presumed to set upon "anything already standing and objective" (OWA1 140–41/HS 14). Rather, the experience of visible and audible 'nearness' to the matter is paralleled by a dynamic and living sense of how the matter 'is,' how the shoes 'are'—terms proper to a determinative approach to truth have become kinetic, underway.

By letting-be the work we find a work of truth *in* the painting that brings its matter (the shoes) *to stand*. Afforded a 'free field,' the 'dark opening' in the artwork thus "opens up in its own way the Being of beings" (OWA 165/GA5 26). Poetizing's distorting measures are straightened by an emergent 'standing' measure. The shoes' opening shows the belonging of the equipment, and, accordingly, the work's opening shows the happening of truth, art as "truth setting itself to work" (165/26). Passing from description to reflection, we realize that Heidegger has allowed the pursuit of the actuality of the work, in terms of its thingly substructure, to highlight the impasse a more determinative poetizing would reach, wherein "we force the work into a preconceived framework by which we obstruct our own access to the work-being of the work" (165/26). Letting-be (as a letting-stand), by contrast, enables "the pure self-subsistence of the work" to display itself (165/26). There is a sense in which our inquiring vision must be opened in a manner commensurate with the openings of the work, an indication that Heidegger's phenomenological mode of questioning, though distinct from representation and willful production, is an exercise in and on faculties commonly associated with the imagination.

But how does a work's standing self-subsistence comprise a happening of truth in which world and earth—traditional touchstones for poetizing measurement writ large—emerge in a manner resistant to representational depiction or mastery? By turning to a *Greek temple*, Heidegger elects to describe an experience in which the viewer is already standing in the ordinary sense, and an architectural work that by its very nature elides all representational mastery over it. Such a work maintains its own tremendous physical standing, its presence as an "all-governing expanse of this open relational context" of its historical world (OWA 167/GA5 28). The temple stands as a unity that is fitted together, and by virtue of its standing "brings to radiance the light of the day" and "makes visible the invisible space of air" (168/28). The work of such a work, then, is to 'illuminate' man's "dwelling [*Wohnen*]" within *physis*, upon the ground of *earth* as the site of all "arising" and "sheltering" (168/28). The opening of the peasant shoes is magnified by this opening of the temple: "The temple-work, standing there, opens up a world and at the same time sets this world back again on earth, which itself only thus emerges as native ground" (168/28). It is vital to note that this opening is, Heidegger continues, what "first gives things their look [*Gesicht*] and [gives] men their outlook on themselves" (168/29). The remark stands in contrast to the 'look' (noted in the N. Lectures) by which man, as subject, looks upon Being as will then represents himself in subjectivity as willful reason. We may also hear a precise instance of letting-be—the work of the temple "lets the god himself be present and thus *is* the god himself" (168/29). As in the case of Hölderlin's gods, the religious context of the temple affords Heidegger a way of speaking of holiness in the openness of the structure's presence. The consecrated presence is not as much contrived as it is discovered. The poet priests of "holy night" find shelter in the consecrated work of the temple, in the "guiding measure" (169–70/30–31) granted by the glowing splendor of this open. A look and a measure are thus *given* in the spatial grandeur of the temple's free field.

Such an event amplifies the happening of truth in poetic naming and founding. Heidegger speaks of the same work obtaining in "linguistic work" such as tragedy—an artistic letting-be that transforms a people's "saying" into a "living word [*wesentlich Wort*]" that contends for the standing of the holy (OWA 168–69/GA5 29). The work of the temple and the work of language transcend subjective createdness and poetizing, and open the *Da* of historical Dasein in the same decisive way. In his first version of the text, Heidegger treats the temple's towering motion in a verbal manner: "the temple opens the there in which a people comes to itself, i.e., enters the decreeing power [*fügende Macht*] of its god" (OWA1 139/HS 12). The crossing of the spatial and verbal in a fugal event recalls Schelling's instantiating word of measure in the jointure. Towering manifests the fuller essence of naming, for

> there occurs in the work of language, the naming and saying through which the Beyng of things first comes to be expressed, and through which the unspeakable enters the world with the speakable. In the poet's naming of this kind, a people's great concepts of beings as a whole are prefigured [*vorgeprägt*]. The work of building, saying, and shaping exacts the there, the diffuse and rooted center in which, and out of which, a people grounds its historical dwelling. (OWA1 139/HS 13)

In his later version of text, Heidegger similarly pairs the gift of the measurable with the sayable. The work-being of the temple is a setting-forth that holds "open the open region of the world," transporting Dasein "into Being" in the same way that the work-being of the poem exercises "the naming power of the word" (OWA 170–71/ GA5 31–2).

Exposure and strife

It is through this sense of a measuring word that the *third constitutive element* derived from our opening passages unfolds: truth's *exposing* work in the work's happening. To elucidate the shape of this event and its broader meaning for philosophical questioning, we must appreciate a more subtle manifestation of seclusion and concealment intrinsic to the towering motion and fugal decree of the temple. As we have begun to note, to the temple's work-being belongs a setting-up of world and a setting-forth of earth (OWA1 137/HS 11). Heidegger calls the accomplishment of these two motions *strife* (OWA1 138/HS 12; OWA 174f/GA5 35f). This does not mean that earth and world emerge (through the work) in a dialectical overcoming of conflict. Neither is setting-up and setting-forth directly commensurate with a play of form and essence. We do better to appreciate this sense of contestation basic to work-being as the artistic disclosure of the 'field of opposedness' and the freedom of the 'open region' noted in "On the Essence of Truth." The path of untwisting the distortions of truth here proceeds by way of a play of "arising" and "sheltering" (OWA 168/GA5 29–30) within the dwelling illuminated by work-being—a sense of constitutive disclosure *and* concealment amid the *physis* of measure-taking. With a view toward these elements, Heidegger's question is thus: "In what way does truth happen in the work-being of the work, which now means to say, how does truth happen in the instigation of strife between world and earth? What is truth" (OWA 175/GA5 36).

With respect to the temple, what is set forth is set forth "into the open region of the work's world" (OWA 171/GA5 32), and with this there obtains a setting back of the work into material that allows the *earth* as the ground of dwelling to emerge. In this sense, the work "moves the earth itself into the open region of a world and keeps it there," but the ensuing disclosure of the earth is also a concealing of the earth from "every attempt to penetrate it" (172/33). This means the production underway is one that also reveals the "impotence of will" in the face of an earth that "shrinks from every disclosure and constantly keeps itself closed up" (172/33). To set forth (*her-stellen*) the earth, Heidegger explains, "means to bring it into the open region as the self-secluding [*Sichverschließbare*]" (173/33). The situation of this manifestation resembles that of letting-be in "On the Essence of Truth," where the disclosedness of beings is also a concealment. It is tempting to regard such setting-forth as a species of *poiesis*, but the sense of production and createdness associated with 'bringing-forth' risks diminishing the nonobjectivity (OWA1 135/HS 9) so crucial to the letting-be and seclusion Heidegger means to preserve. This is why, in the first version of the text, he says that the *Stiftung des Seyns* "is not the bringing-forth of beings" (146/19), and why any lingering terms of production and figuration through work and word are ensconced in a language of violence and upheaval rather than a discourse of intentional formation. *Herstellung* is *herstellend* in a forceful, shattering [*Erschütterung*] way (142/15), not as a creative command of reason but as an insistent resistance to poetizing, to the subjective determinacy that has forgotten its own impotence. In a primordial sense, a "rift" (138/12) arises as world "grounds itself on the earth" and earth "juts through world" (OWA 174/GA5 35). Their kinetic opposition, concretized in the work, allows the elements to "raise each other into the self-assertion of their essential natures" (174/35). Each striving, moreover, is bound to the other by belonging together through the open region, the very site of Dasein's dwelling and corresponding "agitation." Beneath the apparent "repose" of a work of art, then, lies an instigation of strife between world and earth, a revelation of the "intimacy" intrinsic to this strife's elements (173–75/37), and the intimation that the poet's word and the dwelling of Dasein alike stand in the inheritance of this strife.

As for truth, if it is an event unfolding *in* the work-being of the work, then it too is a work of strife—a 'how' and an 'as' of open exposure and not a unity wrought by correct representations. When thus Heidegger asks, "What is truth [*Wahrheit*]?" (OWA 175/ GA5 37), the question is posed from the horizon of a work's 'actuality' as opposed to a metaphysical or transcendental interrogative. The question is a parody in one sense, and a profound retrieval in another. And though any alert reader of "On the Essence of Truth" already knows the question to be a gesture toward aletheia, we must not forget that Heidegger's use of the copula ('is') squares precisely with, and is indebted to, the reformulation Schelling brought to the law of identity. Continuing, Heidegger speaks of the essence of an entity as "what the entity *is* [*ist*] in truth," italicizing the copula so as to remove it from the sense of "conformity of knowledge with the matter" and to reappropriate it under the measure of unconcealment—the showing and standing forth of the entity (176–77/37–8). When he then explains, "The essence of truth which is familiar to us—correctness in representation—stands or falls with truth as the unconcealment [*Unverborgenheit*] of beings" (177/38), the aletheaic trajectory is his own, but the urgency of the matter is a reflection of a path opened up by Schelling's own 'is.' Applying his copula to the principle of ground, Schelling exposed a flash of primordial 'openness' before the generation of unity and understanding. Heidegger's accentuated use of the copula denotes a recovery of this moment from two co-constitutive sides: to say that "[i]n the midst of beings as a whole an open place occurs. There is a clearing [*Lichtung*]" (178/40) is to say that the clearing is to the essence of truth what the open region has been to the essence of the work. The answer to the question of the origin of the work of art lies in our ability to grasp these opens as the same grounding and granting center.

This sense of proximity and difference between Schelling and Heidegger on the dynamism and possibility subsisting within principles of identity and ground begs the larger question: How does Heidegger's arrangement of these elements now stand with respect to dark upheaval afoot within Schelling's fugal account of primordial becoming and creation? On the one hand, there is a similar play of darkness and shining in Heidegger's open region, and darkness and light in Schelling's opening toward unity. Heidegger's emphasis on eventful, agitating motion likewise recalls the movement of yearning in Schelling's account of divine self-revelation, and perhaps even the striving of the genius in aesthetic production. We thus find traces of Schelling amid Heidegger's encounter with Hölderlin. On the other hand, we find several instructive differences. First, Heidegger's leading 'essential' interest concerns the aletheiac essence of truth, a problem Schelling did not take up in a 'straightening' way. Incumbent upon this interest is the concern to recover the 'actual' in the work of art, not the divine *actu* or the nonconscious impulses of the absolute. Second, Heidegger allows the path toward 'actuality' to move through the work as an instigation of this strife, and not beneath the primal will or eternal indifference that, though ontologically profound, conscripted Schelling's impulse (for Heidegger) in an account of justification. Third, primordial, poetic, and artistic strife must be thought in reference to the work-being *of* art as truth underway, not createdness or inspiration, or as a gift of nature or nature's primal potency. Finally, Heidegger's artist, like the poet, is not concerned with resolving this strife from a summit position or in a word of *legein*, but with enabling it to "remain" (OWA 175/GA5 37).

The similarities and differences alike are compelling, especially when we appreciate how Schelling and Heidegger, as thinkers of *measure*, attempting, in their own ways, to twist free of poetizing reason. Even though Heidegger's dialogue with Schelling in OWA and HEP is not direct, allowing the question of measurement to be posed from within a fugal impulse necessarily involves both thinkers in an engagement with elements of the imagination at both the level of inquiry and the level of primordial production. And yet, if and how there is a consequential difference between production in Schelling's work and pro-duction in Heidegger's *ergon*—a difference ultimately bearing on the adherence between createdness in the *reell* and creative measure-taking in thought—is a question not entirely settled. Against the backdrop of the three orienting elements treated previously, we are now able to return to the questionable standing of the imagination in Heidegger's position on the full projective essence of art as poetry.

Poiesis, projection, and the preserving imagination

If the meaning of *poetizing projection* has been underway in the matters charted earlier, ascertaining its distinct essence and resulting implications for the poetic imagination requires some reflection on how Heidegger has advanced his discussion, and how this advance itself informs the shape of projection in a way that reinstates and reinvigorates elements traditionally ascribed to the poetizing imagination. More evident in the full version of Heidegger's text than the first, projection is not only the point of departure *into* the origin of art from the essence of poetry, but is also the point of return after having passed through equipmental being to work-being, and the phenomenological exposure to the strife of the open as the happening of unconcealment and seclusion in truth's own clearing (OWA 178/GA5 40). Why and how does Heidegger double back to the question of poetizing projection after having satisfied his inquiry with the discovery that *art* is the origin of the work of art insofar as "truth happens" in the work "as the primal strife between clearing and concealing" (180/42)? One hint later arises when he dovetails an emphasis on the requisite "preserving [*Bewahrung*]" (191/54) of unconcealment in the work-being of art with the vocation of poetry as a "clearing-projection," which unfolds truth's projection and *figures* it, allowing "the open region [to] bring beings to shine and ring out" (197/60). To understand this preserving work of poetizing projection as a positive *measure* of and for unconcealment, we must take stock of how Heidegger has thus far untwisted poetizing on the side of thought's own attunement, then trace his remarkable reinstatement of elements of the imagination thus far in question.

As we have seen, the original question, "what and how is a work of art?" (OWA 144/ GA 5 2) led to the need to establish how truth happens *in a work*, which in turn required a further elaboration of how truth happens *as unconcealment*. As a result, every term in the question has undergone an essential modification. Even the grammatical form of the question has been uprooted from its elementary guise and transferred to an elemental horizon as we stand in the 'actual' experience of the painting and temple. Thinking may well be "a craft" (144/2) but the at-hand *poetizing* instruments we might use to speak of the essence of these works have been set out of reach. Representation, as either an aesthetic concept or an epistemic function is inadequate, for example; and will—the principle drive in subjective and creative knowing—stands impotent before the active elements of the works. Even so, the fact of these elisions assumes we are not disarmed entirely. Though Heidegger says very little with respect to our 'intentionality' as viewers or thinkers, his discussion consistently assumes our affectivity in receiving what the matter shows us. We are 'exposed', 'placed', faced with beings that stand 'for us,' and the being of the entities (be they the works, earth and world, or truth itself) are phenomena that affect us visually and audibly: truth 'flashes out' (176–77/37), matters 'show themselves', the painter's pigment 'shines forth,' things attain their 'look,' the temple 'figures,'our 'vision' is 'opened,' the painting 'speaks' (173/34, 167–68/29–30, 164/24, 161/21).[18] However truth 'is' at work in the work of art, our ability to apprehend (or rather, undergo) it depends on an affective attunement in our questioning. The work-being is not 'constituted' by our standing position *per se*, but we may at least say that our ability to let-be the being and truth of the artwork must require something like the poetic freedom of the poet who stands in the open region and names what remains. Such a consideration lends justification to the more positive implications noted in the closing sections of the work and the direct return to the essence of poetry. Our general undoing is of course pivotal to recovering the actuality of work-being from beneath all thingly consideration. But with the exposure of object-being and the retrieval of

Offenbarkeit, there is a subtle rebuilding of the poetizing function that allows Heidegger to reinstate its primary terms.

Evidence of this turn first appears when Heidegger speaks of *beauty* to characterize the temple's shining, unconcealing work: "*Beauty is one way in which truth essentially occurs as unconcealment*" (OWA 181/GA5 43). Some twenty pages prior, Heidegger placed beauty in abeyance as the obsession of an aesthetics that cared little for truth (see 162/21–2). The term's return is cautious, but in ascribing it to the luminous event of what is "joined in the work" (181/43) Heidegger initiates a chain of reinstatements that will secure the full sense of poetizing projection. Next, notions of 'creation' and 'efficacy/constancy' (and their cognates), and even *technē* are recovered under the banner of the work's 'belonging' to truth. Heidegger admits that his own delay in addressing the "activity of the artist" and "the essence of the creative process" is "curious" (183/45), and indeed it is. And though we have suspected the presence of these matters under the many allusions to setting-forth (*Herstellung*), the skeptical note concerning 'bringing-forth' (*Hervorbringen, poiesis*) in the text's first version left us in a state of hesitation. Heidegger now comes to the phrase in the form of a question: "We think of creation as a bringing forth [*Hervorbringen*]. . . . But what is it that distinguishes bringing forth as creation [*als Schaffen*] from bringing forth in the mode of making [*Anfertigung*]?" (183/45–6). This is a question we began asking in the last chapter as a way of sheltering the imagination in general, and the poetic imagination more specifically, from the fate of representational willfulness. It is the very question that must be resolved if there is to be a significant difference between the poetizing essence of reason and the poetizing pro-duction (following IM 204/N 145–46) of the poet.

On the basis of what Heidegger has argued thus far, we could say that creation (in an acceptable sense) would be an action of the work-being whereas making is an action of a craftsman. But the action of work-being is itself enabled by the letting-be of the artist, the viewer, and the poet who names. We are speaking from a position 'beyond man,' but of an event of projection that obviously involves man, and even depends on man's craftsmanship with words and workable materials. Heidegger's question thus requires two elements that would appear to be in tension: an aletheiac constitution to bringing-forth and a capacitating *technē* on the side of the artist. His embrace of *technē* is, however, conditional. He argues that it denotes "a mode of knowing" rather than a "practical performance" (OWA 184/GA5 47), thus appropriating the term in its essential (as opposed to ordinary or traditional) aspect. Accordingly, we must expect less of craftsmanship on this score and more of knowing, but a kind of knowing that is rightly attuned to the role of appearance (in the Greek practice) in truth's play of concealment and unconcealment. In this sense, Heidegger recaptures *technē* as "a bringing-forth of beings in that it *brings forth* what is present as such *out of* concealment and specifically *into* the unconcealment of its appearance" (184/47). This semblance is a different craft of knowing and a different notion of 'presence' than that arising through the Kantian creative character of reason. Though we are not speaking of an inspired or mastering subject, Heidegger allows that the artist "a *technitēs*"—one whose skill serves the presencing aspect of unconcealment. *Technē* and bringing-forth thus return to the poetizing fold insofar as "the setting forth of works [*Her-stellen von Werken*] and the setting forth of equipment occur in a bringing forth that causes beings in the first place to come forward and be present in assuming an outward aspect" (184/47). This account of creative production resembles Schelling's 1807 emphasis on the primal potency of nature inasmuch as Heidegger accentuates "the being that surges upward, growing of its own accord, *physis*," but Schelling's spiritual essence of art is outstripped by Heidegger's insistence on the work's essence determining the essence of creation (184/47, 185/48). Art remains the origin of the artist. To characterize creation as "to let something emerge as a thing that has been brought forth" may well suggest an artist who 'lets', but in fact refers us back once more to the essential happening *of* truth ("It all rests in the essence of truth," 185/48). *Poiesis* is party to "the primal strife" of truth wherein "the open region is won within which everything stands and from which everything withholds itself and withdraws itself as a being" (185–86/48–9).

The reinstatement of bringing-forth also has implications for man, the entity instantiated in the open region yet scarcely mentioned in the discussion. The service poesis renders the poetizing projection is incomplete without a commensurate treatment of truth's *establishment,* and the instantiation and constancy of truth in/as the openness of the open region depends on "some being" (OWA 186/GA5 49). This necessity concerns primarily truth's "possession" of the open region (which, in view of *technē,* must afford unconcealed beings with a concrete presencing) and is not a deduction of the need for an artist. But what 'being'? Presumably any being, any entity which, as a "clearing of the There" serves the "*establishing*" of truth (186/49). Heidegger refers the reader to section 44 of *Being and Time,* thus putting us in mind of the *Da* of Da-sein. We should also hear a reference to Da-sein's standing in the world-occurrence of Schelling's jointure, the historical igniting of Da-sein's creative possibilities (see ST 105/GA42 183). The mode of truth's establishment, Heidegger explains, is that it "comes to shine forth [in] the nearness of that which is not simply a being, but the being that is most in being" (OWA 186–87/GA5 49–50). Not incidentally, truth's establishing also happens in "the thinker's questioning, which, as the thinking of Being, names Being in its question-worthiness" (187/50). Together, these modes of establishment underscore the connection between the poet's naming and founding and the work of thought noted in the HEP. The reference is verified when Heidegger, continuing, aligns truth's 'need' for constancy with "the *impulse toward the work,*" an impulse to *bring forth* the openness of beings by way of a work in which truth establishes itself "in a being in such a way, indeed, that this being itself takes possession of the open region of truth [*Offene der Wahrheit*]" (187–88/50–51).

The character of this establishing is, as we have seen, strife. As an instigation of strife, bringing-forth reveals "the hidden necessity of measure and decisiveness" (OWA 188/GA5 51). In plain terms, truth is invested in *poiesis* in part because, through it, truth is able to bring *measure* to the "rift" at the heart of earth and world's unity. And it is on account of such measuring possibility that *createdness (Geschaffensein)* may be reinstated in the essential sense of poetizing projection. Createdness serves the strife of establishing by virtue of accomplishing "truth's being fixed in place in the figure [*Gestalt*]" of the work (189/51). Bringing-forth is thus a way of figuring the measuring essence of truth. But are not fixing and figuring actions proper to the determinative side of poetizing that, as it were, conceal primordial discord and strife? Schelling, we recall, exposed thought to the image of unity coveted by the dark yearning of the ground, yet genuinely accomplished in the word as measure. Heidegger's measure is of like importance and quality, but serves the jointure in a different way. "Figure," he explains, "is the structure in whose shape the rift composes itself. This composed rift is the *fugue* [*Fuge*] of truth's shining" (189/51). The shining of truth is in this sense something different from the imaging of the divine imagination, as is the free bestowal of poetic naming from the proclamation of the word of measure in Schelling.

The advance toward *man* and *questioning* is not lost in this recovery of createdness and fugal measure, but turned back through truth's need for establishment and the work's need for what Heidegger has called "preserving." Bringing-forth pertains to the figuration of truth in the composed rift from one direction, and to the Dasein's "standing within the openness of beings that happens in a work" from another (OWA 191–92/GA5 53–4). The fate of the measure for truth and for thought is decided in their juncture. Why is this so? Preservation concerns the createdness that remains in a work. Further adapting the element of 'efficacy' noted earlier, createdness is "expressly created into the created being" such that it may be discovered and experienced "explicitly in the work" (190/53). Createdness is a point of reference, referring "us" to the *factum est* of artistic bringing-forth as unconcealment, a witness to the "thrust"—the "*that* it is" of the work-being (190/53). It is a point of resistance to the pull of "oblivion" (192/54) otherwise threatening the work and the standing of thought. One could allude to a Cartesian 'hallmark' in this regard, but we have a better precedent in Schelling's own 'remainder'—the eternal subsistence of the dark ground even 'after' the accomplishment of existence and understanding. A *factum est* of divine production in its own sense, this remainder was poised to prevent the reduction of becoming to a cause–effect mechanism of creation, a logical sense of identity casting immanence in a deterministic light. Even if the dark ground remains as a fundamental principle in man, and is sometimes experienced by man in the 'grim step' toward abandonment in the 'depths of life' (NPS 217–18/SW9 218), it was, on Heidegger's view, lost beneath the will to system and justification. Its loss, moreover, spelled the loss for thought of the 'between' so crucial to the jointure. Heidegger's interest in the remainder of createdness is not equivalent to a preservation of the dark, irrational ground, but is nevertheless a means of assuring our continued standing in the event of the fugal rift figured in the "steadfastness [*Beständigkeit*]" of the work (OWA 190/GA5 53). This is a remainder that shines without binding its measure to divine personality, a *poietic* 'offering' of the work-being (like the 'gift' of language and dwelling in poetic saying; see HEP 120/GA4 36–7, 124/42) that abides by transporting us "into the openness of beings" and "out of the realm of the ordinary" (OWA 191/GA5 54). Createdness, to press the matter, *preserves* our standing, our letting-be, and marks the genuine efficacy of the work, which we, in turn, must preserve. The possibility of our dwelling "in the work's truth," our "resoluteness" (*Entschlossenheit*) in the ecstatic "openness of Being" (192/55), and indeed any 'straighter' poetizing depends on this: "To submit to this displacement means to transform our accustomed ties to world and earth and henceforth to restrain all usual doing and prizing, knowing and looking, in order to stay within the truth that is happening in the work. Only the restraint of this staying lets what is created be the work that it is" (191/54). The work of art preserves the *Da* of our standing, our exposedness to truth and Being, and we preserve this capacitating work in our knowing, questioning, and naming.

The larger accomplishment of this reorienting and reinstating a work's efficacy under the rubric of preservation is that it allows the bringing-forth of truth in art to subsist in a mode of "thrownness" (*Geworfenheit*), and it is in this vein that the work's opening of the open region is "projected" (*Entwurf*) (OWA 196–97/GA5 59). *Geworfenheit's* appearance suggests that the motion of truth through the work-being of the artwork resembles the way the Dasein of *Being and Time* was given over to itself in its facticity. And if in the existential character of the human being, *Entwurf* denotes the drive toward possibilities, then we understand the movement of truth in and through the artwork as a becoming of truth in terms of its own possibilities.[19] This is the deeper sense of the work's 'composure,' and insofar as it presents the origin and essence of truth in terms already applicable to Dasein, we may surmise that the *dichtender Entwurf* poses the possibilities of *Being and Time*'s poetic discourse (noted earlier) in a more primordial way. The artwork is a 'thrown project,' which Dasein, as Da-sein, must 'let happen.' This is the basic sense in which all art "as the letting happen of the advent of the truth of beings, is as such, *in essence, poetry*" (197/59). The full poetic essence of truth conspires with the poetizing projection, as a preservation—truth's endurance happens, most decisively, in the *Entschlossenheit* of the poetic imagination.

And yet, Heidegger's culminating discussion interrupts this chain of reinstatements elucidating the *poietic* possibilities of poetizing with a pronounced hesitation. Can the reader bear the difficulty in sheltering this essential work from its traditional association with the "whimsicalities" (OWA 197/GA5 59) of the poetic imagination? This is the point at which the *imagination*, bracketed early in the text's first version, is mentioned in the full version. It is the only mention, a fact which in the very least suggests that it ranks with 'genius' on Heidegger's watch-list of notions that might adversely disorient his discussion. Let us hear the statement again in full:

> If we fix our vision on the essence of the work and its connection [*Bezug*] with the happening of the truth of beings, it becomes questionable [*wird fraglich*] whether the essence of poetry, and this means at the same time the essence of projection [*Entwurfes*], can be adequately thought in terms of the power of imagination [*vonder Imagination und Eindbildungskraft*] (OWA 197/GA5 60)

What does this say? The aim is to understand the essence of *projection*—the tipping point for an authentic mode of poetizing. We now know that projection is precisely what effects the recapacitating of Being as the 'measure' for the truth of beings. We also know that a poetizing projection abhors any flight "into the realm of the unreal" (OWA 197/GA5 60). Thinking projection adequately means standing resolute in the actuality of the work. Heidegger thus situates us in the moment of *viewing* the essence of a work; his pronouns, 'we' and 'our,' are already unusual in the discursive economy of the text. Situated thus, the 'power of imagination' seems like a 'questionable' means to ascertaining what is already a difficult disclosure—the essence of projection. The hesitation has two sides. *First*, to speak of the 'power of imagination' is to make reference by way of Kant to imagination as a transcendental faculty, which, pressed into the service of German Idealism and aesthetic theory, has become a power of so-called Romantic flight. If we are truly interested in *letting* truth *be* in the work and be projected through the work, then we should be cautious of summoning old instruments that delimit the possibilities intrinsic to *Entwurf*—instruments used for ends such as schematizing the manifold for the understanding and determining beauty. On this score, we must admit that Heidegger shrinks back from *Einbildungskraft* and *Ineinsbildung* for specific reasons that mirror his more general resistance to the poetizing essence of reason. *Second*, to say that the imagination's work is 'questionable' in this regard is not to say that all poetic or creative productions or dispositions are *per se* misguided. *Fraglich* denotes a position of doubt or reticence. But, questionability is, as we know, a spur to continued thought: "Each answer remains in force as an answer only so long as it is rooted in questioning" (195/58). Following this remark, Heidegger says that the very essence of poetry is itself "something worthy of questioning [*Frag-würdiges*], something that still has to be thought through" (197/60). It is, thus, one thing to say that the essence of projection is irreducible to elucidation on the basis of imagination as a cognitive faculty, but must this preclude us (or Heidegger) from continuing to think through imagination as a more pro-ductive, projective, poetizing power? Has not our whole affective entry into the work-being of the artwork and the *Ereignis* of *aletheia*—the very path of disclosing the full essence of poetry—already assumed a reorientation of the imagination from the fate of poetizing reason to the possibilities of poetizing projection?[20]

If we are to continue speaking of the imagination in the context of Heidegger's essential sense of poetizing in this period, then it must be on the side of language's projective work in and from the clearing "*as*" of *Ereignis* and not under the determinative 'is' to which *Einbildungskraft* succumbs at the impasse of poetizing reason. The imagination, that is, may no longer be allowed to furnish the representational mastery thought to justify reason's command over standing beings or being as a whole. *Einbildungskraft*, to be sure, brought the manifold of intuition into the mediating occurrence of schematism, but language alone, says Heidegger "brings beings as beings into the open for the first time" (OWA 198/GA5 61). If imagination is to be ascribed to the work of poetry and the instantiating experience of work-being, then it must be grasped in terms of the way truth "directs itself into work" (199/62) and happens in the clearing of language, not in terms of the way beings stand against the cognizing subject, or spirit's eternal archetypes come to stand and shine through the absolute's *Ineinsbildung*. The conclusion of OWA thus returns to the impulse of HEP, to the sense in which the saying of poetry is a founding and preserving of truth, a clearing in language that encompasses the "special poetizing" (199/62) of art. A poetic imagination, moreover, would have to evoke the manner in which the creative bestowing of poetry, and the instigating work of work-being, accentuate 'founding' as a 'beginning.' The poetic imagination would be an attunement to the beginning as a thrust of measure through the site of dwelling, a "fixing in place of truth in a figure" that "lets truth originate" (200–02/64–5).

Da-sein and the domain of imagination

Though we have been speaking in a purposefully artistic register, the movement of the imagination in Heidegger's thought perhaps already evokes a broader, more encompassing framework. Notwithstanding the tensions attached to the status of poetizing production and projection (to all that is questionable or question-worthy in the echoes of *Einbildungskraft*), the turn toward the measure of poetic saying and the work-being of artistic works entails a deeper effort to retrieve and sustain the impulse toward the being of the ground and the experience of the 'between' in the open occurrence of the primordial jointure. Heidegger's path for philosophical questioning is one that turns from the impasse of willful production and ontology to the aletheiac event of truth, the instantiation of Dasein amidst the clearing of beings, and the strife of thought arising in the strife of earth and world. Poetizing reason stands down, apprenticing itself to poetizing projection (*dichtender Entwurf*), and thereby returning through the creative remainder of works to a bringing-forth that is genuinely productive and resolute in preserving. But there is yet a further advance in this course of reflection, one in which the domain of imagination and the *Da* of Da-sein appear to be reinstated, still more remarkably, in the *Da* of *Ereignis*. One should consider, first, a moment in Heidegger's difficult yet penetrating work of 1936–38, *Contributions to Philosophy (Of the Event)*. Section 192, entitled *Da-sein*, reads as follows:

> To the usual view directed toward 'beings,' Da-sein, as grounding the openness of self-concealing, appears as nonbeing and imagined [*eingebildet*]. In fact, *Da-sein, as the projecting-thrown grounding, is the highest reality in the domain of imagination* [*im Bereich der Einbildung*], assuming we understand the latter not simply as a faculty of the soul and not simply as something transcendental (cf. Kant book), but as the *event* itself, wherein all *transfiguration* oscillates [*worin alle Verklärung schwingt*].
>
> 'Imagination' as an occurrence of the *clearing* [*Lichtung*] itself. Yet 'imagination,' *imaginatio*, is a name that names from the viewpoint of the immediate apprehending of ὄν [that which is] and of beings. Calculated in those terms, all beyng and its opening constitute a *formedimage*[*Gebilde*] that is added to what supposedly stands on its own. But all this is inverted: what is 'imagined' ['*eingebildet*'] in the usual sense is always the so-called 'really' present at hand, for that is what is brought to an image, i.e., brought into the clearing, into the 'there,' so as to appear. (CP247/ GA65 §192)

What does this passage say and what relationship does this 'imagination' have to the tense standing of *Einbildungskraft* and *Ereignis* noted in the art discussion? Though we do not have space for the kind of full textual study the work deserves, a few technical remarks will illuminate the specific advance Heidegger is testing for what could be termed as the 'appropriated imagination.'

That Dasein has become Da-sein signifies how, in a larger turn of his thought, Heidegger is ever more resolved to focus not on the entity (to whom we might traditionally ascribe faculties or properties), but rather on the site or place of this being as it arises amid the advent of truth in *Ereignis*. Let us admit that it is difficult, disarming even, to think in this way. Da-sein, one could say, suggests a clearing that is at once affective, ontological, and disclosive—something not unlike the open region projected in a work of art. In the *Beiträge*'s preceding section Heidegger calls Da-sein "the pivot in the turning of the event [*Wendungspunkt in der Kehre des Ereignisses*], the self-opening center of the counterplay between call and appurtenance [*Zu-gehörigen*], the 'domain of what is proper' [*Eigen-tum*, 'property']." He likens Da-sein to "the 'domain of a prince' [*Fürsten-tum*, 'principality'], the sovereign center of the appropriating eventuation as the assignment, of the one who is appurtenant, to the event and at the same time to *himself*: becoming a self" (CP 246–47/GA65 §191). The translation does an able job of signaling the work of language afoot in this description, but the original terms make this work more explicit as a play of jointure and resonance. As *Wendungspunkt*,[21] Da-sein is or ought to be a structural pivot-point on which *Ereignis* turns through *Zuruf* (call, directive) to a domain of *hören* (hearing) and *gehörig* (belonging, fitting). As *Fürsten-tum*, Da-sein is itself a privileged yet subordinate domain, something kindred and obedient to its lord. 'Appurtenance' rightly amplifies the instrumental sense of Da-sein's domain, as well as the legal sense of a property, a right of way for the appropriating event (*Er-eignung*). Further, *Zu-gehörigen zum Ereignis* also positions Da-sein's *Selbstwerdung* as a pivot that is underway—not yet settled—in the *Eigentum* of Beyng. Unless Da-sein attends the call as a way toward a sounding of belonging, then it is not yet itself in the event but an instrument without assignment.

Returning to our preceding passage, the opening sentence is an admission that the ordinary view—the *view* of the traditionally metaphysical guiding question (*Leitfrage*) and the customary *ear* for representation—will not hear this description of Da-sein as pivot-point, but will instead hasten to view or grasp it as something imagined. The ordinary view wants to see beings, objects, and thus cannot listen for a domain of hearing and belonging. *Eingebildet* is thus a term of failure, of literally missing the 'point.' Then, as if surprised by the insinuation of *eingebildet* in his discourse, Heidegger suddenly turns to *Einbildung* in a formal sense and instates it as a domain in which Da-sein's reality is superlative, much the same as abandonment was the superlative experience in the domain of plight. This, and every ensuing statement, presents a play of reinstatement and caution, as though *Einbildung* is itself so tangled in the knot of what is guiding and what is the basic that the matter simply will not yield to a 'straightened' disclosure. *First*, the domain of imagination, Heidegger continues, is not to be confused as a transcendental faculty, but is rather *Ereignis* understood as the site of transfiguring motion. *Schwingt* immediately recalls the *Kehre des Ereignisses*, and also echoes the trembling strife of earth and world in the truth of the temple's rift. *Verklärung* overwhelms the mode 'appearing' supposed by the guiding question and its poetizing reason. In his notes for a 1941 course on Schelling's *Freedom Essay*, Heidegger pauses on this term—*Verklärung*—and emphasizes it as "not dissolution (evaporation), [but] rather the dark as the dark allows itself to appear [*erscheinen*, shine forth] in the light" (GA49 126); this later emphasis accentuates the disclosure of the abyssal in the very *Einbildung* of *Ereignis*. The sense of the play is that: if we let-be the imagination as a domain of Da-sein and bestow upon this domain the name of *Eriegnis*, then we allow *Einbildungskraft* to leap from the field of schematizing cognition into the open of

Beyng. *Second*, placing *Einbildung* in quotes captures the identity of the matter as being underway, in motion in the text just as the copula "is" is so often found. But here again a caution: *imaginatio*, though en route to comportment with Beyng's word, is always already a 'name' (i.e., a founding) deployed in the service of the same apprehending command that conflates Beyng with Being as the category of beingness. Lest we allow Da-sein to be stood under the authority of such a name, a 'reversal' is required.

Hence, the *third* and most ambiguous play of reinstatement and caution: the usual sense (of the 'usual view') regards its imagined objects as most extant, thereby borrowing its determinative capital from the supposed immediacy between that which appears and that which is. But the very presence necessary to extantness owes its domain to a clearing (*Lichtung*), and appearing owes its disclosure to a bringing-forth of imagination (*hereingebildet*). The implication is that imagination names the conditions of possibility for usual viewing and usual naming, but when the standpoint for these actions tries to subsume 'imagination' into its command structure, it is already too late to hear the constitutive work of bringing-forth proper to imagination. The section, for all intents and purposes, ends with this point, though it is not a conclusive point. On the surface, these brief remarks have treated imagination so as to disclose the projection of Da-sein into an oscillating event of transfiguration. Da-sein's positional counter play is the primary concern; the imagination is a secondary matter arising in the work of this concern. This is a correct, though not complete, reading. More closely regarded, the 'counterplay between call and appurtenance' is enacted in the motion of Heidegger's statements—he brings thought to participate in the oscillation between transfiguration and naming. Imagination 'is' the thrust and counter-thrust of thought's measures in *Ereignis*. To say that imagination is reinstated in Heidegger's discourse on this score, is to say that it is recovered *in* the labor of language to perform the counterplay that Da-sein 'is.' The transfiguration proper to *Ereignis* 'oscillates' in the space between viewing and hearing, naming and bringing, and to stand these modes together in the turning work of the clearing Heidegger allows 'imagination' to name itself. Imagination as occurrence, like the distress of a lack of distress, must 'get out' (CP 92–4/GA65 §56), translation adapted) from beneath the plight of *imaginatio*. Indeed, Da-sein as pivot-point is a thrown-grounding for transfiguration because Da-sein is already thrown into the recapacitating measures of distress. Imagination breaks forth from concealment by standing in the shelter of the clearing, even as it brings the matters for transfiguration into the clearing. In *On Time and Being,* Heidegger returns to this same emphasis on the clearing as "the open for everything that is present and absent." Contrasting the nature of the clearing to the usual privileging of presence, he insists that the opening "is not only free for brightness and darkness, but also for resonance and echo."[22] To conjoin the elements of sight and sound under the free, unconcealing domain of the clearing is to underscore what he has done in the *Beiträge* concerning how transfiguration is brought into *Eriegnis* as the domain of imagination. Under every guise in which we have found it, imagination is a work of freedom, and, in this case, it is the freedom of the clearing at work in the grounding play of the *Da*. If the work of the *Beiträge* is to apprentice thought to a hearing of Beyng's word—*Ereignis*—and to thereby transform thought's questioning into an inceptual saying of Beyng, then Heidegger's word of 'imagination' marks the first term in the poetics of the crossing or leap to another beginning in philosophy. It names both the essential dwelling of Da-sein in the open and the measuring work of thought in and as this dwelling.

The dimensional imagination

On the basis of the preceding elucidations, *Beiträge* §192 is a marker for the continued question-worthiness of imagination as a way of thinking the clearing as a creative expanse of possibility. Da-sein stands within the domain of imagination just as humans, Heidegger elsewhere notes, "always already stand within philosophy because they do so essentially" (IP 1/GA50 90). In its standing, Da-sein "is the *between*: between humans (as *grounding* of history) and the gods (in their history)" (CP247/§191).[23] What is true of philosophy, we may surmise, is true of imagination—that it is a realm of "sojourn" (IP 2/GA50 91). Sojourn (*Aufenthalt*) implies an abiding decision to name a path of thinking and a site of dwelling. That this sojourn may pass steadfast into a space of resonant transfiguration is by no means guaranteed by bestowing the name *Ereignis* upon the domain of imagination. The jointure of Beyng promises no apotheosis of *Einbildung*. It does, however, compose itself by measures that have elided the distinction between the sensible and intelligible, and have exposed the command of poetizing production to the spatial expanse of *poietic* projection. The domain of human being, if we may allow ourselves to speak in this way, is fundamentally a site of creative measure. *Ereignis* is Beyng's word, and what Heidegger states in his 1944/45 course, "Thinking and Poetizing," here applies to Da-sein as the 'between'—that "what is peculiar to the thinker and the poet is that they receive their meditation [*Sinnen*] from the word and shelter it in saying, such that thinkers and poets are the genuine preservers of the word in language" (IP 5/GA50 94). Owing to their distinct "awareness" and "thoughtful guarding" of Beyng, thinkers and poets "produce [*hervorbringen*] us in our essence" (IP 5/GA50 94, 15/105, 12/102); they bring forth this "*highest reality in the domain of imagination*" (CP247/§192) by virtue of being "the ones who reflectively speak and the ones who verbally reflect" (IP 59/GA50 156). The genuine preservation of the word and the essential production of Da-sein comprise the guiding and founding measures to be taken in the domain of imagination. This means that the word, as the work of imagination and for the sake of man's sojourn and dwelling, again springs forth as it did in Schelling's impulse and in Hölderlin's impetus, only now with a weight of inceptual significance that concentrates the worthiness of the poetic imagination still more decisively in the matter of measure and measure-setting.

Accordingly, Heidegger's "Poetically Man Dwells" (1951) sustains and sharpens the sense of *measure* and, so doing, performs an expansion of the thoughts initiated in §192 of that text. Heidegger recovers the project initiated in "Hölderlin and the Essence of Poetry" by distilling the question of essence into the question of the necessary relationship between poetic measure-taking and human dwelling. As in "The Origin of the Work of Art," he pairs a diagnosis of the contemporary and customary horizon of poetic reception and standardization with a penetrating entry into the work-character of a specific work. But lest we assume this text to be a brief diagnostic treatise in the 'philosophy of poetry' or a mere critique of the plight of dwelling in a time of machination, we must first be very clear about the standpoint from which the thought of the text unfolds. This standpoint is signaled on the opening page, where the text's title also names its task: to *hear* the *resonance* of Hölderlin's phrase ("poetically, man dwells") from within the poem's own fugal work. Our standpoint before the poem, then, mirrors our standing as Da-sein at the threshold of the other beginning—the rebuilding of the space of open projection, the silent steadfast anticipation of the transfiguring sound of Beyng's word. Hölderlin's phrase *assigns* thought the task of gathering itself into the relationship of poetry and dwelling, much the same as Da-sein, as *Wendungspunkt*, is assigned the task of carrying the *Kehre* of *Ereignis* through call, hearing, and belonging (*Zuruf, hören, gehörig.* Unless we appreciate how Heidegger's thought issues from *within* the imaginative occurrence of the clearing, we will fail to grasp the singular scope of measure-taking (*Maß-nehmen*) he means to retrieve through the poem's work.

Heidegger's leading concern is to take the strangeness of Hölderlin's phrase as an invitation to restore the phrase to the poem, to then hear the phrase in its full standing, and thus discover "dwelling and poetry in terms of their essential nature" (PMD 212/GA7 192). The initial work of restoration vies on the one hand with a literary establishment that overly schematizes poetic meaning, and on the other with the common opinion that the poetic imagination practices a dream-like flight from the actual; both obstacles parallel the default postures critiqued in the Origin of the Work of Art. Accordingly, the first mark of removing these scientific and customary concealments is that we listen for the experience of Hölderlin's own poetic vision. Says Heidegger: "When Hölderlin speaks of dwelling, he has before his eyes the basic character of human existence. He sees the 'poetic,' moreover, by way of its relation to this dwelling, thus understood essentially" (213/193). As in the case of our repositioning in the leap and creative work in the site of the open, the relationship of the poetic to dwelling is not reducible to a *poiesis* understood as mere *machen*. Dwelling does, however, include building: "Poetry is what really lets us dwell. But through what do we attain to a dwelling place? Through building [*das Bauen*]. Poetic creation, which lets us dwell, is a kind of building" (213/193). It is important to note that this distinction (and those to come) does not result from an argumentative assertion Heidegger stamps on his theme. Rather, he finds traction for the 'essential' question (for our hearing) by drawing distinctions from the passage. In this way he moves to and from Hölderlin's words, spacing their constitutive elements in the silence of our reflection. If we want to know what horizon Heidegger is reading from and for, the emergence of 'building' suggests that he is hearing Hölderlin's poem from the arising foyer of the blocks quarried for the space of inceptual resonance.

Between our attempt, with Heidegger, to let the fragment 'be' in the context of the poem's jointure, and Hölderlin's attempt to display the "nature of poetry as a letting-dwell [*Wohenlassen*]" (PMD 213/GA7 193), there thus arises this heightened sense of the mutual belonging between building and language. Just as the nature of building must be sheltered from making, Heidegger submits all human speaking to the antecedent appeal of language itself—the "telling of language [*Zuspruch der*

Sprache]" (213/193). Notably, this step reminds us that though we are speaking here of 'man's' dwelling, we may only do so essentially with an ear toward what is beyond man. "For, strictly, it is language that speaks. Man first speaks when, and only when, he responds to language by listening [*hört*] to its appeal" (214/194).[24] This responsiveness before a directive bears specifically, as in the *Beiträge*, on the originary emergence of beings before the occlusions of 'beingness' set upon them.[25] Language "beckons us [*winkt uns*]" toward a response, which is also an authentic 'listening' for a thing's nature (214/194). Presumably, if we are to build in/as our dwelling, then the materials and laborers must be sheltered in their own essence, not manipulated in the service of design. As meritous, poetic dwelling attunes us to "another way" of building, a building that listens from the *earth* as a scene of bestowal and exposure (215/195–96). The distorting notion of poetic 'flight' stands undone by the discovery that poetry "is what first brings man onto the earth, making him belong to it, and thus brings him into dwelling" (216/197). But what service does this earthly standing render dwelling and its poetic constitution? In "The Origin of the Work of Art", the emergent strife between earth and world marked the opening of truth's clearing and the site in which philosophical questioning took root on a path of strife and composure.

In the present discussion Heidegger opts not to revisit this specific discourse, but hastens through a "parenthetical remark" to bring forth a reflection on identity in this earth-bound position. This reflection has two sides. First, there is a jointure between poetry and thinking provided "they remain distinctly in the distinctness of their nature" (PMD 216/GA7 197)—their nature, it would seem, when rooted in the earth. He calls this jointure, following the life of Schelling's copula, "a gathering by way of difference" that holds what is distinct in an "original being-at-one" irreducible to "mere uniformity" (216–17/197–98). Second, from the position of the poem itself and its hearing, this gathering is composed and thus enables us to "come nearer to thinking the same as what the poet composes in his poem" (217/198). What is composed in the earthly standing of the poet (the gathering of poetry and thinking) is thus enacted in the event of the poem. The result is that our hearing becomes all the more alert to the gathering of thought and poetry in words of dwelling said from an earthly position.

Thus far, Heidegger has emphasized the acoustic manner of our encounter with Hölderlin's poem and has exercised our visual comportment only in the subtle gesture toward the field of the poet's vision as opposed to the ordinary view of poetry itself. This accords with the preparation for resonance in the *Beiträge*, itself a counterthrust to the visual course of poetizing representation. Still, if Hölderlin is now our chief 'necessity' in this interim time of plight and coming projection, and if (as suggested) Heidegger's thought in this text issues forth from the site of 'imagination' as an occurrence of the clearing, then we are justified in expecting from Heidegger (i) a clarifying comment on the status of vision and bringing in poetic dwelling and (ii) a trace of the constitutive experience of distress so crucial to forming being-historical hearing and saying. Proceeding with the poem, Heidegger satisfies both expectations by stressing the positional dimension of dwelling as a 'between' (*zwischen*) in which 'measures' are taken. *First*, there is a *toil* (*Mühe*) before all merit (*Verdienst*), an earthly term that concretizes the historical condition of plight. In this toil, moreover, there is a work of vision. Heidegger explains:

> The upward glance passes aloft to the sky, and yet it remains below on the earth. The upward glance spans the between of sky and earth. This between is measured out for the dwelling of man. We now call the span thus meted out the dimension [*die Dimension*].
>
> (PMD 218/GA7 198)

The poet, for whom thought and poetry are essentially gathered, looks upward through the space of resonance. Odd as it may seem, in listening to the poem we are to hear the motion of this glance, a further manifestation of the scene's silence and a passage of the eye, so to speak, through the larger dimension of dwelling. A mere glance intimates the movement of "what is brought to an image" (CP247/ GA65 §192) of the *Beiträge*. *Second*, the dimensional field of the glance accentuates the 'between' as a living site of measure. To stress the dimensional over the spatial in this regard is to accentuate the poet's measuring glance as a work of dwelling that is already and immediately a primordial work of grounding, much like the standing of thought before the originary mystery of Plato's *khora*. Measurement, moreover, is not an instrumentalizing practice of man, but 'is' man's essential mode of dwelling: "According to Hölderlin's words, man spans the dimension by measuring himself against the heavenly. Man does not undertake this spanning just now and then; rather, man is man at all only in such spanning" (PMD 218/GA7 199). The verbal sense of 'spanning' amplifies the dynamic identity of poetry and thought (noted earlier) and thus elides the need to name or "disfigure" (218/199) man's essential condition under a static nominative domain. Spanning, or measure-taking, would appear to mirror the motion of Beyng in *Ereignis*, as well as the sense of 'standing' in a leap.

Why focus on the 'heavenly' and the "godhead [*der Gottheit*]" (PMD 218/GA7 199) in lieu of the *Abgrund* or *Ereignis*? In an obvious sense, Heidegger has bound his discussion to Hölderlin's terms, and Hölderlin has allowed the heavenly to stand in question. But Heidegger, echoing the later Schelling, has done this as well in the *Beiträge*, and it is evident that what is audible in the poem accords with the predicament of (and possibility for) measure-taking in Heidegger's own terms.[26] The station of the heavenly as a point of measure amplifies the sense of abandonment and withdrawal ascribed to both Beyng and to the uncertain passing of the gods. "Man, as man," says Heidegger, "has always measured himself with and against something heavenly" (218/199). The specific, and indeed most important, point in this turn of the discussion is the field of (and necessity for) this measure-taking. To measure 'with' and 'against' the heavenly is a statement of description, not an allusion to moral standing or a confusion of guiding and basic questions. Man, for whom poetry and thought are gathered in dwelling, is thrown into a measure-taking necessity. In fact, beneath this description lies a distinction between such measuring and the customary measuring of Being and beings in terms of beingness; Hölderlin's scene of measure already assumes a terrain of belonging on which dwelling depends. Heidegger states:

The godhead is the 'measure' with which man measure's out his dwelling, his stay on the earth beneath the sky. Only insofar as man takes the measure of his dwelling in this way is he able to be commensurately with his nature. Man's dwelling depends on an upward-looking measure-taking of the dimension, in which the sky belongs just as much as the earth. (PMD 218–19/GA7 199)

But how, exactly, is the godhead the 'measure,' and what is the meaning of setting dwelling in a scene of elemental belonging? Even as we allow that Heidegger is 'saying' what he 'hears' in Hölderlin's verse, we do well to hear *in* Heidegger an echo of Schelling's own fugal word in the *Freedom Essay*. It is an echo of vital difference. Schelling, we recall, advanced the question of measure in accordance with the need for unity in the ultimate work of ground and existence, and in the work of man as the bearer of this measuring word. Heidegger, though inspired by this attention, protested that Schelling failed to sustain the bare necessity of measure, and instead sheltered the fate of measure-taking under the wings of divine personality. This misdirection was indicative of the larger failure to remain in the moment 'between' darkness and light, yearning and understanding. Together, these missed opportunities spelled an impasse indicative of the retreat into poetizing willfulness and representation. In Hölderlin, Heidegger finds the *asystic, a-pseudos* resolve (entertained in the later Schelling, though unnoted in Heidegger's reading) to stand in the moment of the between wherein man enjoys no assurances of divine actuality but instead faces a heavenly concealment.[27] In the present text, Heidegger's concern is to contrast Hölderlin's sense of measure to ordinary and scientific measurement (as calculation), though his statements to this effect bear equally on the impulse he hoped Schelling would sustain. Earthbound and upward, measure-taking "gauges [*ermiβt*] the between, which brings the two, heaven and earth, to one another. This measure-taking has its own *metron*, and thus its own metric" (PMD 219/GA7 199).[28] To be sure, such gauging is not on par with man's immoral self-assertion or yearning's covetous clinging to the image of divine unity. It is a measure-taking shorn of all directive *ideas* and archetypes, which nonetheless affords man his "security" and 'endurance' (219/199)—terms evoking the constancy of Beyng and the steadfastness of Da-sein. Poetry is this measure-taking, an essential activity resembling creative bestowal in which the measure is taken by way of reception from the dimensions of the between:

> In poetry there takes place what all measuring is in the ground of its being. Hence it is necessary to pay heed to the basic act of measuring. That consists in man's first of all taking the measure which then is applied to every measuring act. In poetry, the taking of measure occurs. To write poetry is measure-taking, understood in the strict sense of the word, by which man first receives the measure for the breadth of his being. (PMD 219/GA7 199; cf. CP 247/§192)[29]

Every measuring act. With this statement the Kantian creative character of reason is recalled to its roots. The measure, moreover, is received, and then applied first and foremost to man's being, not to beings under the commanding lens of beingness. The birth of all measuring resides in poetic measure-taking. The taking is an event of basic reception, recalling the basic disposition in which a decision is made for the question-worthiness of Beyng. The scene of the decision is mortal not transcendental, and the dimension is between earth and sky not will or indifference (Schelling). The 'telling' of language says as much through the responding words of the poet. And if we listen to the glance of these words we hear again the name of the 'godhead' as the upward edge of a projective concealment. What resonates in this dimension is not yet the saying of Beyng but the word 'godhead' as a name for the withholding that nevertheless apportions man his means of bringing-forth. For Hölderlin, Heidegger explains, "God, as the one who he is, is unknown and it is just as *this Unknown One* [*Unbekannte*] that he is the measure [*das Maβ*] for the poet" (PMD 220/GA7 201). To take 'seriously' the abyssal depth beneath the root of representation is to rebound to a height in which finding and letting-be the superlative concealment furnishes a point of departure for measure. Heidegger's elucidation is not a theological pronouncement; Hölderlin's voice is neither atheistic nor agnostic. Even if we, following the typology of the *Kehre*, are inclined to gather this event into the mysteries of meditative *thought*, the very work of thought here remains phenomenological in the strict sense of allowing what is concealed to manifest itself as such. To be sure, there is also no recourse to transcendental constitution of the ego in this concealedness, but instead a letting-be of the godhead against the elemental 'as' of the sky. Measuring works according to appearances, to an appearing, which, following §192 of the *Beiträge*, happens by virtue of something brought to image into the clearing. The unknown god is brought to image 'as' unknown in the clearing between sky and earth and by the dimensions of this expanse, and this bringing affords man the measure for every measuring work. Heidegger explains:

> What is the measure for human measuring? God? No. The sky? No. The manifestness of the sky? No. The measure consists in the way in which the god who remains unknown, is revealed *as* such by the sky. God's appearance through the sky consists in a disclosing that lets us see what conceals itself, but lets us see it not by seeking to wrest what is concealed out of its concealedness, but only by guarding the concealed in its self-concealment. Thus the unknown god appears as the unknown by way of the sky's manifestness. This appearance is the measure against which man measure's himself. (PMD 220–21/GA7 201)

It is with this sense of 'guarding' that Heidegger registers a terrific pause in Schelling's rush to account for the principled basis of man's capacity for evil. To be sure, a moral drama or not, poetizing reason has shown the forgetful efficacy of the disposition to 'wrest' what 'is' from out of concealment. But before consigning the yearning of the ground to a covetousness of the image of existence, there is this poetic decision to guard the image of the unknown and to indeed receive this imaging as an impetus for measuring. As the work of truth in art is to be 'preserved,' the measure taken is to be guarded. The appearance of concealment is not a denial on the godhead's part, but is the manner by which "the unknown imparts itself, in order to remain guarded within it as unknown" (PMD 223/GA7 204). The "hands" that measure and build, like the words of the poet in pro-ducing and founding, do not belong to *ideas* of presence and do not serve the security of categorical knowing, but are hands extending from the gathering of poetry and thought—hands "guided by gestures befitting the measure here to be taken . . . a gathered taking-in, that remains a listening [*Hören*]" (221/201–02). The hands of the sculptor, Heidegger later observes, follow these same gestures and manifest this same gathering:

> Gathering plays in a place, in the sense of the freeing sheltering of things in their region [*Gegend*]. The older form of the word is 'that-which-regions' [*Gegnet*]. It names the free expanse. Through it, the open is urged to let each thing unfold into its resting in itself. But this means at the same time: preserving [*Verwahren*], the gathering of things in their belonging-together. . . . Sculpture: the embodiment of the truth of Being in its work of instituting places. (AS 308–09/GA13 207–08)

Concealment—resting—is not a challenge to reason's will, but a summons to *gauge* "the very nature of man" (PMD 221/GA7 201). Poetry stands in the immediacy of this summons, and if thought belongs 'by way of difference' with poetry then in every measuring act of thought the gauging of the measure reverberates. In this way, our listening to Hölderlin's words brings us to a *decision* as to whether we "are really prepared to make our stay in the domain of poetry's being" (222/203), the domain of the dimensional measured forth as the dwelling of man. This state of affairs is precisely the same as the point of culminating decision in the *Beiträge*: the resonance we hear through Hölderlin as the call to decision for poetic dwelling is the resonance we hear in the leap as the call to decision for Da-sein to be the 'there' of the clearing.

Finally, there is a spirit of submission in this guarding and gauging that reveals the *dimensional* bearing of Heidegger's Hölderlin to be the *domain of imagination* for the *Beiträge's* Da-sein. Poetry exemplifies the originary course of making not as a willful manipulation, but as a "saying [of] the sights of heaven in such a way that he submits to its appearances as to the alien element to which the unknown god has 'yielded'" (PMD 223/GA7 204). Together, the modes of sighting and saying bring forth an image, in which case something imaged is simply something made seen.[30] The poetic imagination, then, is the domain of measure that projects by way of submission, producing "imaginings [*Ein-Bildungen*] that are visible inclusions of the alien in the sight of the familiar" (223–24/205). The imagination is an event for transfiguration because it hosts a "twilight" (224/205) measure, a measuring that allows concealment to traverse the field of figuration. This is something altogether different from a mimetic or inspired imagination, and the product of this measuring is an "admission of dwelling" not a "frantic calculation" (225–26/206–07). That submission becomes traversal, and sojourn dwelling, is what distinguishes Hölderlin's imaginative domain for Heidegger in the *Beiträge*: "Hölderlin is the most futural, because he approaches from the longest distance and in this distance *traverses* and transforms what is greatest" (CP318/§252). If poetry speaks in images and if we are to "remain heedful of the poetic," then this means the pivot-point that is Da-sein is the site of sounds transfigured—a domain of composition in which the imagination is 'appropriated' (PMD 226/GA7 207) to its measure.

For Kant and Schelling alike the experience of the beautiful summoned the imagination toward an affective drive—be it pleasure, tranquility, or moral readiness. Heidegger concludes his hearing of Hölderlin in like manner by speaking with the poet of "kindness" (from the Greek, *charis*). It is a strange turn of emphasis to find in Heidegger.[31] He does not mean a practical moral duty, but rather kindness as the structure of a call that gathers sound and hearing in a configuring work. Kindness, Sophocles notes, calls forth kindness (PMD 226/GA7 207). The yielding of the godhead calls forth the ascent and assent of measure-taking—the "appeal of the measure to the heart in such a way that the heart turns to give heed to the measure" (227/208).

In sum, what these elements of domain and dimension, imagination and measure, evidence is for the Heidegger of the late 1930s onward an apprenticeship of thought to the character of poetic work. The 'heed' given poetic measure in "Poetically Man Dwells" draws the work of thought into the precise dimension of configuration, where the domain of human dwelling is a field of projection and submission, decision and letting-be. Certainly more may be said regarding the ongoing ascendance of language at the helm of being-historical thinking. But in the *heeding* and *taking* of measure, much like the creative bestowal of Beyng's truth in the work of art, there is a profound accomplishment of the imagination that enriches our guiding thematic and distills the leading ambitions of Heidegger's project at this time. To speak of Heidegger's turn toward inceptual thinking is, most precisely, to speak of a turn within the problematic of poetizing. His is a passage through the entanglements of poetizing production to the attunements of poetizing projection as a path of recovering the proper domain of imagination. There is a repositioning of philosophical questioning, a recalibration of the representational gauge, a recapitulation of basic measures in which renewed creative measures for thoughtful construction and figuration may be found. *Einbildung* and *Ereignis* share in common a fidelity to measure. But to dwell in the dimensional life of *Ereignis* is to yield the instrumental and systematizing imagination to a *poietic* refinement. *Ereignis* appropriates the projective creativity of reason reflected in Kant's root and Schelling's ground, but exchanges the commanding assurance of system and assertion for the integrity of the between—for bringing-forth the figures and images, names and remains, by which humans dwell. All told, this is a long way to go to positioning thought in a crossing that resists the imagination in one guise and reinstates it in another. To be sure, Heidegger did not venture the discipline of being-historical thinking in the name of imagination, but with each advance in his elemental work the character of *Ereignis* is manifest as a *poietic* movement whose metric is best named the poetic imagination.

Conclusion

It is a precarious thing to conclude a project in which the thinkers examined have taught us to hesitate before presumptions of philosophical conclusiveness. We began this project, after all, by recalling Heidegger's early observation concerning the 'fluctuating' nature of philosophical concepts, and the essential standing we, as humans, always already have in the field of philosophical assumptions and ambitions. And while we have also performed this study under the echo of Schelling's call to know things "according to their pure necessity," none of the standpoints visited in this journey has won for us an assured point of view anchored outside the field of rational construction and ecstatic experience; some standpoints—perhaps the best of them—have in fact shown such a point of remove to be provisional at best, illusory at worst.

We have, however, sought the poetic imagination in a variety of discourses and elucidated its catalyzing function without needing to isolate it as a static conceptual entity against which the needs of thought would measure themselves or make their final case. We have sought it at the roots of Kant's transcendental architecture, at the heights and depths of Schelling's idealism, and in the critical retrievals and needful attunements of Heidegger's fundamental orientations. We have found its traces in the grounds for ontological synthesis, the work of intuition, the life of identity, the questions of essence and jointure, the task of measure, and the dimensions of poetic dwelling. We have witnessed the poetic imagination in moments of promise and peril, pseudos and doxa as well as disclosure and decision. And we have tried to honor the adhesive quality of the imagination—the way in which it cannot be subtracted or isolated from the more explicit matters that render it problematic or productive for Schelling and Heidegger's paths of thinking. Nowhere have we held that the imagination must be understood as a matter under consistent, unflagging progress—as though it were a secure baton passed from Kant to Schelling to Heidegger. We have, rather, three different sets of hands and even more manifestations of the matter they grasp. Without forgetting what Schelling and Heidegger have brought to the meaning of 'identity' in any statement purporting to categorize or define, we may say the poetic imagination names the point at which the creative basis of thought comports with the creative possibilities of human existence. It is the matter that stands astride the theoretical and practical domains, the work of reflection and works of art, the strife of questioning and the mystery of being. It is persistent and explosive, an impulse and impasse, the elemental compass in one sense and the brink of enthusiasm in another. Plato's position remains telling: he knew enough to withhold credence from the poetic arts, but what he knew 'well' he knew on the basis of a poetic imagination.

Still, even at this 'conclusive' stage, one might wonder whether the imagination is any better off for having been run through the mill of Schelling and Heidegger's philosophies. The theme itself (as Kant discovered) is already unwieldy—why multiply the confusion by rooting it out in two thinkers proficient in stylistic obscurities? And why chase it down in two texts (the *Freiheitschrift*, the *Beiträge*) stationed at the far outskirts of rational coherence? Does calling the imagination 'poetic' clarify the issue or underscore the problem? And why press the matter with Schelling and Heidegger, when other established earmarks serve them better? Two replies. First, if clarity is the issue then I must hasten to accept the blame that cannot, properly speaking, be theirs. Philosophy is difficult, the more so when the matter concerned is born in philosophical self-criticism and harbored in the strenuous tasks of system completion, metaphysical closure, phenomenological possibility, and essential retrieval. Second, I do hope to have shown the imagination to be of central importance to Schelling and Heidegger—neither an afterthought in their itineraries nor, as it were, a candidate for flights of fancy in our readings of their signature works. Neither the inner dynamics of Schelling's idealism nor Heidegger's ontological questioning can, I believe, be understood properly without appreciating the formative role of the imagination in their projects and the corresponding creative transformations of inquiry they bring about in conjunction with this theme. In fact, by way of providing a brief resume of our discussion, I would like to borrow two tropes (that are obviously more than tropes) from these thinkers and apply them to our theme: the poetic imagination, as it appears in the thought of Schelling and Heidegger, has proven to be something of an irreducible *remainder*, a matter caught up in the play of *unconcealment* and *withdrawal* at the limits of metaphysics and in the primordial scene of phenomenological beginnings. Let us revisit the leading insights we have uncovered in order to show how this is the case.

First, in Schelling's early preoccupation with furnishing an unconditional principle for transcendental knowing and a system of absolute identity wrought on the basis of productive intuition, the power of imagination provided a clue to the activity of spirit in the genesis of consciousness, nature, and history. By modeling intuitive acts on the striving of spirit, and anchoring both in the fundamental movement of will, the mediating and sensuous character of imagination brought the prize of identity within reach of idealism and brought philosophical abstraction through a decidedly aesthetic and poetic turn. In his *System* (1800) Schelling redoubled his emphasis on the productive imagination by appealing to the creative imagination to characterize the generative mediation of the whole of nature and intelligence, and, more specifically, the function of aesthetic intuition in revealing the harmony between conscious and unconscious forces for the immediacy of reason. His ensuing writings, even while seeking to refine the meaning of absolute identity and the standpoint of absolute reason, deferred to imagination as intuition's primordial potentiality and accentuated the life of the absolute as a movement of *Ineinsbildung* throughout the whole and in the vocation of artistic creation. The result was an ontological system of the absolute in which the poetry of thought sought to mirror the imaginative life of the whole.

Second, Schelling's 1809 *Freedom Essay* signaled the harrowing problems of creation and ground arising in the aftermath of the identity philosophy, and with them the question of the fate of imagination at a time in which matters of essence exerted remarkable strain upon the ambitions of system. Here it seemed as if a discourse of origins and becoming, existence and evil, would eclipse the primacy of intuition and the celebrated status of imagination in both the character of the absolute and the quality of systematizing reason. What, if any, place would arise for imagination in the problem of necessity and freedom and the standpoint assumed for articulating its resolution? In the midst of this radical venture, we observed that the increasingly elemental depth of Schelling's inquiry led to a new concentration on the generative work of the divine (or 'true') imagination in the exchange between ground and existence, there manifesting a creative mediation commensurate with a new emphasis on difference in the principle of identity. We also noted an incisive critique of the inquiring imagination, and thus a tension between the creativity that buttresses the bonded unity of the whole and the creative abstractions that handicap reason's traditional account of this *poietic* drama. To reason through imagination's generative ontological function, then, Schelling had to exercise the science of inquiry in a manner appropriate to thought's inspired, measuring vocation. His account of divine and human becoming, that is, revealed imagination to be engaged in the primordial, capacitating, work of bringing-forth, and his dialogical enactment of a resolute, poetic inquiry illustrated a parallel work of bringing-forth in reason itself. The imagination—intrinsic to divine self-revelation and human reason alike—was firmly placed in service to the *word*.

If, then, *Einbildungskraft* was something of a 'remainder' to Kant's critical project, each of the above ventures in Schelling's thought, in different ways, established the imagination as the very ground of being and becoming such that without it there would be no logos of the whole and no secure footing for the work of understanding. If the idealist system, extended even to the depths of the irrational ground, is to be 'of' the absolute or God in both senses of the genitive, then the manner in which knowledge is a knowing of the life of the whole and a knowing from the finite standpoint (the 'summit') of this whole amounts to a belonging-together constituted by the imagination.

But it is at this apparent highpoint of the imagination—this poeticizing of thought— that our theme fell into a state of withdrawal; or rather, it became manifest as a concealing force. This state of affairs arose through our third consideration, Heidegger's 1936 course on the *Freedom Essay*. Our task would have been easier had Heidegger simply celebrated Schelling's attention to, and use of, the poetic imagination in the same spirit he magnified its importance in Kant. But this was not the case. Heidegger indeed not only celebrated a certain 'impulse' in Schelling, but also identified a metaphysical 'impasse' that implicated the imagination. Following his lectures on Nietzsche from this period, we discovered that Schelling's impasse was not simply an unwillingness to jettison the cargo of a systematizing, onto-theological agenda, but was, still more specifically, a failure to relinquish the purported command of a *poetizing essence* (from *dichtender*) in reason itself. Even if Schelling problematized the habits of the inquiring imagination, Heidegger found that his appeals to representation, will, and the productive work of subjectivist thought persisted to the extent that Schelling could not hear the cautionary tale written in his own accounts of identity and ground. The impasse, then, echoed the failure of Heidegger's Kant to let imagination upset the reign of pure reason in light of Kant's own disclosures regarding the fundamental ground of ontological synthesis. That all great thinkers 'think the same' was true then in the following way: with Kant and beyond Kant Heidegger insisted the transcendental standpoint be ontological; with Schelling and beyond Schelling Heidegger insisted the essential standpoint be fugal. In each thinker Heidegger found an advocate for thinking the inner and originary by way of questioning and critique, thereby allowing the manifestation of primordial productivity to reorient the very shape of thought. But Kant recoiled at the expense of imagination and Schelling's work shattered on account of it. The drama of impulse and impasse, applied to our theme, could thus be summarized in this period by saying that, for Heidegger, the imagination that had been so promising becomes blameworthy.

In view of this critical balance we might have been justified in consigning the imagination to the last great strides of the idealist tradition, then presenting Heidegger's turn to the essence of truth in art and poetry (contemporaneous with his Schelling course) as a deliberate alternative to the creative character of reason envisioned by Kant but ever destined for contamination. We might have been justified, that is, in announcing for Heidegger that there was an essential work of the imagination glimpsed in one era, but there must now be an essential retrieval of poetry in the next. Such a summation, to be sure, comes close to the state of affairs, but not close enough. And the clarity won by embracing its rigidity would have wrecked the more penetrating insights to be had by working through Heidegger's exact relation to the poetizing imagination. In the play of impulse and impasse Heidegger allows the imagination to pass into a state of withdrawal. But at the same time it persists as a remainder, undergoing a sustained reorientation in his own essential inquiries into art and poetry—inquiries to a large extent performed in the name of the impulse he found in Schelling.

Our fourth primary consideration, then, was to examine the work of thought underway in Heidegger's "The Origin of the Work of Art" and "Hölderlin and the Essence of Poetry." With the status of the imagination necessarily in question, we charted the difference between *production* in the eidetic, mimetic, and representational sense, and *projection* (*Entwurf*) in a sense corresponding to the aletheiac essence of truth and the work-being of poetic works. The difference proved vital to the potentialities within poetizing, the status of which had to do precisely with the fate of imagination. Though Heidegger was careful in avoiding the thematization of the imagination in these texts (for the most part), his conceptions of poetic founding, saying, preservation, and creative bestowal advanced a case for elemental bringing-forth commensurate with the work hitherto ascribed to the primordial productivity of imagination. The difference between production and projection signaled a passage underway from the poetizing imagination to the measuring work of art, from the primacy of will to the openness of *Hervorbringen*, from *Einbildung* and its legacy to *Ereignis* and its poetic figurations. Heidegger conveyed a sense in which the 'work' of truth was the work of being in the poetic essence of art. In so doing, the touchstones of the Kantian and Schellingian imaginations—activity, motion, pro-duction, illumination, and occurrence—came to be reinscribed in the projective quality of a 'special poetizing.' Without neglecting the 'obtrusions' of production subtracted from these elements or the broader conscription of imagination in the will to system Heidegger assailed, we allowed the phrase 'poetic imagination' to return to the fore. This was not to reduce Heidegger's insights to a repetition of what came before, but to underscore the reorientation of imagination underway in his work even as the term 'imagination' itself could not carry the weight of what was at stake. In these texts, I argued, Heidegger was venturing forth from the site of Schelling's impasse—allowing the imagination together with the creative character of reason to shatter outward toward projection and the creative work of thought. This broadening expanse, I argued, could then be cited in two later attempts to displace Dasein itself from the standpoint of determinations based on beingness to the position of Da-sein in the decisive, constructive, and configuring site of Beyng's fugal clearing. Corresponding to this repositioning was a recalibration of the representational gauge, confirming my view that the turn of poetizing takes shape as a turn of the measuring imagination. Heidegger's explicit, though brief, treatment of the imagination in the *Beiträge* marked a moment in which the theme became manifest once again, thus indicating its presence as an abiding remainder in his thought even while bracketed in a position of questionability. Moreover, in view of "Poetically Man Dwells," we observed how imagination now operated as the mode of measure-taking and letting-be in the impetus and outworking of poetic dwelling. To complete the relationship between the aletheiac essence of truth and the instantiation of Da-sein in the fugal rift of Beyng, the poetic imagination in its refined state was summoned to capture the creative possibilities intrinsic to Da-sein and Beyng alike.

Whether or not the poetic imagination affords a useful rubric for the ongoing work of interpreting Schelling and Heidegger's broader provocations is a decision their readers must make. I hope only to have shown that it is by no means incidental, but rather imperative to those more established reference points to which we turn in understanding them. It is inseparable from Schelling's treatments of intuition, identity, ground, and freedom; it names the most specific focal point of Heidegger's turn in the 1930s; and it clarifies the impetus drawing both thinkers into a study of artistic origins and meaning that would reflect upon, retrieve, and transform the creative character of philosophical reason.

Notes

Introduction

1 Heidegger continues: "We do not even think about the fact that philosophy and art could themselves be the realms of the sojourn of the human" (IP 2/GA50 91).

2 The analogy appears famously in the 1943 'Postscript' to Heidegger's "What is Metaphysics?" (1929), and may also be found in §256 of his *Beiträge zur Philosophie (Vom Ereignis)* (1936–38).

3 It is worth recalling that the word "aesthetics" did not come to name a discipline that treats works of art and beauty with respect to a judging and contemplating 'ego' until the eighteenth century. My use of the term in this project not only includes this recent history but also looks beyond its purview to the Greek and medieval emphasis on more *poietic* meditation—reflections on artistic production, not simply aesthetic judgment (see Jacques Taminiaux, *Poetics, Speculation, and Judgment*, 57). In Schelling and Heidegger we will find a certain reorientation of the *poietic* emphasis, joining it with variations of ontological inquiry that, I believe, still offer much to contemporary aesthetics.

4 See Victor Hugo, *Les Misérables*, 87, 92, 112.

5 For a thoroughgoing account of the problem of imagination in the tradition of Western metaphysics see John Sallis, *Delimitations: Phenomenology and the End of Metaphysics*, 1–29. See also Richard Kearney, *The Wake of Imagination*, 79–189; and James Engell, *The Creative Imagination: Enlightenment to Romanticism*, 3–64.

6 John Sallis speaks of a "loss of anterior signification" concerning imagination—a sense in which "[o]ne can no longer take it for granted that what imagination is as such is established anterior to all discourse on imagination, that *imagination* has a predetermined sense to which that which is called imagination—that to which *imagination* refers—would conform in its concrete determinativeness." See Sallis, *Force of Imagination: The Sense of the Elemental*, 45–6.

7 The tension surrounding imitation, and the distinction between the work of painters and craftsmen, artists and artisans, comes down to the Greek notion of *poiēsis*. This term shall remain of vital significance throughout this project. *Poiēsis*, following Taminiaux, denotes productive activity—be it in the artisan or artist. Though Plato may well have thought "the true poet is the artisan," he held that the artisan in the basic sense of craftsman devoted his productive work to the imitation of the Ideas, whereas painters, sculptors, and poets do not attain the contemplation of Ideas in their imitative work. See Taminiaux, *Poetics, Speculation, and Judgment*, 2–3.

8 See Sallis, *Force of Imagination*, 46–7.

9 Ibid., 48–9.

10 See Friedrich Schiller, *On the Aesthetic Education of Man, in a Series of Letters* (1794–95), 63–5. Schelling will treat the matter with similar consternation from the outset of his career.

11 See paraphrase by Thomas Aquinas, in *Aquinas: Selected Philosophical Writings*, 39.

12 See Aristotle, *On the Soul (De Anima)*, Book Γ, 428a1–4; 428a13 (p. 47).

13 See *Plutarch's Lives Volume IV*, 433.

14 See David Hume, *A Treatise of Human Nature* (1739–1740).

15 Ibid., 252–4, 260, 262.

16 Ibid., 633.

17 See Immanuel Kant, *Prolegomena to Any Future Metaphysics* (1950/1783), 8/260.

18 See Immanuel Kant, *Anthropology from a Pragmatic Point of View* (2006/1798), 74/180–181, my emphasis.

19 Ibid., 220/318n.

20 See Kant, *Prolegomena*, 26/278–9, 63/315–6.

Chapter 1

1 Quite the contrary, what transcendental argumentation appreciates is the manner in which reason, says Kant, ideally aims "at complete determination in accordance with *a priori* rules. Accordingly it thinks for itself an object which it regards as being completely determinable in accordance with principles" (CPR A571/B599). Schiller observes: "In this, as in everything else, critical philosophy has opened up the way whereby empiricism can be led back to principles, and speculation back to experience" (*Letters*, 103n).

2 See J. Sallis, *Spacings: Of Reason and Imagination in Texts of Kant, Fichte, Hegel*, 4. See also CPR, A707/B735.

3 Namely "the language of concept and judgment." See B. Freydberg, *Imagination and Depth in Kant's Critique of Pure Reason*, 18, 16.

4 See Sallis, *Spacings*, 5.

5 See Freydberg, *Imagination and Depth*, 5.

6 Following Freydberg, *Imagination and Depth*, 7.

7 This observation that we are scarcely conscious of the imagination in its workings is echoed in Kant's *Anthropology From a Pragmatic Point of View*, 22.

8 This passage does not appear in the B edition of CPR, a revision we will have cause to wonder about.

9 Freydberg, *Imagination and Depth*, 16.

10 Sensibility and understanding, he continues, "must stand in necessary relation with each other through the mediation of this transcendental function of imagination" if there is to be empirical knowledge and experience (CPR A124).

11 Though I am working principally from the level of close textual comparison, a historical note is in order insofar as it bears on the motivations informing Kant's A and B Deductions. As is well known, in 1782 there appeared the rather scathing 'Göttingen Review' of the first *Critique*. The review, appearing anonymously in the *Zugabe zu den Göttinger gelehrte Anzeigen*, was attributed to Christian Garve and edited at length by his associate, J. G. Feder. Garve charged Kant's idealism with succumbing to a Berkeleyian reduction of "the world and ourselves into mere representations" (see Beiser, *German Idealism: The Struggle Against Subjectivism 1781–1801*, 89). Kant's purported distinctions between the spatiotemporal reality of things and the determinative faculties of subjective representation amounted, so it goes, to an unconvincing difference that did little to overcome the otherwise apparent "identification of the objects of consciousness with ideas" (89). This is not the place to investigate the dispute in the detail it deserves, but it is worth

noting that Kant replied to the review rather bitterly in a 1783 Appendix to his *Prolegomena*. Among his concerns is that the charge of subjective idealism overlooks the core question of synthetic *a priori* judgments, a question that any careful reading of the Transcendental Deduction would evidence. The association with Berkeley, regardless, was potentially devastating to the effect that Kant's work, says Beiser, "would be dismissed as a radical solipsism or *Egoismus* that doubts or denies the existence of everything except one's own self" (90). Given this concern, and given the precarious association of 'imagination' with subjective idealism, it is safe to assume that when Kant set out to author the B version of the Deduction he took pains to minimize his treatment of the representative power and thereby remove some of the basis for the Göttingen misreading, and those likewise prejudiced. This context clearly informs the 'ambiguity' I attribute to the comparison of the two versions, but does not explain it in full or decide outright the question of *Einbildungskraft*, which remains before us.

12 I have adapted Smith's translation of: "*Einbildungskraft* is das Vermögen, einen Gegenstand auch ohne dessen Gegenwart in der Anschauung vorzustellen" (CPR B151).

13 Kant will later attribute the apprehension of appearances to "their reception in the synthesis of imagination" (CPR A190/B235).

14 See Aristotle, *De Anima* I 1.403a8, III 7.431a16.

15 See Aristotle, *De Memoria et Reminiscentia*, 449a30–450a10, at Aquinas, *Aquinas: Selected Philosophical Writings* 138–39.

16 Ibid.

17 Ibid.

18 In *De Anima* Aristotle entertains the dialectical premise that imagination is "a species of motion . . . produced by the activity of sense." See *De Anima*, pp. 48–9, 428a11–12–429a1, and Apostle's commentary at p. 148 notes 33–5.

19 Sallis, *Spacings*, 94–5.

20 See F. Marti's "Translators Introduction" to Schelling, LDC, 152; see also Alfred Denker, "Three Men Standing over a Dead Dog: The Absolute as Fundamental Problem of German Idealism" in Christoph Asmuth, Alfred Denker, and Michael Vater. *Schelling: Between Fichte and Hegel/Zwischen Fichte Und Hegel*. The unconditioned principle is central to Fichte's *Wissenschaftslehre* as a "science of scientific principles" (see Denker, 386). As he remarks in 1794: "It should express that Act that neither is, nor can be, found among the empirical determinations of our consciousness and alone makes it possible" (Fichte, GA 1, 2, p. 255, at Denker, 387). Denker explains: "The first, unconditioned and absolute principle can neither be deduced from a higher principle, nor be proven in any science. Factically, the I posits its own being" (388).

21 See Frederick C. Beiser, *German Idealism: The Struggle Against Subjectivism 1781–1801*.

22 Fichte explains the character of intellectual intuition as follows: It is "the intuiting of himself that is required of the philosopher, in performing the Act whereby the I arises for him. It is immediate consciousness that I act and what I enact: it is that whereby I know something because I do it. We cannot prove from concepts that this power of intuition exists, nor evolve from them what it may be. Everyone must discover it immediately in himself, or else he will never make its acquaintance" (Fichte, SW1, 463 at Denker, 389). Schelling, in this early period, agrees with the necessity for the original self-positing I, but appreciates this necessity more as a principle of unity than an act of freedom in the exercise of science.

23 Kant, notes Theodore George, refers to the 'absolute' in the first *Critique* as that which isolates the "special organizing *telos* of reason." See George, "A Monstrous Absolute," 137 with reference to CPR A326/B383.

24 See Beiser, *German Idealism: The Struggle Against Subjectivism (1781–1801).*

25 More basically: "Intuition [*Anschauung*] as such is usually explained as the most immediate experience; correctly so, as far as it goes. Yet the more immediate the experience, the closer to disappearance" (LDC 185/SW1 325).

26 For clarification on the meaning of *Schwärmerei* in Schelling see F. Marti's helpful discussion at LDC 215–16n.69.

27 Here, in his Ninth Letter, Schelling also makes a statement that is a remarkable anticipation of his later work on *freedom*: "He who has reflected upon freedom and necessity has found for himself that these two principles must be *united* in the absolute: *freedom*, because the absolute acts by unconditional autonomy [*Selbstmacht*], and *necessity*, because it acts only according to the laws of its own being, the inner necessity of its essence" (LDC 189/SW1 331–32.).

28 Privileging imagination in such a way is a point likewise pertinent to Schelling's interest in the poetic arts, especially Greek tragedy. See George, "A Monstrous Absolute," 141–42, and Taminiaux, *Poetics, Speculation, and Judgment,* 27.

29 See Heidegger, PIK 292/GA25 430–31.

30 Slavoj Žižek thus emphasizes what, for Heidegger, is lost in Kant's otherwise penetrating insight: "One can see clearly, now, why Heidegger focuses on transcendental *imagination*: the unique character of imagination lies in the fact that it undermines the opposition between receptivity/finitude (of man as an empirical being caught in the phenomenal causal network) and spontaneity (i.e., the self-originating activity of man as a free agent, bearer of noumenal freedom): imagination is simultaneously receptive and positing, 'passive' (in it, we are affected by sensible images) and 'active' (the subject himself freely gives birth to these images, so that this affection is self-affection)." See Žižek, *The Ticklish Subject: The Absent Centre of Political Ontology,* 27–8.

31 In the Preface to the second edition of KPM (1950) Heidegger allows that readers "have taken constant offense at the violence of my interpretations. Their allegation of violence can indeed be supported by this text" (18).

32 See also Heidegger's comments in *The Essence of Reasons* (1928), such as ER 97/GA9 161–62.

33 In *The Essence of Reasons* Heidegger refers to Kant's CPR section on "Supreme Principle of All Synthetic Judgments" (cf. A154/B193): "This second 'principle' explains what, at a transcendental level [*überhaupt*], i.e., within the range and on the level of Kant's ontological inquiry, belongs *to the Being* of being—'being' here understood as that which is accessible in experience. It gives a positive definition of transcendental truth, which is to say that it defines the inner possibility of transcendental truth through the unity of time, the faculty of imagination, and the 'I think'" (ER 31–33/GA9 136).

34 Heidegger explains: "If the essence of transcendence is grounded in the pure power of imagination, or more originally in temporality, then precisely the idea of the 'Transcendental Logic' is something inconceivable, especially if, contrary to Kant's original intention, it is autonomous and is taken absolutely" (KPM 166/GA3 236–37).

35 See Heidegger, KPM 154/GA3 219–20.

36 Hugo, *Les Misérables,* 622.

Chapter 2

1   I am aware the formal starting point for Schelling's so-called "identity system"
    is commonly dated with the appearance of his 1801 "Presentation of My System
    of Philosophy." See, for example, Antoon Braeckman, "From the Work of Art
    to Absolute Reason: Schelling's Journey Toward Absolute Idealism," In *Review
    of Metaphysics* 57, 3 (1 March 2004): 551. As I will indicate, this is so because
    the *Darstellung* contains a deductive rationale for 'absolute identity' that is self-
    consciously post-Fichtean, and therefore a ready point of orientation for Schelling's
    more singular system. However, Schelling is already preoccupied with the question of
    identity and the problem of system—both with and against Fichte—in the late 1790s.
    I have broadened the period of these issues accordingly.

2   Maurice Merleau-Ponty, *Nature: Course Notes from the Collège de France*
    (1956–1957), 49.

3   From "Earliest Program of German Idealism" (1797) at US xii–xiii. The authorship
    of this brief text has been variously attributed to Schelling, Hegel, and Hölderlin.
    Though indications are the text was a collaborative effort among the three, the
    authorship proper appears to belong to Hegel and is in his handwriting. See
    Christoph Jamme and Helmut Schneider, *Mythologie der Vernunft: Hegels ältestes
    Systemprogramm des deutschen Idealismus*. Among the primary aims of the text,
    according to Krell, are "to understand the supreme act of reason as an *aesthetic*
    act and *beauty* as the supreme idea of reason," and to provide "a polytheism of the
    imagination conjoined with a monotheism of reason and the heart" (Krell, *The
    Tragic Absolute*, 3).

4   "Earliest Program" at US xii–xiii.

5   This faculty, he continues, "equally capable of activity and passivity, is the only one
    capable of comprising and exhibiting in one communal product the negative and
    positive activities" (T 72/SW1 357).

6   SW2 7, at US x–xi, 1797.

7   Shelling conceives the meaning of the 'whole' in terms of imagination in his
    1802–1803 *Lectures on Art*: "The splendid German word '*imagination*'
    (*Einbildungskraft*) actually means the power of mutual informing into unity
    (*Ineinsbildung*) upon which all creation is based. It is the power whereby something
    ideal is simultaneously something real, the soul simultaneously the body, the power
    of individuation that is the real creative power" (ART 32/SW5 386).

8   James Dodd, "Philosophy and Art in Schelling's *System des transzendentalen
    Idealismus*," 3.

9   The aim of this question, echoing Kant, is to solidify that preconceptual grounding
    center that ultimately "prevents *my own self* from drowning in the stream of
    representations" and "carries me from act to act, from thought to thought, from time
    to time (on invisible wings, as it were)" (T 103/SW1 402).

10 For a contextualization of this theoretical/practical impulse in terms of uncertainties
    left standing in Kant's thought, see Denker, "Three Men Standing over a Dead Dog,"
    383–85.

11 Since the matter is arbitrated by theoretical reason in the first *Critique*, Kant, says
    Schelling, could not help but *symbolize* "this supersensible ground of all sensibility"
    and as a result "leaves *unexplained* all that could be explained only through *this
    primordial, inner principle of all representation* (which he nowhere attempts to
    determine)" (T 106–07/SW1 406–07).

12 SW1 348n, at US xi.

13 Any "true system," he again declares in STI, "must contain the ground of its subsistence within *itself*" (STI 15/SW3 352–53). To track Schelling's continuity on this point see P 350/SW4 116, P 344/SW4 108, US 9/SW5 215.

14 The problem of analysis and separation is more nuanced as Schelling comes to frame the principle of identity within the scope of absolute totality. See P 357/SW4 126, and US 14/SW5 220, 68/274, 154/128–29.

15 Fichte, II, 3:300 at Pfau, *Idealism and the Endgame of Theory*, 21.

16 Fichte writes: "The (productive) imagination is itself a faculty of the Self. Couldn't it be the only grounding faculty (*Grundvermögen*) of the Self?" (II, 3:298 at Pfau, 22). In a sense, yes, but Schelling is already moving beyond the 'I', beneath the Fichtean subjectivity of the subject. He holds, for example, that unity "cannot be produced, let alone be recognized, by an exclusively theoretical consciousness" (Pfau's paraphrase, 25). He is interested, rather, in "a Being which precedes all thinking and imagining" (I, 167/75 at Pfau, 25).

17 Pfau, 26–7.

18 Ibid., 27.

19 It is important to note that, prior to Schelling, Herder makes extensive use of '*Geist*' in compiling his general history of cultures, arts, and the achievements of the human species. Herder's usage typically comports with a story of how "Providence carried along the thread of development." See Johann Gottfried Herder, *Another Philosophy of History* (1774), 11. Schelling's usage may have a similar appreciation of 'providence' in view, but is more focused along lines of the constitution of consciousness and the play of the infinite and finite.

20 Pfau, 28.

21 See Marx, *The Philosophy of F. W. J. Schelling: History, System, and Freedom*, 12–13.

22 For Schelling's sense of the tensions surrounding the status of 'spirit' see T 78/SW1 367n.C.

23 "Earliest Program of German Idealism (1797)," at *US* xiii. That the productive imagination is itself an activity of spirit is further evident in Schelling's assertion that "the world is truly nothing other than our *productive spirit* in its finite productions and reproductions" (T 74/SW1 360, my emphasis). These are the very activities Schelling has in mind when, in the *System*, he observes that "knowledge proper presupposes a concurrence of opposites, whose convergence can only be a *mediated* one" (STI 15/SW3 353). Indeed, insofar as "no world exists unless a spirit is to form knowledge of it" and "nothing can be real unless there is a spirit to know it" (T 72–3/ SW1 357–58), there is reason to believe that the viability of knowledge and world depend on imagination as a production of spirit in the depths of intuition.

24 The force of Schelling's *System*, and indeed the central tension between intuition and abstraction that comprises the difficulty at the heart of attaining the absolute standpoint via intellectual intuition, operates in the aftermath of this vital clarification.

25 See also STI 49/SW3 397.

26 Identity, to be clear, names the relationship between representation and object that must obtain if philosophical truth claims are to have any basis in the real. Schelling formulates the predicament of subject/object identity as a principle in need of recovery.

27 Schelling's tone is contemptuous; though it is not clear he believes the handicap was unavoidable.

28 Schelling's more forceful account of this unity is found in his 1801 *Presentation*. It is here that the specific discoveries of the *Treatise* and *System* allow him to work from the standpoint of *absolute reason* (the position of absolute identity and absolute totality, which will be assumed through the act of intellectual intuition), and to raise the present matter of 'identity' into the 'indifference' expressed in the proposition A = A. Absolute reason, he explains, is "reason insofar as it is conceived as the total indifference of the subjective and objective," and is a philosophical "standpoint" (P 349–50/SW4 114–15) that has recovered the notion (more primordial than correspondence models) that *"Being belongs equally to the essence of reason and to that of absolute identity"* (352/118). The error lodged within the correspondence model of truth is the same as that which shows itself more readily in formal logic and strictly inferential reasoning: the divorce of form and content, and the empirical sundering of absolute reality from absolute ideality—what is assumed in any "antithesis between subjectivity and objectivity" (see US 63–8/SW5 269–75).

29 That is not to suggest that self-consciousness and spirit are the same. The reflective agent and the intuiting spirit are not reducible to a relationship of part and whole, nor a Fichtean 'I' or judging subject, but rather the intended self-consciousness of absolute identity belongs to both the inquiring subject and the spiritual subject.

30 It is in the passage of spirit through a state of objectification that consciousness first arises. We have already observed this motion, in reduced form, in the understanding's *formal* imitation of the imagination's *material* figuration, thereby constituting consciousness of an individual object. Schelling now combines his logic of necessity with a metaphysical extension of the activity/passivity principle discovered in the productive imagination.

31 In simple terms, spirit's essence is toward self-intuition but to become "conscious of itself" it must become "*finite* for itself" (T 88–9/SW1 380–82).

32 See T 81/SW1 370.

33 "Only now," he explains, "through our abstraction, does the product of our activity become an *object*" (T 81/SW1 370).

34 See T 81/SW1 370. The price of becoming *conscious* of an intuited product is that I must *abstract* from it, and the price of becoming conscious of my *freedom* is that "I feel restricted with respect to the object" (T 81/SW1 371).

35 Fichte, I, 3:298–300 at Pfau, 21–2.

36 See 1797 "The Earliest Program of German Idealism" at US xii–xiii.

37 Cf. T 92–3/SW1 386–87.

38 Velkley, "Realizing Nature in the Self," 153.

39 Velkley, 153.

40 In 1801 Schelling will imply that the imagination is the productive capital of reason (cf. P 349n.15/SW4 115), for it is an element shared by what may be called spiritual productivity, as well as by intuitive intellectual insight (in the sense of *Erkennen*).

41 See STI 15/SW3 352–53.

42 Though such a move may seem to collapse 'knowing' into 'being,' Schelling is not taking up the dogmatic line that privileges being as fundamental, but rather pressing the Spinozistic trajectory toward its natural conclusion in transcendental philosophy; the principle of identity (here named 'nature') is treated as a principle within knowledge itself (STI 19/SW3 358–59), which means nature is taken in such a way that it shares in knowledge the unconditional ground heretofore characterized as 'freedom.'

43 Xavier Tilliette, *Schelling: une philosophie en devenir*, Biblioteque d'histoire de la philosophie, (Vrin 1992) at Dodd, 13.

44 Schelling further notes: "Only what art brings forth is simply and *solely* possible through genius, since in every task that art has charged, an infinite contradiction is reconciled" (STI 228/SW3 623).

45 In 1802 he speaks of the need for the philosopher to "penetrate into the very workshop of its [the absolute law's] creations" (US 148/SW5 349). The artist, moreover, "is a genius insofar as he expresses the highest law, and it is precisely this absolute law that philosophy recognizes in him, for philosophy is not only autonomous itself but also seeks to penetrate to the very *principle* of autonomy" (US 148/SW5 349).

46 Tilliette at Dodd, 13.

47 The larger identity of intelligence and nature is also at work in the revelatory unity of the work. See Dodd, 11.

48 Cf. 1797 "Earliest Program of German Idealism," at US xiii.

49 Cf. ART 37.

50 See, for example, P 349/SW4 115, 352/118.

51 In which case: "*Everything that is, is absolute identity itself*" (P 352/SW4 119).

52 Schelling will radicalize this position on the law of identity in his 1809 *Freedom Essay*, a crucial ontological development we will discuss in Chapters 3 and 4.

53 One's emphasis on "infinite knowing" or "infinite being" depends on which propositional 'A' is in question (P 365–66/SW4 137–38).

54 See Vater's note at P 343 on terms, and Schelling at P 344–45/SW4 108–9.

55 The trope of the 'mirror' will continue to figure in Schelling's thought at least until 1821, and will enter into Heidegger's discourse in a limited way in the 1930s (see our Chapter 5). Readers will recognize it–*katoptron*–as a theme from Plato's *Republic*, Book X. For Plato, *katoptron* denotes the imitative possibilities of artistic activity. But the mirror also signals a limit situation—the artist may imitate appearances, but cannot engage in the same level of ontological production enjoyed by the artisan (who fabricates). Suffice it to say, Schelling does not take artistry (in the form of mythology, tragedy, poetry, or painting) to be limited to the imitation of appearances, as Plato would have it, but rather weds artistry to the inspired corroboration of speculation and creation.

56 I am grateful to my colleague, Mark Thomas, for alerting me to this latter point.

57 The conception of creation remains framed within Schelling's abiding appreciation for the tension between the ideal and the phenomenal—the absolute standpoint (embodied in A=A, 1801) and the finite standpoint (accounted as A=B, 1801). But his ambitious embrace of 'absolute reason' in 1801 is now tempered by a more qualitative characterization of the unconscious, irrational, and harrowingly 'actual' absolute. See ART 36–7/SW5 393 and P 361/SW4 131.

58 We are reminded of how, in the *Treatise*, the human spirit was that being in which spirit's eternal becoming was individuated; furthermore, Schelling's analogy of 'flow' appeared in the *System* as a way of capturing the return motion of philosophy to its source in poetry (see STI 232/SW3 628–29).

59 Not unlike Kant's position in the *Critique of Judgment*, Schelling explains that *nature* contains touchstones of this kind, for, as he noted in his Jena lectures, the student of philosophy "learns to recognize . . . forms in works of art as sensuous images which have their origin in nature and which are her symbols" (US 151/SW5 351–52). Compare ART 90/SW5 468.

60 This is true provided one makes the colossal element in nature "into a symbol of the absolutely colossal" (ART 87/SW5 463).

61 See Vater, 217–19. A common interpretation regards the two *Presentations* and *Philosophy and Religion* (1804) as evidencing a retreat from Schelling's earlier interest in art and aesthetic intuition.

62 Cf. Shiller, *Letters*, 57–9.

63 See, for example, FP 378/SW4 364, 381/367, 381/368.

64 See B 151/SW3 251, 158/258, 167/267–68.

Chapter 3

1 Translators' note at F 82, my emphasis.

2 The weight of this problem may be compared to the question of what reality inheres in representations—the formative question of his early period. The problem is, more broadly, a primary catalyst for what will be Schelling's so-called turn toward a more 'positive' philosophy.

3 Friedrich Heinrich Jacobi, *Über die Lehre des Spinoza in Briefen an den Herrn Moses Mendelssohn*, ed. Marion Lauschke (Hamburg: Felix Meiner Verlag, 2000) 23–36 and Lessing, *Werke VIII*, 565–71. Love and Schmidt include Jacobi's text, "On Human Freedom," as an appendix to *Freedom*, and the passage in question may be found at F 120, my emphasis.

4 Franz Xavier von Baader, *Sämmtliche Werke*, 33–8. Love and Schmidt include von Baader's text, "On the Assertion that there can be no Wicked Use of Reason," as an appendix, and the passage in question may be found at F 101.

5 See translators' comments on *Wesen* at F xxxiii–xxxv. Boehme states that "every essence is an *arcanum* or a *mysterium* of a whole being" (at F 88). The description by no means answers our question, but is indicative of what will be Schelling's orientation in the *Freedom Essay*. Love and Schmidt include an excerpt from Jakob Boehme's *Mysterium Pansophicum* as an appendix to *Freedom*. See Boehme, *Sämliche Schriften*, ed. Will-Erich Peukert, vol 4 (Stuttgart: Frohmann-Holzboog [Reprint], 1955–1960), 97–111. For commentary on Schelling's relationship to Boehme see Robert F. Brown, *The Later Philosophy of Schelling: The Influence of Boehme on the Works of 1809–1815*.

6 See B. Freydberg, *Schelling's Dialogical Freedom Essay*, 95.

7 Freydberg, 9, see 88.

8 See Freydberg, 110, 89. In the *Beiträge*, Heidegger presses still further beyond the scope of traditional *Erklärung* in order to reconfigure philosophical questioning as an alertness to Beyng's word: *Ereignis*. So doing, he will also radicalize the Schellingian question of *Wesen* as a grounding question (*Grundfrage*) of *Wesung*.

9 Schelling added this note, and others, in the 1809 publication of the text: Schelling, *Philosophic Papers*, vol. 1 (Landshut 1809).

10 Here one may be tempted to charge Schelling and his 'line' of indifference as deadening absolute identity in a similar way, though this is far less evident than the fact that his philosophy of nature was already in place and readily assumed at the time of the *Presentations*.

11 In context, Schelling is chiding a methodology of art criticism that "strives to proceed from form to essence," a mistake Schelling calls the "mere intensification of the relative" (PA 328/SW3 396).

12 In his 1801 *Presentation* he allowed that identity as essentially A = A could be viewed as A = B from the standpoint of being and production, in which case one could focus on beings and form relative to the indivisible line of identity provided one maintain that the relative or formal is such only by virtue of a different modality of the same primary 'A.' To inquire by way of abstraction is to privilege the 'B' term, and indeed isolate it from the life of the 'A.'

13 Here the closest approximation to anything like disobedience or sin is the betrayal of essence in the misguided appeal to form.

14 Necessity and freedom, says Schelling "are in one another as one being [*Ein Wesen*] that appears as one or the other only when considered from different sides, in itself freedom, formally necessity" (F 50/SW7 385).

15 The *Erklärung* for freedom and evil will concern nature, though without mechanistic reduction, and God, though without metaphysical dogmatism.

16 In the *Treatise* (1797) he privileged the act of will as "the *supreme condition of self-consciousness*" (T 98/SW1 395).

17 Schelling believes that Descartes, Leibniz, and even Spinoza all failed to draw idealism and realism into a "living whole" (F 26/SW7 356).

18 Boehme considers "an eternal being in two mysteries" (at F 89).

19 Failure to attend to the necessity of divine self-revelation and the efficacy of divine imagination is, it would seem, one reason why 'systems' subjugate all beings "under a blind, thoughtless necessity" (F 19/SW7 348).

20 See Schelling LDC 184/SW1 324.

21 The etymological clarification belongs to Fiona Steinkamp in her translator's notes to Schelling's unfinished novel, *Clara: Or on the Relationship Between Nature and the Spirit World* (1810), 95n.1, cf. 67/SW4 92.

22 See also F 28/SW7 358–59 and C 54/SW4 75.

23 We will discuss the significance of *die Sehnsucht* (yearning) as we proceed. Warnek understands it to mean "unruly longing before all willing" (Warnek, "Reading Schelling after Heidegger," 166). Krell takes a somewhat different tack, rendering *Sehnsucht* "languor," and notes that Heidegger will use *Regung* (bestirring) to capture the meaning of *Sehnsucht* (see Krell, *The Tragic Absolute*, 84–90, 101n. 25).

24 See Freydberg, 47–8. At the same time, we must bear in mind that the excessive ground "is the living genesis of all things, but is not itself a 'thing' and can never be exhausted by its animating function" (Freydberg, 48). As well, the notion of the unruly remainder is new since the *Presentation*. This qualification is one reason Schelling prefers to speak of 'becoming' and not immanence as the basis for apprehending the nature of things. Immanence stands overwrought, reduced to a "dead containment of things in God" (F 28/SW7 358), and thus incommensurate with the circle of eternal activity noted between God as *prius* and *actu*. Becoming accords with the standpoint attuned to genesis as differentiation.

25 One should also consider the mythological component at work in these discursive maneuvers. See, for example, Schelling's 1815 treatise on "The Deities of Samothrace" (trans. Robert F. Brown, *AAR Studies in Religion*, 12 (Missoula, MT: Scholars Press, 1977, 1974)).

26 What distinguishes the *Freedom Essay* is the interest in qualities of this irrational ground *in* God, a new approach to the nature of the absolute that will ultimately yield a conception of divine personality and hence a different accent on the life of the system and the creative vocation of philosophy.

27 Though the generative passage from darkness to light was noted in the *Plastic Arts* address, this sense of an anarchic remainder would seem to complicate the stability

of eternal ideas or prototypes. Schelling, however, is working at a greater depth of ground, a depth from which he means to recast the story of how the bond of understanding and love emerges between God and man. Further, darkness and anarchy do not imply estrangement in the strict sense; they are the conditions of yearning; yearning is the quality of the ground in God; and the ground is the motion of all emergence; the seed of birth into light and understanding. Here one may charge Schelling and his metaphors (his "human terms," F 28/SW7 359) with mystical enthusiasm. But a better observation is that the elements arrayed at the level of origins are found to be in perpetual, productive motion; and precisely the same case was found, albeit under a different discourse and with different ambitions, in the transcendental imagination.

28 Continuing, Heidegger reports: "The true creation [*Das eigenliche Geschöpf*] is that which is properly in itself separated from God yet remains for and thus in God— Human kind. Not independence from, but rather that which is within Creation, is most free; 'human freedom' and the quality of being like [the quality of being a precise-image] the Absolute. The true Creation of 'God': that which God, as himself, allows to become" (GA49 125–26).

29 Schelling is drawing on Boehme. Boehme describes a state of revolt in which the imagination of craving seizes upon the mirror of unity, "guides it into its imagination," effectively breaking the mirror through an act of "*turba* [disruption/ discordance] as a dying of the seized life" (at F 90). Within the realm of "the eternal nature" (at F 90), then: "*With creation is fury [Grimm] brought into motion*" (at F 89). But the motion is necessary to awakening the disclosure of the primal essence: "And it is known well to us how the *imagination* of the eternal nature has thus the *turba* in the craving, in the *mysterium*, but how it is impossible to wake it up unless the creature as the mirror of eternity should wake it up itself as the fury that lies hidden in eternity in the *mysterium*" (at F 90).

30 We will encounter a different conception of 'transfiguration' in Chapter 5 when we consider §192 of Heidegger's *Beiträge*.

31 The issue of the *word*, for Schelling, of course, stands at the center of this question of motion and genesis. We cannot provide a full discussion of this matter here, as it would entail a prolonged study of how Schelling understands and employs the Trinitarian Johanine conception of *logos*, as well as a deeper consideration of the relationship between the voice of language and the unity of nature. But we may at least note that Schelling is alert to the unity accomplished between the silence of God (the consonant) and, so to speak, the sound of nature (the vowel). Language belongs to the word, completing the 'image' in both its unruly freedom and its ruly measure. My thanks to Jason Wirth for helping me appreciate the depth and difficulty of this issue.

32 Boehme's sense of profanation is similar. He describes his own "*mysterium*," like Schelling's 'whole,' as "a miracle in figures" (at F 92). The 'magic' of this mysterium yields place to evil, but does not cause it. The relationship of evil to word is similar. With regard to will in the essence of the whole being, "The word is its *centrum* or residence and stands in the middle as a heart" (at F 88). But in the division and multiplication of wills there arises the fury for oneness wherein each will "seeks again the ONE [*das EINE*]" (at F 91) in a violent *turba*. The result is a multiplicity of languages detached from the "the nature-language that is the root in all languages" (at F 93).

33 Plato uses the phrase in his *Timaeus* (49a2, 52b2) to underscore the difficulty one faces when trying to speak or reason about the nature of the cosmogonical site

or paradigmatic receptacle of all origins, *khōra*. The problem for Socrates and his interlocutors is that *khōra* 'is' in the mode of withdrawal and cannot be predicated of directly. *Khōra* is a site (*topos*) of eternal, generative work, but its mode of birthing beginnings and spatializing being comprises a third *genos* to which a kind of *logos* that is neither *nous* nor right opinion must comport itself. In this Platonic sense, a *logismo notho* is necessary and involves a species of imaging and recollection. Schelling's usage likewise arises within a context of generation and imagination set at a distance from conceptual abstractions.

34 Schelling explains: "The first beginning for the creation is the yearning of the One to give birth to itself or the will of the ground. The second is the will of love, whereby the word is spoken out into nature and though which God makes himself personal" (F 59/SW7 395).

35 See also PA 355–56/SW3 426, 364n. 8 for precedent.

36 See Freydberg, 98–9.

37 Ibid.

38 The temptation to align *Indifferenz* with primal will is understandable, but is a slippage we should be cautious of. Hellmers, for example, holds: "The purest and most absolute form of will for Schelling is the *Ungrund*, a presently absent version of the absolute in which the primal will that grounds both nature and the good is wholly indifferent to any particularity, an opaque unity that is only complete in providing a primordial indifference that divides from itself for difference to emerge as good and evil" (Hellmers, 143). The necessity for differentiation is right, but it is not clear that Schelling means *Indifferenz* as the superlative form of *will*.

39 Boehme at F 85.

40 Boehme at F 89.

41 Boehme at F 88, 85.

42 In later chapters we will discover in Heidegger a similar concentration on 'measure' but an altogether different mode of inspiration and dimension of truth.

Chapter 4

1 In her translation, Stambaugh includes an appendix containing manuscript and course notes for Heidegger's seminars on Schelling 1941–43. Hereafter ST2/GA49. In both cases pagination appears as English/German, though when referencing GA49 passages not provided in Stambaugh translations are my own.

2 Letter to Jaspers on April 24, 1926. See *Martin Heidegger & Karl Jaspers: Briefwechsel 1920–1963*, 62. As quoted in Theodore Kisiel, "Schelling's Treatise on Freedom and Heidegger's *Sein und Zeit*," in *Schelling: Zwischen Fichte und Hegel*, pp. 287–302: 293n. 8

3 There is, of course, a broader context for this specific focus of fundamental ontology: Heidegger's departure from the focus on 'consciousness' not only in Kant and German Idealism, but as well in Husserl's doctrine of intentionality. Consciousness is no longer of central importance to Schelling by the time of the *Freedom Essay*, and this is perhaps one reason why Heidegger privileges the text.

4 He continues: "In *Being and Time*, on the basis of the question of the truth of Being, no longer the question of the truth of beings, an attempt is made to determine the essence of man solely in terms of his relationship to Being. That essence was described in a firmly delineated sense as *Da-sein*" (N4 141/GA48 260).

5 According to the 1927 course, the dialectic of self-consciousness furnished idealism with an apparent means of getting "behind the mode of being of the subject and of mind" (BPP 152/GA24 217). When Fichte says "Gentlemen, think the wall, and then think the one who thinks the wall" (at 162/231), the appeal to self-consciousness assumes an ontological distinction between *res cogitans* and *res extensa* (ego and non-ego) such that thought is capacitated to reflect on the thinking subject in spite of the "contexture" to which thinker and wall belong. Heidegger will make use of this same example when underscoring the significance of ontological difference in 1944–45 (see IP 37/GA50 129–30).

6 See ER 63f/GA9 148f, 74–75/152–53.

7 Intuition, in this sense, assumes the standpoint of a knowing prefiguration belonging to the Absolute, a knowing *of* the Absolute "in the double sense that the Absolute is the knower and the known, neither only the one nor only the other, but both the one and the other in an original unity" (ST 47/GA42 81).

8 Thought through to its end, however, even this position of reason already signals a drive "to know and grasp a prefigured whole in its prefiguration from the very basis and more primordially" (ST 50/GA42 87).

9 Heidegger stresses the interconnected play of the theological (the ground of beings as a whole) and ontological (the essence of beings as such) in Schelling's inquiry, but hastens to add that Schelling's discussion of pantheism necessarily highlights the questionable status of "ontotheology" (ST 66/GA42 113–14).

10 "Dasein . . . is ontically distinguished by the fact that, in its very Being, that Being is an *issue* for it" (BT 32/GA2 16).

11 This is by no means the first time Heidegger thematizes the law of identity as a matter for investigation. See, for example, Part One chapter Four of BPP (179–226/GA24 225–320).

12 In his *Nihilism* course, Heidegger notes the Platonic background to this formulation: "Plato therefore says that Being as presence in the unconcealed is *idea*, visibleness. *Because Being is presence of what endures in the unconcealed, Plato can therefore interpret Being*, ousia (*beingness*), as idea. 'Idea' is not the name for 'representations' that we as 'I-subjects' have in our consciousness. . . . Idea is the name for Being itself. The 'ideas' are *proteron tēiphysei*, the previous as presencing" (N4 162/GA48 293–94).

13 Two instructive repetitions of this point occur in Heidegger's Nietzsche Lectures. In *The Will to Power as Art* the ontological primacy of the will is a clear heuristic for Heidegger's understanding of the metaphysical tradition: "The conception of the Being of all beings as will is very much in line with the best and greatest tradition in German philosophy" (N134/GA43 42). In Heidegger's lecture, "Who is Nietzsche's Zarathustra?" (1953) he names Schelling's *Freedom Essay* as the site in which "the essential coinage of Being comes to language" in Schelling's statement: "Will is primal Being" (*Wollen ist Urseyn*) (at N2 222/113) (the lecture was published originally as "Wer ist Nietzsches Zarathustra?" in *Vorträge und Aufsätz* (Pfullingen: G. Neske, 1954) pp. 101–26, and Krell includes it as a supplement to N2). The verbal motion ('comes to language') conveys something more than a decision—something, rather, of a necessary though limited movement of the matter of Being into language. The vital difference is that Heidegger does not believe the matter of 'will' is settled, exhausted. He means to draw this coinage and appearance back toward the deeper necessity and agency of Being, in which man "is held" (N2 223/114). Where Schelling goes astray, Heidegger believes, is in assuming the authority of predicating

Being (will) as 'eternal' and 'independent from time' (N2 225/117), and thus settled as a matter for thought in a way incommensurate with the dynamism otherwise granted the identity principle.

14 Though Stambaugh translates *das Grundgefüge* as "jointure" I believe 'structure' is more appropriate. Heidegger does at times use *Fuge* in his Schelling course, but it is not clear his full thematization of 'jointure' is yet in place. This thematization occurs more fully in the *Beiträge*.

15 Following Schelling's impulse means taking up "the necessity of an essential returning to a great basic mood [*eine große Grundstimmung*]" (ST 105/GA42 183–84).

16 The original reads: "Und es ist in diesem Zusammenhang von Bedeutung, den hier gar zu leicht sich vordrängenden Gedanken des Herstellens fernzuhalten" (GA42 207).

17 Schelling's subject matter "is the Absolute, creation, nature, the essential factors of Being, pantheism, and idealism," and yet "all of this speaks only of man, and the highest determinations are gained from an analogy to man" (ST 162/GA42 282).

18 See Freydberg, 97–108 for one avenue of critique.

19 Kiesel, "Schelling's Treatise on Freedom and Heidegger's *Sein und Zeit*," 296, in reference to GA49 54.

20 See for example Žižek, *The Ticklish Subject*, 22–23.

21 As, for example, '*Machenschaft*' will be for Heidegger contemporaneous to these reflections.

22 See Kiesel, "Schelling's Treatise on Freedom and Heidegger's *Sein und Zeit*," 296.

23 See Heidegger's important clarification of this predicament at N4 170–71/GA48 303 and 174/305–06.

24 See Krell's discussion of this point in his "Analysis" following N3-N4, 255f.

25 Ibid., 256–57.

26 Ibid., 259.

27 See KPM xv (1973 Preface).

28 See Schelling, US 61–62/SW5 267–68, STI 232/SW3 628.

29 Schelling's critique of such questioning anticipates a long-standing Heideggerian preoccupation with what he will call the 'guiding question' (*Leitfrage*) of the metaphysical tradition. Schelling's work upon/against such questioning resembles what Heidegger will later call "reflection" (*Besinnung*) (see IP 36f/GA50 128f). In a representative later passage Heidegger observes: "'*Essenz*' is the abbreviation for the name of a key concept in Western metaphysics: *essentia*. Whenever it is asked—and thinkers of metaphysics are continually inquiring in this way—*quid est ens?* 'what are beings?', *essentia* provides the answer to the *quid-esse* of beings. . . . The word that has become the standard in German for '*essenz*' and *essentia*, the whatness [*Wassein*], is 'essence' [*Wesen*]. The German word 'essence,' which verbally means the being of beings, is immediately interpreted in the traditional sense of metaphysics, which we can better signify with the name 'substance' [*Wesenheit*]" (IP 36/GA50 128). The question, of course, is whether Schelling's *Besinnung* on the approachability of the infinite 'principle' remains invested in an 'essential' basis for system.

30 Still, Schelling's position regarding the 'self' in this passage is worthy in its own right, and anticipates the laudable 'danger' Heidegger will ascribe to poets.

31 Schelling, *The Ages of the World* (1815), at xxxviii.

32 I am obviously speculating, since Heidegger comments little on these texts. But I am speculating in the interests of a clarifying comparison.

33 Heidegger refers the reader to BT §44 and §60, and OET. (IM 22–23/N 16).
34 See Taminiaux, *Heidegger and the Project of Fundamental Ontology*, 215.
35 In Heidegger's "The Age of the World Picture" (1938) Parmenides' statement is rendered: "the apprehension of beings belongs to Being." See *The Heidegger Reader*, AWP 219/GA5 90–91.
36 For clarification of *offenbar* and *das Offene* see Sallis' notes to OET at *Pathmarks*, 372n. 7.
37 In "The Age of the World Picture" Heidegger's broader diagnosis of the standardization of beingness includes a similar emphasis on this neglected possibility. See AWP 218–19/GA5 89–91.
38 To avoid confusion, when I speak of 'pro-duction' or of truth as 'pro-duced' in this chapter and the next, I have in mind this poetic work of *ergon*, as opposed to the 'production' of poetizing in the concealing and willful sense of representation. By the same token, I will at times contrast 'poetizing command' or 'poetizing production' with 'poetizing production' or 'poetizing projection.' The difference between these modalities will become more pronounced in the following chapter.

Chapter 5

1 I will also refer to Heidegger's "On The Origin of the Work of Art: First Version" (1935), the translation of which is by Jerome Veith and appears in *The Heidegger Reader*.
2 Alert readers will note that Heidegger's mention of the 'visible' echoes his emphasis on *Lichtung* in *Being and Time*. See Richard Capobianco, *Engaging Heidegger*, 90–91, with reference to 177 of BT.
3 Daniil Kharms, "Letter to K.V. Pugacheva, October 16, 1933," in *Today I Wrote Nothing*, 13.
4 From Hölderlin, "Bread and Wine," in *Hyperion and Selected Poems*, 178–79.
5 This element of playfulness is not incidental. Heidegger will advance through it toward the foreboding yet expansive scene of *der Spielraum* in the *Beiträge* and the spirit of 'gathering' evoked in "Poetically Man Dwells." Indeed, artistic 'play' has an important history for the milieu in which Hölderlin writes, as we have noted in Kant's understanding of taste.
6 Cf. Parmenides' statement at IM 154–55/N 111, noted earlier.
7 This distinction appears in *Introduction to Metaphysics*: "Being, in contradistinction to becoming, is enduring [*das Bleiben*]" (IM 216/N 15). My point is that Heidegger's understanding of the poetizing event amounts to an elucidation of this distinction.
8 Roman mythology offers one instance of this tension between what is fleeting and what is founded. See *The Aeneid of Virgil*, Book III, lines 579–89, pp. 71–2, and Book VI, lines 105–08, pp. 135–36.
9 In a supporting contrast, Hölderlin's Hyperion says of his despair: "as I am now I have no names for things and all before me is uncertainty" (*Hyperion*, 126).
10 Hölderlin, *Hyperion*, 54.
11 Heidegger will echo this conception of 'gift' in both structure and quality when, at the conclusion of "Poetically Man Dwells," he speaks of 'kindness.'
12 Hölderlin, *Hyperion*, 51.
13 This 'time' is the deeper sense of the time marking the standpoint of thought in the *Beiträge*, the time of plight and the being-historical moment on the verge of another beginning.

14 Pertinent to this point, Gosetti-Ferencei understands projection (*Entwerfen*) as "the activity of interpretation of the given, which is aided by discourse (*Rede*) as a creative relation of poetical Dasein to its world" (see Gosetti-Ferencei, 247). In general, however, she believes that "a reconception of the poetical imagination" is "neglected in the post-metaphysical poetics" of Heidegger (25), and that "we need to expand the sketch of poetical Dasein to include creative production and its ontological spontaneity" (251). It is not clear to me whether such a 'need' is stated on the basis of what Heidegger begins or as a remedy to his shortcomings. But I believe the 'reconception of the poetical imagination' is underway in Heidegger, though at times implicit.

15 Heidegger's usage of *Ursprung* (origin) is of decisive importance to our discussion. It does not mean 'cause.' See Miguel Beistegui, *Thinking With Heidegger: Displacements*. See also Desmond, *Art, Origins, Otherness*, 229.

16 On the contrary, notes Sallis, "In a work of art there is essentially something more than its being produced by a certain kind of activity, something more than its correlation with the productive artist, an excess that opens the circle [of artist and work of art]." See Sallis, *Echoes: After Heidegger*, 173.

17 Heidegger may have this wrong. Jacques Derrida believes the shoes are in fact Van Gogh's (see Derrida, *The Truth in Painting*). I do not believe the question disturbs Heidegger's reading, for either way we may surmise the shoes were 'worn' by one who 'toiled.'

18 These terms do not imply representation or mimesis, even if an 'imaging' is afoot.

19 See translator note at OWA 196–97.

20 See also Sallis, *Echoes*, 185–86.

21 Compare Schelling's usage of *Gipfel* and *Scheidepunkt* to convey man's station, and the *Mittelpunkte* from which an inquiry into the *lebindigen Grund* arises (F 41/SW7 374, 9/336). *Wendung*, from verb *wenden*, of course conveys a sense of 'turning' which accords with the sense of a *Kehre* within the event of Beyng, and also echoes the necessary turning of need or distress in *notwendig(keit)*. Schelling's terms reflect the more determinate sense of an accomplishment, a height, and a basis.

22 Martin Heidegger, "The End of Philosophy and the Task of Thinking," in *On Time and Being*, 65.

23 For a discussion of Heidegger's conception of the 'between' (*zwischen*) see Eveline Cioflec, *Der Begriff des "Zwischen" bei Martin Heidegger: Eine Erörterung ausgehend von "Sein und Zeit."*

24 For an interesting comparison of such listening with the *call of conscience* discussed in *BT* see Steven Crowell, "Measure-taking: Meaning and Normativity in Heidegger's Philosophy," *Continental Philosophy Review* 41(2008): 261–76.

25 Looking forward in Heidegger's oeuvre, we find a similar turn toward the appeal of language in the context of a specific artistic matter. In "Art and Space" (1969) his focus on the experience and meaning of visual art (*bildende Kunst*), especially sculpture, consists in allowing the meaning of *space* to become question worthy. See AS 306–07/GA13 205–06).

26 God or godhead in this regard is not to be confused as another name for Beyng. See CP 207/GA65 §143, 20–24/§7, 321/§253.

27 See also AS 307/GA13 206.

28 "To speak of a 'metric,'" Crowell explains, "is not to invoke a standard that may be applied to the way one lives; if poetizing is measuring, measuring cannot be the application of a rule" (Crowell, 272).

29 Sculpture evokes a similar measuring motion specified in terms of *granting* a place for the standing of entities. See AS 308/GA13 207.

30 See PMD 223–24/GA7 205.

31 Schelling, as well, alludes to *charis* in his 1807 address on the *Plastic Arts* (see PA 342e/SW3 410–11). Where Schelling's reference is qualitative, celebrating the love and goodness manifest in the experience of archetypal beauty, Heidegger's usage is a more structural analogy to the conversational nature of call/hearing. One could go so far as to associate PMD's closing allusion to *charis* with KPM's closing allusion to *philia*—where *philia* denoted the disposition of thinking with respect to the essential depth of *Einbildung, charis* denotes the disposition of dwelling and measuring in the dimensional realm of the between. Together, the Greek terms name the dispositional depth and height of Heidegger's thinking on the poetic imagination.

Selected Bibliography

Schelling

Schellings Sämmtliche Werke. Ed. Karl Friedrich August Schelling. Stuttgart-Augsburg: J. G. Cotta, 1856–1861. (Reprinted by the Wissenschaftliche Buchgesellschaft in Darmstadt).

Ausgewählte Schriften, six volumes. Ed. Manfred Frank. Frankfurt am Main: Suhrkamp, 1985.

Schellings Werke: Nach der Originalausgabe in neuer Anordnung. Ed. Manfred Schröter. Munich: C. H. Beck, 1927–1959 and 1962–1971.

Werke: Historisch-Kritische Ausgabe. Eds. Hans Michael Baumgartner, Wilhelm G. Jacobs, Hermann Krings and Hermann Zeltner. Stuttgart-Bad Cannstatt: Frommann-Holzboog, 1976–present.

In translation

The Ages of the World (1815). Trans. Jason Wirth. Albany, NY: SUNY Press, 2000.

Bruno, or, On the Natural and the Divine Principle of Things (1802). Ed. and Trans. Michael G. Vater. Albany, NY: SUNY Press, 1984.

Clara: Or on the Relationship Between Nature and the Spirit World (1810). Trans. Fiona Steinkamp. Albany, NY: SUNY Press, 2002.

The Deities of Samothrace. Trans. Robert F. Brown, *AAR Studies in Religion 12.* Missoula, MT: Scholars Press, 1977, 1974.

First Outline of a System of the Philosophy of Nature. Trans. Keith R. Peterson. Albany, NY: SUNY Press, 2004.

The Grounding of Positive Philosophy: The Berlin Lectures. Trans. Bruce Matthews. Albany, NY: SUNY Press, 2008.

Historical-critical Introduction to the Philosophy of Mythology (1842). Trans. Mason Richey and Markus Zisselsberger. Albany, NY: SUNY Press, 2007.

On the History of Modern Philosophy (1827). Trans. Andrew Bowie. Cambridge: Cambridge University Press, 1994.

On the Nature of Philosophy as Science (1821). Trans. Marcus Weigelt. In *German Idealist Philosophy.* Ed. Rudiger Bubner. London: Penguin Books, 1997.

Philosophical Investigations into the Essence of Human Freedom (1809). Trans. Jeff Love and Johannes Schmidt. Albany, NY: SUNY Press, 2006. The latest critical edition in German is: Ed. Thomas Buchheim. Hamburg: Felix Meiner Verlag, 1997.

Philosophical Letters on Dogmatism and Criticism. (1795); *Of the I as a Principle of Philosophy, or On the Unconditional in Human Knowledge* (1795). Trans. Fritz Marti. In *The Unconditional in Human Knowledge: Four Early Essays (1794–1796).* Lewisburg: Bucknell University Press, 1980.

The Philosophy of Art (1802–1803). Trans and ed. Douglass Stott. Vol. 58 of *The Theory and History of Literature*. Minneapolis: University of Minnesota Press, 1989.

Concerning the Relation of the Plastic Arts to Nature (1807). Trans. Michael Bullock as an appendix to Herbert Read. *The True Voice of Feeling: Studies in English Romantic Poetry*. New York: Pantheon Books, 1953.

"Presentation of My System of Philosophy" (1801). Trans. Michael Vater. In *The Philosophical Forum*, XXXII, 4: (Winter 2001).

"Further Presentations from the System of Philosophy" (1802). Trans. Michael Vater. In *The Philosophical Forum*, XXXII, 4: (Winter 2001).

Stuttgart Seminars (1810). In *Idealism and the Endgame of Theory: Three Essays by F. W. J. Schelling*. Ed. & Trans. Thomas Pfau. Albany, NY: SUNY Press, 1994.

System of Philosophy in General and of the Philosophy of Nature in Particular (1804). In *Idealism and the Endgame of Theory: Three Essays by F. W. J. Schelling*. Ed. & Trans. Thomas Pfau. Albany, NY: SUNY Press, 1994.

System of Transcendental Idealism (1800). Trans. Peter Heath. Charlottesville: University of Virginia Press, 1978.

Treatise Explicatory of the Idealism in the Science of Knowledge (1797). In *Idealism and the Endgame of Theory: Three Essays by F. W. J. Schelling*. Ed. & Trans. Thomas Pfau. Albany, NY: SUNY Press, 1994.

On University Studies (1803). Trans. E. S. Morgan. Ed. Norbert Gutterman. Athens, OH: Ohio University Press, 1966.

Heidegger

Gesamtausgabe, Vol. 1: *Sein und Zeit* (1927). Ed. F.-W. von Herrmann. Frankfurt: V. Klostermann, 1977. See also Ed. Max Niemeyer. Tübigen. 15th edn. (1984).

Gesamtausgabe, Vol. 3: *Kant und das Problem der Metaphysik* (1929). Ed. F.-W. von Herrmann, Frankfurt: V. Klostermann, 1991, and 2nd edn. (2010).

Gesamtausgabe, Vol. 4: *Erläuterungen zu Hölderlins Dichtung* (1936–1968). Ed. F.-W. von Herrmann, Frankfurt: V. Klostermann, 1981.

Gesamtausgabe, Vol. 6.1: *Nietzsche* I (1936–1939). Ed. Brigitte Schillbach, Frankfurt: V. Klostermann, 1996.

Gesamtausgabe, Vol. 6.2: *Nietzsche* II (1939–1946). Ed. Brigitte Schillbach, Frankfurt: V. Klostermann, 1997.

Gesamtausgabe, Vol. 7: *Vorträge und Aufsätze* (1936–1953). Ed. F.-W. von Herrmann, Frankfurt: V. Klostermann, 2000. Contains, among others: "Die Frage nach der Technik" (1953); "Wer ist Nietzsches Zarathustra?" (1953); "Was heißt Denken?" (1952); "'. . . dichterisch wohnet der Mensch . . . '" (1951).

Gesamtausgabe, Vol. 9: *Wegmarken* (1919–1961). Ed. F.-W. von Herrmann, Frankfurt: V. Klostermann, 1976, 1996 (rev. edn).

Gesamtausgabe, Vol. 10: *Der Satz vom Grund* (1955–1956). Ed. Petra Jaeger, Frankfurt: V. Klostermann, 1997.

Gesamtausgabe, Vol. 13: *Aus der Erfahrung des Denkens* (1910–1976). Ed. Hermann Heidegger, Frankfurt: V. Klostermann, 1983, 2002 (rev. edn).

Gesamtausgabe, Vol. 20: *Prolegomena zur Geschichte des Zeitbegriffs* (1925). Ed. Petra Jaeger, Frankfurt: V. Klostermann, 1979, 1988 (2nd, rev. edn), 1994 (3rd, rev. edn).

Gesamtausgabe, Vol. 24: *Die Grundprobleme der Phänomenologie* (1927). Ed. F.-W. von Herrmann, Frankfurt: V. Klostermann, 1975.

Gesamtausgabe, Vol. 25: *Phänomenologische Interpretation von Kants Kritik der reinen Vernunft* (1927–28). Ed. Ingtraud Görland, Frankfurt: V. Klostermann, 1977.

Gesamtausgabe, Vol. 26: *Metaphysische Anfangsgründe der Logik im Ausgang von Leibniz* (1928). Ed. Klaus Held, Frankfurt: V. Klostermann, 1978, 1990 (2nd rev. edn), 2007 (3rd rev. edn).

Gesamtausgabe, Vol. 28: *Der deutsche Idealismus (Fichte, Schelling, Hegel) und die philosophische Problemlage der Gegenwart* (1929). Appendix: "Einführung in das akademische Studium" (1929). Ed. Claudius Strube, Frankfurt: V. Klostermann, 1997.

Gesamtausgabe, Vol. 31: *Vom Wesen der menschlichen Freiheit. Einleitung in die Philosophie* (1930). Ed. Hartmut Tietjen, Frankfurt: V. Klostermann, 1982, 1994 (rev. edn).

Gesamtausgabe, Vol. 40: *Einführung in die Metaphysik* (1935).Ed. Petra Jaeger, Frankfurt: V. Klostermann, 1983. Also published separately by Max Niemeyer, Tübingen.

Gesamtausgabe, Vol. 42: *Schelling: Vom Wesen der menschlichen Freiheit (1809)* (1936). Ed. Ingrid Schüßler, Frankfurt: V. Klostermann, 1988.

Gesamtausgabe, Vol. 43: *Nietzsche: Der Wille zur Macht als Kunst* (1936–37). Ed. B. Heimbüchel, Frankfurt: V. Klostermann, 1985.

Gesamtausgabe, Vol. 44: *Nietzsches metaphysische Grundstellung im abendländischen Denken: Die ewige Wiederkehr des Gleichen* (1937). Ed. Marion Heinz, Frankfurt: V. Klostermann, 1986.

Gesamtausgabe, Vol. 45: *Grundfragen der Philosophie. Ausgewählte "Probleme" der "Logik"* (1937–38). Ed. F.-W. von Herrmann, Frankfurt: V. Klostermann, 1984.

Gesamtausgabe, Vol. 47: *Nietzsches Lehre vom Willen zur Macht als Erkenntnis* (1939). Ed. Eberhard Hanser, Frankfurt: V. Klostermann, 1989.

Gesamtausgabe, Vol. 49: *Die Metaphysik des deutschen Idealismus. Zur erneuten Auslegung von Schelling: "Philosophische Untersuchungen über das Wesen der menschlichen Freiheit und die damit zusammenhängenden Gegenstände" (1809)* (1941). Ed. Günter Seubold, Frankfurt: V. Klostermann, 1991, 2006 (2nd rev. edn).

Gesamtausgabe, Vol. 50: *Nietzsches Metaphysik* (announced for 1941–42); *Einleitung in die Philosophie—Denken und Dichten* (1944–45). Ed. Petra Jaeger, 1990, 2007 (2nd rev. edn).

Gesamtausgabe, Vol. 65: *Beiträge zur Philosophie (Vom Ereignis)* (1936–1938). Ed. F.-W von Herrmann, Frankfurt: V. Klostermann, 1989, 1994 (rev. edn).

Gesamtausgabe, Vol. 86: *Seminare: Hegel – Schelling* (1927–1957). Ed. Peter Trawny, Frankfurt: V. Klostermann, 2011.

Martin Heidegger & Karl Jaspers: Briefwechsel 1920–1963. Eds. Walter Biemel and Hans Saner. Frankfurt, V. Klostermann: 1990.

In translation

"The Age of the World Picture" (1938). In *The Heidegger Reader*. Ed. Günter Figal. Trans. Jerome Veith. Bloomington, Indianapolis: Indiana University Press, 2009.

"Art and Space". In *The Heidegger Reader*, Ed. Günter Figal. Trans. Jerome Veith. Bloomington, Indianapolis: Indiana University Press, 2009.

The Basic Problems of Phenomenology (1927). Trans. Albert Hofstadter. Bloomington, Indianapolis: Indiana University Press, 1988.

Basic Questions of Philosophy: Selected "Problems" of "Logic" (1937–38). Trans. Richard
    Rojcewicz and Andre Shuwer. Bloomington, Indianapolis: Indiana University Press, 1994.
Basic Writings. Ed. David Farrell Krell. New York: Harper Perennial Modern Classics, 2008.
Becoming Heidegger: On the Trail of his Early Occasional Writings, 1910–1927. Eds. Theodore
    Kisiel and Thomas Sheehan. Evanston Ill.: Northwestern University Press, 2007.
Being and Time (1927). Trans. John Macquarrie and Edward Robinson. San Francisco:
    HarperSanfrancisco, 1972.
Contributions to Philosophy (Of the Event) (1936–1938). Trans. Richard Rojcewicz and
    Daniela Vallega-Neu. Bloomington, Indianapolis: Indiana University Press, 2011.
The Essence of Human Freedom (1930). Trans. Ted Sadler. London & New York:
    Continuum, 2002.
The Essence of Reasons (1929). Trans. Terrence Malick. Evanston, IL: Northwestern
    University Press, 1969.
"On the Essence of Truth" (1930). Trans. John Sallis. In *Martin Heidegger: Pathmarks.*
    Ed. William McNeill. Cambridge: Cambridge University Press, 1998.
Four Seminars (1966–73). Trans. Andrew Mitchell and Francois Raffoul. Bloomington,
    Indianapolis: Indiana University Press, 2003.
The Heidegger-Jaspers Correspondence (1920–1963). Eds. Walter Biemel and Hans Saner.
    Trans. Gary E. Aylesworth. Amherst, NY: Humanity Books, 2003.
The Heidegger Reader. Ed. Günter Figal. Trans. Jerome Veith. Bloomington, Indianapolis:
    Indiana University Press, 2009.
History of the Concept of Time (1925). Trans. Theodore Kisiel. Bloomington, Indianapolis:
    Indiana University Press, 1992.
"Hölderlin and the Essence of Poetry" (1936). In *The Heidegger Reader.* Ed. Günter Figal.
    Trans. Jerome Veith. Bloomington, Indianapolis: Indiana University Press, 2009.
Introduction to Philosophy—Thinking and Poetizing (1944–45) Trans. Phillip Jacques
    Braunstein. Bloomington, Indianapolis: Indiana University Press, 2011.
Introduction to Metaphysics (1935). Trans. Gregory Fried and Richard Polt. New Haven &
    London: Yale University Press, 2000. The translation is based on the 1953 edition of
    Einführung in die Metaphysik (Tübingen: Max Niemeyer).
Kant and the Problem of Metaphysics (1929). Trans. Richard Taft. Bloomington,
    Indianapolis: Indiana University Press, 1990.
The Metaphysical Foundations of Logic (1928). Trans. Michael Heim. Bloomington,
    Indianapolis: Indiana University Press, 1992.
Nietzsche, Volume I: The Will to Power as Art (1936–1937). Trans. David Farrell Krell. San
    Francisco: Harper & Row, 1979.
Nietzsche, Volume II: The Eternal Recurrence of the Same (1937). Trans. David Farrell Krell.
    San Francisco: Harper & Row, 1984.
Nietzsche, Volume III: The Will to Power as Knowledge and as Metaphysics (1940). Trans.
    Joan Stambaugh, David Farrell Krell, Frank A. Capuzzi. Ed. David Farrell Krell. San
    Francisco: HarperSanFrancisco, 1987, 1982.
Nietzsche, Volume IV: Nihilism (1940, 1944–46). Trans. Frank A. Capuzzi. Ed. David
    Farrell Krell. San Francisco: HarperSanFrancisco, 1987, 1982.
"The Origin of the Work of Art" (1935/36). In *Poetry, Language, Thought.* Trans. Albert
    Hofstadter. New York: Perennial Classics, 2001.
"On the Origin of the Work of Art: First Version" (1935). In *The Heidegger Reader.*
    Ed. Günter Figal. Trans. Jerome Veith. Bloomington, Indianapolis: Indiana University
    Press, 2009. Veith's translation follows the edition of the text appearing in *Heidegger
    Studies* 5, (1989): 5–22.

Pathmarks. Ed. William McNeill. Cambridge: Cambridge University Press, 1998.

Phenomenological Interpretation of Kant's Critique of Pure Reason. Trans. Parvis Emad and Kenneth Maly. Bloomington, Indianapolis: Indiana University Press, 1997.

The Phenomenology of Religious Life. Trans. Matthias Fritsch and Jennifer Anna Gosetti-Ferencei. Bloomington, Indianapolis: Indiana University Press, 2010.

"Poetically Man Dwells" (1951). In *Poetry, Language, Thought*. Trans. A. Hofstadter. New York: Perennial Classics, 2001.

Poetry, Language, Thought. Trans. Albert Hofstadter. New York: Perennial Classics, 2001.

"What are Poets For?" (1946). In *Poetry, Language, Thought*. Trans. A. Hofstadter. New York: Perennial Classics, 2001.

The Question Concerning Technology, and Other Essays. Trans. William Lovitt. New York: Harper & Row, 1977.

Schelling's Treatise on the Essence of Human Freedom (1936). Trans. Joan Stambaugh. Athens, OH: Ohio University Press, 1985.

On Time and Being. Trans. Joan Stambaugh. Chicago & London: University of Chicago Press, 2002.

General

Aquinas, Thomas. "On Natural Science, Mathematics, and Metaphysics." In *Aquinas: Selected Philosophical Writings* Trans. and ed. Timothy McDermott. Oxford: Oxford University Press, 1993.

Aristotle. *Aristotle's Metaphysics*. Bloomington, Indianapolis: Indiana University Press, 1966.

—. *Aristotle's On the Soul (De Anima)*. Trans. Hippocrates G. Apostle. Grinnell, Iowa: Peripatetic Press, 1981.

—. *Aristotle: Introductory Readings*. Trans. Terence Irwin and Gail Fine. Indianapolis, IN: Hackett Publishing, 1996.

Asmuth, Christoph, Alfred Denker and Michael Vater. *Schelling: Between Fichte and Hegel/Zwischen Fichte Und Hegel (Bochumer Studien Zur Philosophie, 32)*. Amsterdam/Philadelphia: Br Gruner Pub Co, 2001.

Beiser, Frederick. *German Idealism: The Struggle against Subjectivism, 1781–1801*. Cambridge, MA: Harvard University Press, 2008.

—. *The Fate of Reason : German Philosophy from Kant to Fichte*. Cambridge, MA: Harvard University Press, 1993.

—. *The Romantic Imperative: The Concept of Early German Romanticism*. Cambridge, MA: Harvard University Press, 2006.

Beistegui, Miguel de. *Thinking with Heidegger: Displacements*. Bloomington, Indianapolis: Indiana University Press, 2003.

Benz, Ernst. *Schelling: Werden und Wirken seines Denkens*. Zürich and Stuttgart: Rhein-Verlag, 1955.

Bernasconi, Robert. *The Question of Language in Heidegger's History of Being*. Atlantic Highlands, NJ: Humanities Press, 1989.

Bowie, Andrew. *Schelling and Modern European Philosophy: An Introduction*. London & New York: Routledge, 1993.

—. *From Romanticism to Critical Theory: The Philosophy of German Literary Theory*. London & New York: Routledge, 1997.

Braeckman, Antoon. "From the Work of Art to Absolute Reason: Schelling's Journey toward Absolute Idealism." In *Review of Metaphysics* 57, 3 (1 March 2004): 551–69.

Capobianco, Richard. *Engaging Heidegger*. Toronto: University of Toronto Press, 2010.

Cioflec, Eveline. *Der Begriff des "Zwischen" bei Martin Heidegger: Eine Erörterung ausgehend von "Sein und Zeit."* Freiburg i.Br: Alber Verlag, 2012.

Crawford, Donald W. "Kant's Theory of Creative Imagination." In *Essays in Kant's Aesthetics*, Eds. Ted Cohen and Paul Guyer. Chicago and London: University of Chicago Press, 1982.

Crowell, Steven. "Measure-Taking: Meaning and Normativity in Heidegger's Philosophy." In *Continental Philosophy Review* 41, 3 (2008): 261–76.

Derrida, Jacques. *The Truth in Painting*. Trans. Geoff Bennington and Ian McLeod. Chicago and London: University of Chicago Press, (1978) 1987.

Desmond, William. *Art, Origins, Otherness: Between Philosophy and Art*. Albany, NY: SUNY Press, 2003.

Dodd, James. "Expression in Schelling's Early Philosophy." In *Graduate Faculty Philosophy Journal* 27, 2 (1 January 2006): 109–39.

—. "Philosophy and Art in Schelling's *System des transzendentalen Idealismus*." *Review of Metaphysics* 52, 1 (1998): 51–85.

Engell, James. *Creative Imagination: Enlightenment to Romanticism*. London & Cambridge: Harvard University Press, 1999.

Evrigenis, Ioannis. *Johann Gottfried Herder: Another Philosophy of History and Selected Political Writings*. Indianapolis, IN: Hackett Publishing, 2004.

Ferrarin, Alfredo. "Kant's Productive Imagination and Its Alleged Antecedents." *Graduate Faculty Philosophy Journal* 18, 1 (1 January 1995): 65–92.

Fichte, Johann Gottlieb. *The Science Of Knowing: J. G. Fichte's 1804 Lectures On The Wissenschaftslehre*. Albany, NY: SUNY Press, 2005.

—. *The Science of Knowledge*. Eds. Peter Heath and J. Lachs. Cambridge: Cambridge University Press, 1982.

Findler, Richard. "A Sketch of Schelling's Appropriation of the Kantian Imagination in the *System of Transcendental Idealism*: Schelling's Divergence from Fichte," In Asmuth, Denker, and Vater eds, *Schelling: Between Fichte and Hegel/Zwischen Fichte Und Hegel (Bochumer Studien Zur Philosophie, 32)*. Br Gruner Pub Co, 2001.

Freydberg, Bernard. *Imagination and Depth in Kant's Critique of Pure Reason*. New York: P. Lang, 1994.

—. *Schelling's Dialogical Freedom Essay: Provocative Philosophy Then and Now*. Albany, NY: SUNY Press, 2008.

George, Theodore D. "A Monstrous Absolute: Schelling, Kant, and the Poetic Turn in Philosophy." *Schelling Now: Contemporary Readings* (1 January 2005).

Gosetti-Ferencei, Jennifer Anna. *Heidegger, Hölderlin, and the Subject of Poetic Language*. New york: Fordham University Press, 2009.

Hegel, Georg. *The Difference Between Fichte's and Schelling's System of Philosophy*. Albany, NY: SUNY Press, 1977.

Hellmers, Ryan S. "Reading in 'Ereignis': Schelling's System of Freedom and the 'Beiträge.'" *Epoche: A Journal for the History of Philosophy* 13, 1 (2008): 133–62.

Herder, Johann Gottfried. *Another Philosophy of History* (1774). Trans. Ioannis D. Evrigenis and Daniel Pellerin. Indianapolis & Cambridge: Hackett Publishing Company, 2004.

Hesiod. *Hesiod's Theogony*. Trans. Richard S. Caldwell. Cambridge, MA: Focus Information Group, 1987.

Hölderlin, Friedrich. *Friedrich Hölderlin: Essays and Letters on Theory*. Albany, NY: SUNY Press, 1987.

—. *Hyperion and Selected Poems*. Ed. Eric L. Santner. Trans. Willard R. Trask and adapted by David Schwarz. New York: Continuum, 1994.

Hugo, Victor. *Les Misérables*. New York: Signet Classics, 1987.

Hume, David. *A Treatise of Human Nature* (1739–1740). Ed. L. A. Selby-Bigge. Oxford: Clarendon Press, 1987, 1978.

Inwood, M. *A Heidegger Dictionary*. Malden, MA: Blackwell Publishers, 2000.

Jähnig, Dieter. *Schelling: Die Kunst in der Philosophie*. 2 vols. Pfullingen: Neske, 1966 and 1969.

Jamme, Christoph and Helmut Schneider. *Mythologie der Vernunft: Hegels ältestes Systemprogramm des deutschen Idealismus*. Frankfurt am Main: Surkamp, 1984.

Jaspers, Karl. *Schelling. Grösse und Verhängnis*. Munich: R. Piper, 1955.

Johnston, Adrian. "The Soul of Dasein: Schelling's Doctrine of the Soul and Heidegger's Analytic of Dasein." *Philosophy Today* 47, 3 (2003): 227–51.

Kant, Immanuel. *Anthropology From a Pragmatic Point of View* (1798). Edited and Trans. Robert B. Louden. Cambridge: Cambridge University Press, 2006.

—. *Critique of Judgment* (1790). Trans. Werner S. Pluhar. Indianapolis & Cambridge: Hackett Pub. Company, 1987.

—. *Critique of Pure Reason* (1781/1787). Trans. Norman Kemp Smith. Bedford: St. Martins Press, 1969.

—. *Prolegomena to any Future Metaphysics* (1783). Trans. Carus (revised) Indianapolis: Bobbs-Merril Educational Publishing, 1950.

Kearney, Richard. *Poetics of Imagining: Modern and Post-Modern*. 2nd edn. New york: Fordham University Press, 1998.

—. *The Wake of Imagination*. London: Routledge, 1998.

Kharms, Daniil. *Today I Wrote Nothing: The Selected Writings of Daniil Kharms*. Trans. and Ed. Matvei Yankelevich. New York & London: Duckworth, 2009.

—. *Fear and Trembling*. Eds. C. Stephen Evens and Sylvia Walsh. Trans. Sylvia Walsh. Cambridge: Cambridge University Press, 2006.

Klemm, David. *Figuring the Self: Subject, Absolute, and Others in Classical German philosophy*. Albany, NY: SUNY Press, 1997.

Krell, David. *The Tragic Absolute: German Idealism and the Languishing of God*. Bloomington, Indianapolis: Indiana University Press, 2005.

—. "The Crisis of Reason in the Nineteenth Century." In *The Collegium Phaenomenologicum* Eds. J. C. Sallis, G. Moneta, and J. Taminiaux. Dordrecht: Kluwer Academic, 1988, pp. 13–32.

Lawrence, Joseph P. "Spinoza in Schelling: Appropriation through Critique." *Idealistic Studies: An Interdisciplinary Journal of Philosophy* 33, 2–3 (1 June 2003): 175–93.

—. "Art and Philosophy in Schelling." *Owl of Minerva* 20, 1 (1988): 5–19.

—. "Schelling: A New Beginning." *Idealistic Studies: An Interdisciplinary Journal of Philosophy* 19, 3 (1989): 189–201.

—. Trans. and Jean Grondin. "The A Priori from Kant to Schelling." *Idealistic Studies: An Interdisciplinary Journal of Philosophy* 19, 3 (1989): 202–21.

Linker, Damon. "From Kant to Schelling: Counter-Enlightenment in the Name of Reason." *Review of Metaphysics* 54, 2 (1 December 2000): 337–77.

Makkreel, Rudolf. *Imagination and Interpretation in Kant: The Hermeneutical Import of the Critique of Judgment*. Chicago, IL: University of Chicago Press, 1994.

Marcel, Gabriel. *Coleridge et Schelling*. Paris: Aubier-Montaigne, 1971.

Marx, Werner. *The Philosophy of F. W. J. Schelling: History, System, and Freedom.* Bloomington, Indianapolis: Indiana University Press, 1984.

Merleau-Ponty, Maurice. *Nature: Course Notes from the Collège de France.* Evanston, Ill.: Northwestern University Press, 2003.

Norman, Judith. *The New Schelling.* London & New York: Continuum, 2004.

Plato, G. M. A. Grube and C. D. C. Reeve. *Plato: Republic.* 2nd edn. Indianapolis, IN: Hackett Publishing Company, 1992.

Plutarch. *Plutarch's Lives Vol. IV.* Trans. John Dryden. Ed. A. H. Clough. New York: A. L. Burt, 1864.

Richardson, William. *Heidegger: Through Phenomenology to Thought.* 4th edn. New York: Fordham University Press, 2003.

Rockmore, Tom. *Heidegger, German Idealism & Neo-Kantianism.* Amherst, N.Y.: Humanity Books, 2000.

Ruin, Hans. "The Destiny of Freedom: In Heidegger." *Continental Philosophy Review* 41, 3 (2008): 277–99.

Russon, John. "The Self As Resolution: Heidegger, Derrida and the Intimacy of the Question of the Meaning of Being." *Research in Phenomenology* 38, 1 (1 January 2008): 90–110.

Sallis, John. *Chorology: On Beginning in Plato's Timaeus.* Bloomington, Indianapolis: Indiana University Press, 1999.

—. *Delimitations, Second Expanded Edition: Phenomenology and the End of Metaphysics.* Second Expanded Edition. Bloomington, Indianapolis: Indiana University Press, 1995.

—. *Double Truth (Suny Series in Contemporary Continen.* Albany, NY: SUNY Press, 1994.

—. *Echoes: After Heidegger.* Bloomington, Indianapolis: Indiana University Press, 1990.

—. *Force of Imagination: The Sense of the Elemental.* Bloomington, Indianapolis: Indiana University Press, 2000.

—. *Spacings–of Reason and Imagination: In Texts of Kant, Fichte, Hegel.* 1st edn. Chicago, IL: University of Chicago Press, 1987.

—. *The Gathering Of Reason.* 2nd edn. Albany, NY: SUNY Press, 2005.

—. *The Verge of Philosophy.* Reprint. Chicago, IL: University of Chicago Press, 2009.

—. *Transfigurements: On the True Sense of Art.* Chicago, IL: University of Chicago Press, 2008.

Schalow, Frank. *Heidegger and the Quest for the Sacred: From Thought to the Sanctuary of Faith.* Dordrecht, Boston: Kluwer Academic Publishers, 2001.

—. *The Renewal of the Heidegger-Kant Dialogue: Action, Thought, and Responsibility.* Albany, NY: SUNY Press, 1992.

Schiller, Friedrich. *On the Aesthetic Education of Man: In a Series of Letters. (Über die ästhetische Erziehung des Menschen, in einer Reihe von Briefen)* (1794–95), Oxford, England & New York: Clarendon Press; Oxford Unversity Press, 1982.

Schulz, Walter. *Die Vollendung des deutschen Idealismus in der Spät-philosophie Schellings.* Pfullingen: G. Neske, (1955) 1975.

Scott, Charles E., Susan Schoenbohm, Daniela Vallega-Neu and Alejandro Vallega. *Companion to Heidegger's Contributions to Philosophy:* Bloomington, Indianapolis: Indiana University Press, 2001.

Seidel, George J. "Heidegger's Last God and the Schelling Connection." *Laval Theologique et Philosophique* 55, 1 (1 February 1999): 85–98.

Sheehan, Thomas. "A Paradigm Shift in Heidegger Research." *Continental Philosophy Review* 34, (2001): 183–202.

Smith, F. Joseph. "Heidegger's Kant Interpretation." *Philosophy Today* 11, (1 December 1967): 257–64.

Snow, Dale. *Schelling and the End of Idealism.* Albany: SUNY Press, 1996.

Summerell, Orrin F. "The Theory of the Imagination in Schelling's Philosophy of Identity." *Idealistic Studies: An Interdisciplinary Journal of Philosophy* 34, 1 (1 March 2004): 85–98.

Taminiaux, Jacques. *Heidegger and the Project of Fundamental Ontology.* Trans. Michael Gendre. Albany, NY: SUNY Press, 1991.

—. *Poetics, Speculation, and Judgment: The Shadow of the Work of Art from Kant to Phenomenology.* Translated and Ed. Michael Gendre. Albany, NY: SUNY Press, 1993.

Tilliette, Xavier. *Schelling.* Stuttgart: Klett Cotta Verlag, 2004.

—. *Schelling, une philosophie en devenir (Bibliotheque d'histoire de la philosophie).* 2nd edn. Paris: J. Vrin, 1992.

—. *La mythologie comprise: L'interpretation Schellingienne du paganisme.* Naples: Bibliopolis, 1984.

Vallega-Neu, Daniela. *Heidegger's contributions to philosophy an introduction.* Bloomington, Indianapolis: Indiana University Press, 2003.

Velkley, Richard L. "Realizing Nature in the Self: Schelling on Art and Intellectual Intuition in the *System of Transcendental Idealism.*" In *Figuring the Self: Subject, Absolute, and Others in Classical German Philosophy.* Eds. David E. Klemm and Günter Zöeller. Albany, NY: SUNY Press, 1997, pp. 149–68.

Virgil. *The Aeneid of Virgil: A Verse Translation.* Translated Allen Mandelbaum. Toronto & New York: Bantam Books, 1981.

Warnek, Peter. "Bastard Reasoning in Schelling's *Freiheitsschrift.*" *Epoche: A Journal for the History of Philosophy* 12, 2 (1 March 2008): 249–67.

—. "Reading Schelling after Heidegger: The Freedom of Cryptic Dialogue." *Schelling Now: Contemporary Readings* (1 January 2005).

Wirth, Jason. *The Conspiracy of Life: Meditations on Schelling and his Time.* Albany, NY: SUNY Press, 2003.

—. "Schelling and the Force of Nature." In *Interrogating the Tradition: Hermeneutics and the History of Philosophy.* Eds. Charles E. Scott and John Sallis. Albany, NY: SUNY Press, 2000.

—. (ed). *Schelling Now: Contemporary Readings.* Bloomington, Indianapolis: Indiana University Press, 2005.

Žižek, Slavoj. *The Indivisible Remainder: An Essay on Schelling and Related Matters.* London: Verso, 1996.

—. Trans. F. W. J. von Schelling. *The Abyss of Freedom/Ages of the World.* Ann Arbor: University of Michigan Press, 1997.

—. *The Ticklish Subject: The Absent Centre of Political Ontology.* London: Verso Books, 2000.

Index